Thinking Gender in Transnational Times

Series Editors

Clare Hemmings
Gender Institute
London School of Economics
London, UK

Kimberly Hutchings
School of Politics and International Relations
Queen Mary University of London
London, UK

Hakan Seckinelgin
Gender Institute
London School of Economics
London, UK

Sadie Wearing
Gender Institute
London School of Economics
London, UK

Gender theories have always been important, but no more so than now, when gender is increasingly acknowledged as an essential focus for economics, policy, law and development as well as being central to a range of fields in the humanities and social sciences such as cultural studies, literary criticism, queer studies, ethnic and racial studies, psychoanalytic studies and of course feminist studies. Yet while the growth areas for the field are those that seek to combine interdisciplinary theoretical approaches with transnational arenas of inquiry, or integrate theory and practice, there is currently no book series that foregrounds these exciting set of developments. The series 'Thinking Gender in Transnational Times' aims to redress this balance and to showcase the most innovative new work in this arena. We will be focusing on soliciting manuscripts or edited collections that foreground the following: Interdisciplinary work that pushes at the boundaries of existing knowledge and generates innovative contributions to the field. Transnational perspectives that highlight the relevance of gender theories to the analysis of global flows and practices. Integrative approaches that are attentive to the ways in which gender is linked to other areas of analysis such as 'race', ethnicity, religion, sexuality, violence, or age. The relationship between theory and practice in ways that assume both are important for sustainable transformation. The impact of power relations as felt by individuals and communities, and related concerns, such as those of structure and agency, or ontology and epistemology In particular, we are interested in publishing original work that pushes at the boundaries of existing theories, extends our gendered understanding of global formations, and takes intellectual risks at the level of form or content. We welcome single or multiple-authored work, work from senior and junior scholars, or collections that provide a range of perspectives on a single theme.

More information about this series at
http://www.springer.com/series/14404

Alessandro Castellini

Translating Maternal Violence

The Discursive Construction of Maternal Filicide in 1970s Japan

Alessandro Castellini
Gender Institute
London School of Economics and Political Science
London, United Kingdom

Thinking Gender in Transnational Times
ISBN 978-1-137-53881-9   ISBN 978-1-137-53882-6   (eBook)
DOI 10.1057/978-1-137-53882-6

Library of Congress Control Number: 2016962094

© The Editor(s) (if applicable) and The Author(s) 2017
The author(s) has/have asserted their right(s) to be identified as the author(s) of this work in accordance with the Copyright, Designs and Patents Act 1988.
This work is subject to copyright. All rights are solely and exclusively licensed by the Publisher, whether the whole or part of the material is concerned, specifically the rights of translation, reprinting, reuse of illustrations, recitation, broadcasting, reproduction on microfilms or in any other physical way, and transmission or information storage and retrieval, electronic adaptation, computer software, or by similar or dissimilar methodology now known or hereafter developed.
The use of general descriptive names, registered names, trademarks, service marks, etc. in this publication does not imply, even in the absence of a specific statement, that such names are exempt from the relevant protective laws and regulations and therefore free for general use.
The publisher, the authors and the editors are safe to assume that the advice and information in this book are believed to be true and accurate at the date of publication. Neither the publisher nor the authors or the editors give a warranty, express or implied, with respect to the material contained herein or for any errors or omissions that may have been made. The publisher remains neutral with regard to jurisdictional claims in published maps and institutional affiliations.

Cover image © Maksim Evdokimov / Alamy Stock Photo

Printed on acid-free paper

This Palgrave Macmillan imprint is published by Springer Nature
The registered company is Macmillan Publishers Ltd.
The registered company address is: The Campus, 4 Crinan Street, London, N1 9XW, United Kingdom

To my many mothers

Acknowledgements

This project has been a long way in the making. My first encounter with literary representations of maternal animosity dates back to when I was still an undergraduate student of Japanese studies at Ca' Foscari University (Venice, Italy). I am incredibly grateful to Luisa Bienati for teaching a course on Japanese postwar women's literature and for introducing me to a world of literary imagination and transgression that was going to accompany me for many years to come. With time, the research that made this book possible has taken a life of its own, and it almost feels that I have spent the last few years trying to catch up with it and its many changes of direction. I owe a debt of gratitude to Clare Hemmings and Sadie Wearing for their guidance and encouragement in the painstaking process of giving intelligible form to my intuitions. A deeply felt and special thank you to Marina Franchi and Nicole Shephard for all their love and friendship at various stages of this project and beyond. You know way too well that without your support this book would not have seen the light of the day! I am equally grateful to Francesca, whose enthusiastic spirit and heartfelt words helped me remember why this project was important.

I've been fortunate enough to have a family who taught me what it means to love and be loved. There are no words to thank my mother, Loredana, for her strength and wisdom. She's been a guide, a friend and an incredible companion in our common journey. This book is for her. It took me quite some time (and a slow process of maturation) to realize the incredible amount of love that my father, Maurizio, brought into my life. His actions speak more than a thousand words, and I just want to take this opportunity to remind him of how much I love him. When I was a child, my sister, Micaela (Miki), made me feel safe when I was scared of the dark, and I still treasure the memory of her hand holding mine as I fell asleep. She's an irreplaceable point of reference and my "second" family.

I have benefited tremendously from the financial support of the Gender Institute and the London School of Economics and Political Science. In particular, I am very grateful to my colleagues, friends and students at the Gender Institute for our engaging conversations and for reminding me of the value of what I do. Portions of Chaps. 2 and 3 have appeared in *Feminist Review* 106(1) in earlier form as an article entitled "Silent Voices: Mothers Who Kill Their Children and the Women's Liberation Movement in 1970s Japan." I couldn't have completed *Translating Maternal Violence* without my editor at Palgrave who kindly but firmly chased me down when I was hiding behind my teaching commitments, and the anonymous reviewers who provided encouragement and invaluable advice on early drafts of the manuscript.

This book is written in loving memory of my grandmothers, Amelia and Assunta.

Contents

1 Introduction   1

2 Filicide in the Media: News Coverage of Mothers Who Kill in 1970s Japan   39

3 The Women's Liberation Movement in 1970s Japan   81

4 Contested Meanings: Mothers Who Kill and the Rhetoric of *ūman ribu*   119

5 Filicide and Maternal Animosity in Takahashi Takako's Early Fiction   163

6 Conclusions   219

Bibliography   233

Index   261

List of Tables

Table 1.1	Total number of articles per year	33
Table 2.1	Occurrence of the word *shinjū* in the *Asahi shinbun* and *Yomiuri shinbun*	50
Table 2.2	Mother–child suicides and parent–child suicides committed by someone other than the mother alone	52

1

Introduction

Every language's struggle with the secret, the hidden, the mystery, the inexpressible is above all else the most entrenched incommunicable, initial untranslatable.
(Ricoeur 2006: 33)
What can't be said can't be translated[.]
(Bellos 2012: 149)
Not only is power deeply embedded in the words we use, power is embedded in the words that we do not use; there is power in silence. […] If violence is not named or is not allowed to be named, then its very existence is contested and women's experiences reduced to "unreality."
(Cavanagh et al. 2001: 702–3)

Encountering Maternal Violence: The Kimura Case

On the cold, sunny afternoon of January 29, 1985, about ten days after learning of her husband's affair of three years with another woman, 32-year-old Japanese immigrant Kimura Fumiko walked with her two children along an almost-deserted beach in Santa Monica. She carried in her arms her infant daughter, Yuri, while her four-year-old son Kazutaka ran in front, stopping every so often to play cheerfully with the sand. No one saw the mother pick up both children at the water's edge and wade into the cold waters of Santa Monica Bay. They were found 15 minutes later and pulled from the Pacific Ocean unconscious, still clinging together. The children died, but the mother survived (Dolan 1985; Pound 1985). She was later charged with two counts of first-degree murder and two counts of felony child endangering. The district attorney's office alleged the special circumstance of multiple murder, which meant she could face the death penalty (Boyer 1985; Stewart 1985a).

When charges were first filed against her, however, Kimura did not seem to comprehend that she was accused of murder, as she assumed that her crime was failed suicide: in the attempt to end her life together with that of her children, she thought she was committing what in Japan is known as *oyako shinjū* (parent–child suicide). In the weeks and months to follow, this practice was to become the focus of much public debate. News coverage reported the voices of cultural experts calling attention to the sociological and psychological factors that could have prompted what appeared to many an unfathomable (and unforgivable) gesture.[1] They explained that *oyako shinjū* constituted a frequent albeit tragic occurrence in Japan. But they also prudently added that, despite its high incidence in Japanese society, it was not sanctioned by law or custom and remained illegal, even though it was likely to be treated as involuntary manslaughter and to result in a suspended sentence with supervised probation (Dolan 1985; Hayashi 1985a; Pound 1985).[2]

Kimura's case sparked a media frenzy and gained international publicity. It became a rallying point among Japanese and Japanese-Americans

---

[1] As I will explain in some detail in Chap. 2, the causes behind the practice of *oyako shinjū* were understood to vary, ranging from a mother's perception of her child as part of herself, a desire to spare one's child from the social stigma and discrimination faced in Japan by children with single parents and by adoptive children (to the extent that a mother who killed herself while leaving her child behind was frowned upon and considered cruel) up to a cultural romanticization of suicide as an honourable way of dying and a means to avoid losing face (Dolan 1985; Hayashi 1985a).

[2] In this respect, the article by Katie Kaori Hayashi, herself a Japanese immigrant and a mother and back then a reporter for the student-run newspaper of Santa Monica College *The Corsair*, was consequential in expanding early discussions of *oyako shinjū* and clarifying its cultural dimensions (Hayashi 1985a). Her piece was soon reprinted in the pages of the *Los Angeles Times* under the meaningful headline: "Understanding *shinjū* and the tragedy of Fumiko Kimura" (Hayashi 1985b).

with thousands of people from the United States, Japan and Europe asking for lenient treatment and urging the prosecutor to take Kimura's cultural heritage into account (Jones 1985; Pound 1985). In the end, however, Kimura's defence attorney opted for not emphasizing the cultural factors involved in the case. He chose instead to interpose a temporary insanity defence based on expert psychiatric testimonies according to which Kimura—already tried by a previous failed marriage of eight years and the unfulfilled dream of a music career as a pianist in her home country—had been mentally disturbed at the time of the crime (Feldman 1985; Sams 1986). To the extent that it achieved the best legal outcome, this strategy was deemed successful: Kimura entered a plea bargain and was allowed to plead no contest to two counts of voluntary manslaughter. The court sentenced her to five years' probation with mandatory psychiatric treatment and one year in prison (time she had already served awaiting trial) (Stewart 1985b; Matsumoto 1995).[3]

Quite predictably, if cultural evidence was not formally admitted into court, news coverage of the Kimura case did unfold according to a highly polarized interpretative framework evidenced in headlines such as "Two Cultures Collide Over Act of Despair" (Dolan 1985), "Mother Who Killed Children Trapped in a Culture Conflict" (Jones 1985) and "Mother's Tragic Crime Exposes a Culture Gap" (Pound 1985).[4] It did not seem to matter significantly that Kimura had been living in the

---

[3] Despite the fact that a formal cultural defence, that is, the use of the defendant's cultural tradition to excuse her actions and negate or mitigate her criminal responsibility, was not raised in court, it has been argued that cultural evidence was in fact used to better contextualize Kimura's actions and further substantiate her mental instability at the time of the offence. In other words, even though culture was not taken into consideration as a mitigating factor, there was an understanding that Kimura's cultural background had made her more vulnerable to the kind of psychotic conditions which eventually led to the crime (Matsumoto 1995; Kim 1997). This has led some scholars to draw critical attention to the dangers and ethical implications of a pathologization of cultural difference (Reddy 2002; Goel 2004).

[4] Rashmi Goel (2004) has called attention to the fact that, by refusing to formally engage in a meditation on cultural difference and its implications for a conception of justice, both prosecution and defence contributed to relegating the discussion of cultural factors to newspapers, magazines and television, entrusting them with an accurate representation of Japanese culture while disregarding the extent to which the news media thrives on sensationalistic reporting and often indulges in problematic stereotyping. We can easily recognize such an attitude in the extent to which misinformed reporters slipped into outright misrepresentations of cultural difference, especially in the early stages of such extensive media coverage, arriving to describe Kimura's *oyako shinjū* as the "ceremonial drowning" (Dolan 1985) or the "ritualistic slaying" of her two children according to "an ancient Japanese custom" (Jones 1985).

United States for 14 years when she committed her dramatic gesture or that, upon her arrival from Japan, she had studied for two years in a community college (albeit without graduating). The mass media emphatically described her as a woman who had "*remained Japanese* in her thinking and life style," and preferred to focus on those daily practices that could be deemed "unquestionably traditional" such as sleeping "on Japanese mats *instead of* beds" or not wearing shoes indoors, but "*faithfully*" leaving them by the door (Dolan 1985; my emphasis).[5] A persistent cultural essentialism permeated lengthy descriptions of the Kimuras' Japanese traditions that were formulated in exotic undertones and then fed to the orientalist gaze of an avid readership.[6] Kimura was even said to be "trapped in [a] cultural time warp" (Jones 1985), thus implicitly conjuring a hegemonic conception of (US) modernity and progress against a (Japanese) pre-modern temporality (Butler 2008).

The portrayal of Japanese culture as an intractable alterity was further marked by a distinct linguistic dimension. To begin with, Kimura's defence attorney Gerald Klausner pointed at the fact that, after 14 years in the United States and despite her college education, Kimura had still not mastered English and that Japanese was the language spoken at home. Translations, mistranslations and disputed translations also took a special relevance at different stages of the legal proceedings. The Fumiko Kimura Fair Trial Committee, established by the Japanese-American commu-

---

[5] The media also reported about how Kimura would compose poetry in her prison cell and how she would write "in pencil in Japanese script about her love for the sea and her love for music" (Dolan 1985), thus buying into long-standing stereotypes of a highly poetic Japanese sentimentality.

[6] References to her commitment to Japanese cultural and religious practices came to signal Kimura's "authentic" Japanese identity. Dolan's (1985) article in the *Los Angeles Times* arguably provides one of the earliest and most obvious examples of this trend where mourning takes the form of a time-honoured tradition and where the words of Kimura's husband further reinforce the idea of a Japanese cultural identity so deeply entrenched that it does not seem to warrant discussions of any sort:

> With the deaths of the children, another tradition became a part of the Kimura home. Three times a day, meals for the souls of the children are set out on a small, low coffee table that serves as an altar. On a recent day, two small bowls of noodles sat untouched. A photograph of Kazutaka, the couple's son, dressed in a little black-and-white kimono, has been placed next to his favorite cars, trucks and paper planes. There is also a photograph of the couple's daughter, Yuri, wearing a pink dress. Two pink rattles and jars of baby food have been placed beside her picture. Between two small candles is a vase of white carnations. [Husband] Itsuroku Kimura said he does not discuss the altar with his wife but he is certain she knows it exists. "She would expect it," he said.

nity to raise awareness of the cultural specificities of Kimura's actions and to petition for a lenient sentence, criticized, for example, the way in which she had initially been questioned through police interpreters and doubted that she had fully understood her rights under federal and state law (Wetherall 1986). In a similar vein, Kimura's defence attorney also asked that her statement to investigators be excluded from evidence on the grounds that the police officer had mistranslated her rights to her (Boyer 1985). Furthermore, while gathering the testimony (by means of an interpreter) of Yoko Hirose, a Japanese neighbour of the Kimuras', Klausner repeatedly asked her whether she believed the defendant was sane on the night before the crime, but the proceedings were delayed because "two interpreters argued over the proper translation of the word." It was reported that, in the end, Hirose never replied directly to the question and that Kimura's defence attorney "was not satisfied with the translations of his questions and Hirose's answers" (Stewart 1985a).

It is worth noting that, while linguistic issues and translational difficulties punctuated the unfolding of the case, the paramount role of translation in promoting intercultural understanding was never fully or sufficiently explored. This was emblematic, for example, of the distinctive ambiguity that surrounded attempts at understanding Kimura's dramatic gesture and to provide a degree of discursive and cultural intelligibility to the violence she perpetrated. On the one hand, the foreign expression *oyako shinjū* took centre stage and became synecdoche for an assumed intractable cultural alterity. On the other hand, the rendering of the Japanese original with the English expression "parent–child suicide" arguably functioned as a form of (unproblematic?) cultural translation that implicitly claimed to introduce a notion deemed culturally specific (and thus, in principle, alien to Western conceptualizations) into a Western cultural landscape. Granted, "it may be necessary to enter into a field of translation [for a concept or analytical category] to make itself communicable beyond the community of those who speak the idiom" (Butler 2014: 7). But we should also take notice of the fact that the substitution of *oyako shinjū* with the expression "parent–child suicide" was hardly ever critically addressed and appeared to rely instead on a simplistic understanding of translation as a straightforward process of "restitution of meaning" or "restoration of an original" rooted in a dream of perfect equivalence or in what Derrida (2001: 195) ironically described as "the transfer of an intact signified through the inconsequential vehicle of any signifier whatsoever." But was that rendering to be understood as a translation without residues or was something indeed lost (and gained?) in the process of translation? And if so, what did the loss (and gain) consist of and what, if any, were their consequences for an intercultural understanding of a maternal potential for violence?

Words and Silences: The Discursive Construction of Maternal Filicide

Of all possible beginnings an account of the Kimura case offers a useful entry point into the intellectual project at the heart of *Translating Maternal Violence*. At its most basic, the Kimura case constituted an important moment of confrontation of a Western audience with cultural alterity in the form of a differential understanding of maternal violence. Yet, as my cursory account attempted to show, such encounter came to be portrayed as a conflict between cultures rooted in a sense of *unassimilable alterity*. Not only was the Kimura case the emblematic example of an encounter steeped in an essentialist and monadic conception of culture(s), but it also implicitly projected an overly simplistic understanding of Japanese culture as *internally homogeneous* in its engagements with maternal violence. These, I argue, are forms of understanding that refuse—or, rather, pre-empt—any chance of a truly dialogic exchange that could be transformative of the ways we apprehend, recognize and represent a maternal potential for violence.

Translating Maternal Violence disputes this assumed polarity between two cultures and two linguistic communities that were implicitly portrayed as impermeable to one another,[7] and challenges the all-too-familiar dichotomy of "the West and the Rest of the World" that undergirds it. Its writing was motivated by a desire to provide the occasion for *a renewed*

---

[7] For reason of simplicity I will not engage here with the deeply questionable assumption of a homogeneous linguistic community in the United States, an issue that Judith Butler and Gayatri C. Spivak acutely raised in their *Who Sings the Nation State?: Language, Politics, Belonging* (2007).

encounter with Japanese conceptualizations of maternal violence that could offer a more nuanced appreciation of the internal complexity of local modes of representation. Despite its Japanese focus, however, this book is not meant to be confined to the geographical and linguistic specificities that often characterize area studies but is driven, instead, by a broader desire to open up a dialogic space with the material it makes available in the first place. A crucial feature of this project is thus the adoption of translation as both a theoretical and a methodological tool to prompt a *decentring* of the West as the privileged origin of (feminist) theorizations of the maternal and to enable a transnational and transcultural dialogue conducive of new ways of imagining motherhood's violent potential.

The following pages offer the first book-length investigation in English language of the *multiple* and often *contradictory* ways in which mothers who killed their children came to be portrayed in late postwar Japan, and call attention to the underlying tensions that marked the ways in which ideas about a maternal potential for violence entered (or failed to enter) a realm of discursive representability and cultural intelligibility. By drawing on close readings of a wide range of original archival materials in Japanese, the book explores three discursive sites that emerged in the early 1970s where the image of the murderous mother assumed a distinctive visibility: (1) mainstream media coverage of cases of maternal filicide; (2) the rhetoric about mothers who killed their children elaborated by a newly emerging women's liberation movement known as *ūman ribu* (woman lib) or simply *ribu* (lib); (3) works of fiction by Japanese woman writer Takahashi Takako (1932–2013) whom I take here as emblematic of a broader fictional concern with the "dark side" of the maternal.

It seems useful to recall here how alternative ways of framing Kimura's murderous actions competed to make sense of a crime that had dramatically shattered cultural idealizations of motherhood as essentially nurturing, gentle and non-violent (although *which* culture remained a contentious issue). In that respect, "the epistemological problem raised by this issue of framing," as Judith Butler (2010: 1) aptly describes it, calls for the elucidation of the schemas of intelligibility that determined the conditions of appearance and modes of recognition of a maternal potential for violence within public discourse (we can think, for example, of how Kimura's maternal violence was apprehended differently according to a shifting reliance on the analytic categories of "murder" and "suicide"). In similar fashion, a first aim of *Translating Maternal Violence* is to provide a snapshot of a historical and social moment in late postwar Japan when motherhood and the maternal were renegotiated and rearticulated at the very site where maternal violence disrupted social norms of acceptable maternal behaviour. The book explores the modalities whereby knowledge about mothers who killed their children was produced, circulated and contested in the framework of a complex strategic configuration of discourses that made it possible to think of maternal filicide in the first place. In the process, it documents and charts those schemas of intelligibility that governed the conditions of appearance of maternal murderous violence in the discursive field. In particular, it exposes *ūman ribu*'s rhetoric in solidarity with filicidal mothers and Takahashi Takako's fictional representations of maternal animosity as powerful counter-discourses that opposed the obdurate monsterization and stigmatization so common in dominant discourses about filicidal mothers (notwithstanding a degree of cultural tolerance towards what will be shown to be highly regulated forms of maternal violence).

Foucauldian theorizations of the relations between discourse, power and resistance clearly inform the way I understand how a variety of cultural representations of murderous motherhood surfaced in late postwar Japan according to relations of *proximity, continuity, utter rejection* or *concealed displacement.* In their participation in what Foucault calls "the field of discursive events" (1992 [1972]: 27), the three archives I explore provide suggestive indications of how maternal filicide was "created" and variously contested qua object of discourse at a specific moment in time and space. This is by no means to suggest that filicide was not real or that it was performatively brought into being by an identifiable set of discursive practices. The material consequences of "real" maternal filicide for the child who was killed, for the mother who killed and for society (fathers included) are clearly too important to be downplayed as the result of textual exaggerations that produced something short of a moral panic (Cohen 2002). However, an engagement with these consequences demands a fundamentally different kind of investigation that is beyond the scope of this book. While certainly aimed at neither justifying crimes of filicide nor devaluing the suffering of children, this book approaches maternal filicide from a perspective that privileges a broader mechanism of knowledge production: it explores the linguistic and textual strategies whereby knowledge about mothers who killed their children was produced, circulated and contested in the framework of a complex strategic configuration of discourses that made it possible to think of maternal filicide in the first place. In so doing it foregrounds the epistemological and cognitive dimensions of the discursive strategies employed in late postwar Japan to talk about maternal violence.[8]

In this book I intend to raise objection to a claim made by sociologist and criminologist Lizzie Seal according to which "although women who kill their own children [...] are not necessarily perceived to embody norms of femininity, they are *not* culturally unthinkable" (2010: 2, my emphasis). As I explore those cultural archives that actively contributed to a discursive proliferation on maternal violence in postwar Japan, I will also try to make it clear why I do not think this is in fact the case. In the process I distinguish between widespread cultural representations of filicidal mothers as either "bad" or "mad"[9] and what I deem to be a deep-seated difficulty in rendering a maternal potential for violence *truly* intelligible, by which I mean a certain refusal (conscious or unconscious) to confront the fact that the maternal experience might indeed harbour violent and yet deeply human possibilities and dangers. Informing my research is a fundamental understanding of this difficulty as it forcefully emerges (qua silencing and erasure, but also in the form of resistance or ambivalence)

---

[8] Even though we should be wary of simplistically conflating Foucault's conception(s) of discourse with an overemphasis on textuality, for the purposes of my investigation the three discursive arenas I will be exploring clearly presuppose the materiality of the written page and are characterized by distinctive modalities of production, conservation, access and recirculation that I will address in the methodological section of this introduction. For two examples of works that openly collapse the textual/material division in their approach to Foucauldian understandings of discourse, see Mary C. Beaudry, Lauren J. Cook and Stephen A. Mrozowski, "Artifacts and Active Voices: Material Culture as Social Discourse" in *Images of the Recent Past: Readings in Historical Archaeology* (Oxford: AltaMira Press, 1996), 272–310, and Derek Hook, "Discourse, Knowledge, Materiality, History: Foucault and Discourse Analysis," *Theory and Psychology* 11(4) (2001): 521–47.

[9] For a selection of studies on the dichotomous (and biased) treatment of murderous mothers as either "mad" or "bad" in the discipline of criminology, see Wilczynski (1991, 1997a, 1997b) and Meyer and Oberman (2001); in journalism, see Goc (2003, 2007, 2008, 2009, 2013), Barnett (2005, 2006, 2007, 2013) and Cavaglion (2008); in legal studies, see Huckerby (2003), Ayres (2004) and Stangle (2008).

in those very instances where *there is* a clear attempt to bring maternal violence into the realm of discourse and cultural representation.[10]

Therefore, among the questions that haunted the writing of this book are the following: what are we to make of silences, of what is denied any form whatever of intelligible articulation? Is silence indeed synonymous with non-intelligibility? More importantly, does silence always imply an irretrievable erasure? And what role can translation play when such erasure is inscribed in the linguistic materiality of the very categories used to talk about motherhood and violence? Once again, Foucault offers an invaluable lesson with his exposure of the opposition between discourse and silence as a false dichotomy. Instead, he advances the suggestive idea that the way things may not be allowed entry into discourse could be equally (if not more) revealing of the power relations that permeate a given discursive field.[11] The translational approach that variously informs my analysis in the following chapters thus emerges as a productive tool that foregrounds the linguistic mechanisms and discursive strategies whereby a maternal potential for violence remains relegated to the fringe

---

[10] To analyse the complex and fraught articulation of a maternal potential for violence in the realm of cultural intelligibility also brings to our attention that the very notion of "maternal filicide," instead of being the single, unproblematic referent that would confer unity to these discourses, may be far less stable than we might have originally assumed. The fantasy of a stable referent admittedly constituted an important, provisional criterion for the selection of the material to be included in my investigation—what Foucault describes as "a provisional division [that operates] as an initial approximation" (1992: 29). Yet, to call attention to the schema of intelligibility and the "field of emergence" (91) that allowed something we may call "maternal filicide" to surface as an object of discourse in 1970s Japan means to untangle a historically specific set of conditions that made possible the materialization of multiple ways of conceptualizing maternal murderous violence—discursive modalities that may have been at odds with each other or could have partially overlapped or simply coexisted side by side, touching each other only fleetingly.

[11] In the first volume of *The History of Sexuality*, Foucault devotes a brief but significant passage to the relationship between discourse and silence:

> Silence itself—the things one declines to say, or is forbidden to name, the discretion that is required between different speakers—is less the absolute limit of discourse, the other side from which it is separated by a strict boundary, than an element that functions alongside the things said, with them and in relation to them within over-all strategies. There is no binary division to be made between what one says and what one does not say; *we must try to determine the different ways of not saying such things*, how those who can and those who cannot speak of them are distributed, which type of discourse is authorized, or which form of discretion is required in either case. *There is not one but many silences, and they are an integral part of the strategies that underlie and permeate discourses.* (1998: 27, my emphasis)

of signification even when murderous mothers appear in discourse with appalling frequency. In the elusive attempt *to translate what cannot be said*, it prompts the reader to reflect on the epistemological and cognitive potential of a transnational/transcultural approach to a maternal potential for violence.

Feminist Encounters with Maternal Violence

A second aim of *Translating Maternal Violence* is to make an intervention in the existing scholarship on *ribu* that sheds light upon a rather underexplored dimension of the movement's ambivalent relationship with motherhood, namely, the importance of the figure of the child-killing *onna* (woman) for *ribu*'s activism and writing. In this respect, the fact that *ribu* is still barely known to a Western audience and the recognition that a comparable engagement with mothers who kill has yet to be found in any strand of Western feminism that I am aware of have motivated the distinctive emphasis placed upon the exploration of *ribu* in the overall economy of the book.[12] The reader will not fail to notice that, in a way that starkly differs from the treatment of news media and Takahashi's fiction, my analysis of *ribu* develops across two chapters, rather than a single one: Chap. 3 offers a broad introduction to and contextualization of the movement, while Chap. 4 engages in a close reading of those texts produced and circulated by *ribu* that directly address maternal filicide. These "twin chapters" are spatially located at the very centre of the book's

---

[12] Until the recent publication of Setsu Shigematsu's monograph *Scream from the Shadows: The Women's Liberation Movement in Japan* (2012) *ribu* has remained a rather unexplored object of enquiry in English-language academic literature on the history of Japanese feminism(s). Arguably, one of the reasons for this gross oversight is the fact that *ribu*'s experience of political contestation has commonly been perceived as short-lived, spanning only the first half of the 1970s (Fujieda and Fujimura-Fanselow 1995: 159), and already waning by the time the UN-sponsored 1975 International Women's Year marked a drastic change in the character of the Japanese women's movement "from one that was targeted at bringing about changes in women's consciousness […] to one seeking visible changes in social institutions" (Tanaka 1995: 348). However, Shigematsu (2012: 172) remains critical of similar interpretations that disregard the significance of *ribu*'s interventions during the 1970s, and she exposes the inaccuracy of traditional periodizations that would locate the end of *ribu* in 1975, thus ignoring the fact that many *ribu* activists remained committed to various forms of political struggle in the following decades (175).

linear development, but they are intended to invite a mode of reading that is not expected to be linear. The central position they occupy (following the analysis of media coverage and right before the chapter on Takahashi) is meant to operate as a second point of departure for the reader: it simultaneously encourages a "backward movement," that is, a "return" to the analysis of news media in Chap. 2 in light of the challenge *ribu* posed to it, and a "forward movement" that approaches the chapter on Takahashi's fiction (Chap. 5) while keeping the insights developed by *ribu* in play. The implicit purpose here is for these insights to facilitate the recognition and the amplification through juxtaposition of those aspects of Takahashi's writing that might be deemed to harbour a "feminist" potential.

In this respect, *Translating Maternal Violence* is meant to be feminist in scope despite the fact that the relationship of both *ribu* and Takahashi with what we might call "feminism" remains somewhat vexed. A first set of problems emerges as we try to identify what we should take as the referent of the word "feminism." Vera Mackie (2003) draws attention to the fact that the Japanese transliteration of the word "feminist" (*feminisuto*) originally denoted "a man who was kind to women, rather than a campaigner for women's political rights" (160). She also observes that it was only in 1977 that the word was reclaimed by the founders of the homonymous journal *Feminisuto*, and with it "the concept of women's militancy as political agents engaged in a project of social transformation" (ibid.). Setsu Shigematsu (2012: 172), on the other hand, is at pains to stress the enormous gap separating *ribu*'s bottom-up, anti-establishment and anti-capitalist spirit from the one animating a magazine like *Feminisuto*, a journal that "was launched by a group of academic and professional women in collaboration with a few (white) American and European feminists" and which was funded "by selling advertising space to [Japanese] corporations." In a similar vein, it has been frequently observed that the Japanese word *feminizumu* (transliteration of the English "feminism") carries academic and foreign associations and maintains an uncertain relationship with *ribu*'s grass-roots activism, stemming from a desire to dissociate itself from the tone of ridicule with which *ribu* was often portrayed in news media.[13] Furthermore, as will become clear in Chap. 3, the relationship of *ribu* with Western (mainly American) feminism and with pre-existent forms of women's political organizing in Japan has always been a heated and contested one.[14]

If *ribu* cannot be simplistically understood as synonymous with feminism, Takahashi's stance vis-à-vis feminism is even more ambiguous in that, even though she did write non-fictional essays on woman's condition, she never did so from an overtly political or activist perspective nor did she ever identify as feminist (in fact, notions of "feminism" or "women's liberation" never appear in her writings). Yet, as we read Takahashi's non-fictional pieces alongside her early works of fiction we are confronted with an undeniable and persistent preoccupation with gender issues. Her readers are introduced to unorthodox interpretations of cultural representations of femininity in (Western) visual arts, in literature (both Western and Japanese) and in the very functioning of the Japanese language. A quest for new, more viable forms of female subjectivity pressured Takahashi into literary and theoretical explorations of woman's potential for violence that she portrayed as stemming symptomatically from an experience of existential starvation, but also as the wilful reclaiming of a novel, fearless sense of integrity. It therefore seems clear that both *ribu* and Takahashi depicted mothers who killed their children in ways that profoundly challenged widely shared assumptions about motherhood and maternal love, and that these portrayals were framed within broader attempts to question society's gender stereotypes and prescriptive ideas of appropriate femininity.[15]

---

[13] Shigematsu (2012: 171–5, 249 note 1), Mackie (2003: 160–1), Fujieda and Fujimura-Fanselow (1995: 158–9).

[14] Such controversies attest to the fact that the distinction between *ribu* and *feminizumu*, as Shigematsu (2012) aptly puts it, is rooted in a specific political history that was crucial in informing how ideas, theories and categories of political contestation travelled and were translated into ever-changing cultures of reception (see Shigematsu 2012: 171–5, 249 note 1; Mackie 2003: 160–1; Fujieda and Fujimura-Fanselow 1995: 158–9). Analogous "translational tensions" and the intersecting of local and global histories of political contestation characterize the adoption of the term "feminism" in China (Dongchao 2005, 2007a, 2007b). On this issue, see also the work of Lin Chun (1997) and Shu-Mei Shih (2002).

[15] See Mori (1994, 1996) and Bullock (2006, 2010) for excellent examples of scholarship that explores the political challenges Takahashi's fiction poses to normative discourses of gender.

To the extent that a preoccupation with cultural representations of motherhood's potential for violence constitutes a defining aspect of this book, the writing of *Translating Maternal Violence* has been influenced and encouraged by the numerical increase in the past decades of academic investigations of the maternal across a wide range of disciplines and theoretical positions.[16] However, this growing literature notwithstanding, we still face a dearth of scholarship that openly engages in an exploration of maternal violence. What is more, that some of the most significant theoretical contributions to this underexplored territory appear to be variously inscribed in the medicalized framework provided by psychoanalysis or (forensic) psychology also becomes reason for suspicion and concern.[17] Behind this noticeable reticence there could be the intuition that such an unorthodox focus might produce accounts of the maternal whose circulation could have detrimental effects upon the lives of many a mother. Explorations of what Adrienne Rich (1979) once called "the heart of maternal darkness" could indeed be used against women to reinstate notions of maternal propriety, strengthen the policing of maternal behaviour and sustain those processes of monsterization and pathologization whereby mothers who kill their children are expunged from the realm of cultural intelligibility and into social abjection. Also, there clearly is very limited usefulness in emphasizing the violent side of the maternal as a direct counter-strategy against cultural idealizations of motherhood. Is there, in fact, any emancipatory potential in "celebratory" accounts of maternal violence? And yet, to shy away from an engagement with a maternal violent potential means to miss the opportunity to work towards a more viable and humane vocabulary capable of articulating conflictual maternal experiences and emotions.

It is true that we do encounter maternal expressions of rage and aggression in that highly popular genre known as "mommy lit" of which Susan

---

[16] Lisa Baraitser and Imogen Tyler (2010: 117) speak to this discursive intensification around motherhood and the maternal body when they acknowledge the "extraordinary proliferation of public representations of maternity" in the last three decades. Tyler (2008: 2) argues that "the maternal has never been so very public, so-hyper visible," but she also points at the profound incoherence that characterizes this multiplicity of commentaries on and portrayals of the maternal experience.

[17] See, for example, Estela Welldon (1988), Roszika Parker (1995), Anna Motz (2001) and Barbara Almond (2010).

Cheever's *As Good as I Could Be* (2001) and Naomi Wolf's *Misconceptions* (2002) constitute two significant examples. And we should not forget those memorable feminist works that paved the way to the popularity of these "coming out" stories of motherhood (Tyler 2008): Adrienne Rich's *Of Woman Born* (1976), Jane Lazarre's *The Mother Knot* (1976) and Ann Oakley's *Becoming a Mother* (1979). For obvious reasons, however, all these landmark texts do not focus specifically on the notion of a maternal potential for violence, but attempt to relay the inherent and often contradictory complexity of the mothering experience.[18] In highlighting the value of these experiential accounts of maternal subjectivity, Tyler (2008: 6) emphasizes the need for women "to communicate what they already know in ways that will make a difference." But I want to contend that the very ability to communicate what one "knows" may rely on the *availability* of categories that must already be in place for us to be able to make sense of our affective landscapes. However, when widespread public condemnation turns the negative side of maternal ambivalence into a full-fledged cultural taboo (Parker 1995; Almond 2010), then the restrictions thus imposed upon the schemas of intelligibility at our disposal will limit what can be admitted as reality. And this exposes us to the risk that women's experiences of violence will be reduced to *unreality* (Cavanagh et al. 2001). In light of these premises, my hope is for the Japanese case study at the heart of *Translating Maternal Violence* to become a possible interlocutor in a transnational/transcultural feminist search for new modes of imagining, apprehending and representing motherhood's violent potential. In the process or as a result of this search, alternative schemes of conceptualization might emerge whose heightened accountability will *not* be predicated upon the denial of motherhood's permeability to violence—a denial that is often assumed as one of motherhood's normative traits. Here it is worth restating how the archives I explore in the following chapters testify to an astonishing proliferation of public

---

[18] Rich's *Of Woman Born* (1976) constitutes perhaps the only exception here as it devotes an entire chapter to the already mentioned "heart of maternal darkness." However, hers remains a rather singular intellectual endeavour that weaves together autobiographical accounts and diary entries with a carefully researched historical, social and feminist account of the maternal. A rather different but much needed perspective is provided by Michelle Oberman and Cheryl L. Meyer in their *When Mothers Kill: Interviews from Prison* (2008).

discourses around maternal murderous violence whose intensity remains, to my knowledge, unparalleled. But they also demonstrate that schemas of intelligibility can also interrupt one another and may "often come up against spectral version of what it is they claim they know" (Butler 2010: 4). *Translating Maternal Violence* thus acquires the status of an intervention in the field of gender and maternal studies, providing us with an opportunity to reflect on the strategies by means of which a maternal potential for violence acquires (limited and highly regulated) discursive and cultural intelligibility, while alerting us to the epistemological possibility harboured by that spectral remainder assiduously relegated to the fringe of our field of vision.

Straddling Disciplinary and Geographical Boundaries

I began this introduction with the claim that this book provided the opportunity for a renewed encounter with Japanese conceptualizations of motherhood's violent potential and I voiced my hope that it would promote forms of dialogue conducive of new ways of apprehending and representing maternal violence. Judith Butler (1990: 15) once observed that "[t]he power relations that condition and limit dialogic possibilities need first to be interrogated" before we can assert that a conversation is indeed taking place. *Translating Maternal Violence* deeply treasures that remark and draws upon a long history of critiques of Western feminism's rather tenacious temptation to ignore, erase or colonize ethnic and cultural differences for its own political purposes.[19] In the process, it makes a conscious effort to avoid reproducing forms of ethnocentric universal-

---

[19] It feels outrageous to even consider the possibility of relegating to the space of a footnote the ever-expanding corpus of feminist scholarship that in the span of several decades has been calling to task the essentialism, white solipsism and universalist pretences of early (and sometimes more recent) Western feminist writing. Important interventions by Cherríe Moraga and Gloria Anzaldúa (1981), Adrienne Rich (1986 [1984]), Gloria Anzaldúa (1987), Gayatri Chakravorty Spivak (1988), Chandra Talpade Mohanty (1988 [1984], 2003), Judith Butler (1992), Inderpal Grewal and Caren Kaplan (1994), Linda Alcoff (1995) and Susan Standford Friedman (1998) may come to mind, but they are offered here as merely indicative, not representative, of a much wider and heterogeneous scholarship (in English!).

ism and Western solipsism,[20] while also attempting to remain at a safe distance from the equally suspicious desire to particularize its investigation as meticulously as possible in the name of cultural pluralism and as a questionable strategy to sidestep the dangers of Orientalism (Spivak [1987] 2012; Chow 1993). In this respect, Rey Chow (1993: 6) has described with perceptive clarity how the fetishization of ethnic markers such as "Japanese" or "Chinese" may indeed reactivate a type of discourse that is both geographically deterministic and culturally essentialist. Ella Shohat helps us rephrase Chow's concerns as an apprehension that such fetishization of cultural difference might reduce and limit non-Western formulations of women's experiences and struggles to the field of area studies. This would fabricate "segregated notions of temporality and spatiality" (Shohat 2002: 77) that are hardly tenable in a world whose global interconnectedness (past and present) is being increasingly appreciated (Sakai 2001, 2005; Shohat and Stam 2014). And it would also oppose Shohat's relational understanding of feminism "as a polysemic site of contradictory positionalities" (2002: 67).[21]

A note of clarification is needed here about the way in which I sometimes employ in this book a highly questionable notion of "Western feminism" as shorthand for a more complex set of historical, genealogical and theoretical considerations that I hope will become clear as I develop my argument. My use of the term "Western feminism" (in the singular) ought not be taken to suggest a monolithic understanding of feminist theorizations and voices as pertaining to a single narrative, although it does explicitly play with the enduring belief in a linear, developmental

---

[20] My use of the expression "Western solipsism" clearly owes to Adrienne Rich's (1978: 299) formulation of the notion of "white solipsism" which she describes as the tendency "to think, imagine, and speak as if whiteness described the world."

[21] A comparable geographical (and cultural) reductionism is recognized by Allaine Cerwonka (2008) in her examination of power relations within the global academic political economy, especially as they concern Western feminist hegemony in Central and Eastern European countries. In that context Cerwonka considers a certain critique of multiculturalism according to which "showcasing the particularity and difference of nondominant cultures in the name of respect" (817) may just preserve cultural hierarchies and leave unchallenged *implicit assumptions of the West as the primary referent*. In her cautious suggestion that the privileging of difference constitutes "an imperfect solution to Western hegemony" (816), Cerwonka's considerations find a parallel in Naoki Sakai's (1997) recognition of the mutually reinforcing nature of universalism and particularism (see especially the chapter "Modernity and its critique: the problem of universalism and particularism," pp. 153–76).

narrative of progress whose directionality has been traditionally assumed to be from the West to the Rest. My use of the term also purposefully conflates (not without a certain distancing irony) "Western feminism" with a constellation of feminist narratives that could be tentatively described as Anglo-(North-)American. While this is not meant to prioritize Anglo-American feminism(s) over and above other theoretical and geographical trajectories, it does intend to foreground the role played by the hegemony of English as the global lingua franca of academic publishing and the fact that "feminist theory produced in an Anglo-American context is always likely to exceed its geography" (Hemmings 2011: 15). Written in English and from a place (however precarious) within UK academia, *Translating Maternal Violence* remains, nonetheless, critical of "the Anglocentric monolingualism of global English" (Bachmann-Medick 2014: 3), while uncomfortably negotiating its very embeddedness in it. The book is an expression of my desire to contribute to what Wang Ning and Sun Yifeng (2008: 12) identify as "the crisis of the monolingual mode" in cultural studies. Crisis that, it is my hope, will also transform the way we do gender studies and feminist theorizing. *Translating Maternal Violence* thus constitutes a tentative first step towards that democratic, transnational conversation that it intends to promote. It sustains a form of intellectual engagement that cuts across the fields of gender and motherhood studies and cautiously inhabits the fraught relationship between cultural and area studies, relentlessly mediating between their respective claims to intellectual legitimacy.

A certain brand of criticism of area studies, for example, draws attention to the epistemological implications of its structure of knowledge production historically rooted in a post-World War II global geopolitical landscape marked by the emergence of the United States as a new imperialist power (Chow 1993; Sakai and Harootunian 1999; Miyoshi and Harootunian 2002; Sakai 2010). Naoki Sakai and Harry D. Harootunian (1999: 596) remind us that the original format of area studies was the "information gathering program for colonial administration." They also observe—with explicit reference to area studies on Japan—how traces of that colonial structure persist in the discipline's primary concern with the acquisition and accumulation of knowledge of the area (preoccupation that, they contend, is accompanied by a certain indifference to generating knowledge that might be of interest for people outside of Japanese studies). Because of its focus on culture-language areas, area studies have been further criticized for reproducing forms of cultural essentialism, for being primarily descriptive and theoretically naïve (i.e. empirical)[22] and for lacking political commitment (Jackson 2003).

It is indisputable that rigorous language training and translation work played a crucial role in the establishment and consolidation of Japanese area studies and that they may have remained for quite some time the single most important methodological tool that promised "unmediated" access to the native (Sakai and Harootunian 1999: 598).[23] A more generous reading of this epistemic and methodological conundrum is advanced by David Szanton (2004) and draws upon Alan Tansman's (2004) expansive conception of translation as coextensive with (Japanese) area studies' commitment to knowing, analysing and interpreting foreign cultures. Without explicitly addressing the work of translation as a site of theoretical and methodological reflexivity, Szanton does, nonetheless, call attention to the fact that by making "the assumptions, meanings, structures and dynamics of another society comprehensible to an outsider," area studies "creates reflexive opportunities to expand, even challenge by contrast, the outsider's understanding of his or her own society and culture," encouraging in this way a process of decentring and deparochialization of knowledge (2004: 1–2).[24]

---

[22] But see Reader (1998) for a review article that explicitly takes to task Sakai and Harootunian's (1999) critique of area studies as anti-theoretical and which draws attention to works of academic scholarship on Japan that make an enriching contribution to sociological theory.

[23] For an excellent account of the question of the native, see Rey Chow's essay "Where Have All the Natives Gone?" in *Writing Diaspora: Tactics of Intervention in Contemporary Cultural Studies* (Bloomington: Indiana University Press, 1993, 27–54). Chow (2014a) further explores questions of identity, hybridity and nativism with a lens that privileges the "psychic, cross-cultural, institutional, and geopolitical effects" of the unequal confrontation between languages and cultures that is at the heart of the (post)colonial experience (Chow 2014b). See Lai (2008) for a rather different account of nativism as an oppositional practice within forms of cultural contestations under global capitalism.

[24] With a move that simultaneously refuses the false belief in translation as the dream of a perfect equivalence without residues and calls into question the suspicion of self-referentiality that Chow (2006) ascribes to area studies, Szanton (2004: 1–2) argues that

> [p]erfect translations are rarely possible, something is almost always lost in translation; rough or partial translations are the best we can expect. Inevitably, translations from or of even very distant languages and cultures will produce some familiar ideas and images, and will support

That "geography [can be] a domain of theoretically significant difference" (Jackson 2003: 5) is an insightful observation that strikes at the heart of this book's intellectual project. But we should remain suspicious of how most discussions of area studies—and this is especially true of Japanese studies—tend to reproduce a problematic distinction between "the East" (or alternatively "Asia" or "Japan") and "the West." Naoki Sakai (2001: 810) consistently voiced a critique of "the culturalist binary schema of the West and the Rest" and repeatedly called into question the distinction between "Asia" and that "mythic construct" known as "the West" (Sakai 2005: 180). According to Sakai, not only is "the West" always and only a putative unity, that is, a unity that is both assumed in advance and retrospectively projected onto an inherent fragmented, internally diverse and dispersed reality, but the idea of "Asia" "would [also] be too arbitrary unless it is paradigmatically opposed to the West (or Europe)" (Sakai 2001: 792). In clear poststructuralist fashion, Sakai argues that the existence of Asia qua sign depends on this very process of mutual exclusivity or what he calls a schema of co-figuration. It is the "positioning [of] Asia 'over there' away from the West 'this side'" that, according to Sakai, "engenders a fleeting sense of a distinction between the West and the Rest" (2001: 797).

> some familiar concepts and propositions. But they will also almost certainly generate some surprises. Merely finding or imposing our own selves, structures, or dynamics in another culture—in effect, reading it as a Rorschach inkblot onto which we project out own experience—only tells us about ourselves. It also probably means that we have missed whatever we might have learned from it. Such failure to understand—or projections onto—other societies and cultures often result from forms of ethnocentrism. [...] When successful, Area Studies research and teaching demonstrates the limitations of fashioning analyses based largely on the particular and contingent histories, structures, power formations, and selective, and often idealized, narrative of "the West."

These and similar reflections have operated as a cautionary tale in the structuring of *Translating Maternal Violence* and have motivated my decision not to introduce an investigation of Japanese material with a detailed account of Western feminism's engagements with maternal violence. I hope to have sidestepped in this way some of the problems inherent in unwittingly making Western feminism(s) into a privileged interpretative lens and a ready-made grid of intelligibility. In fact, the tendency to reduce non-Western local realities and experiences to case studies mostly framed by metropolitan (i.e. Anglo-European) conceptualizations (Connell 2014) does nothing to challenge a global economy of knowledge characterized by the theoretical hegemony of the West or Global North (Connell 2015), but further reinscribes the West as the normative interlocutor.

In its worst manifestations, too rigid a distinction between "East" and "West," between Japan and the Anglo-American world of feminist theorizing, may sclerotize around an obstinate emphasis on dimensions of unbridgeable cultural and linguistic untranslatability, contributing to a sense of immobility that is detrimental to processes of transnational/transcultural communication and understanding.[25] This would also pre-empt the possibility of envisaging epistemic borders not as allegedly insuperable cognitive boundaries, but rather as *filters* always marked by a degree of porosity and permeability (Sakai 2014). Sakai describes translation as such a filter as opposed to a representation of translation that foregrounds the separation and incommensurability of two linguistic communities conceived as autonomous and internally homogeneous. The notion of translation-as-filter urges us not to content ourselves with identifying what does or does not pass through the filter, but to ask instead about *the conditions under which more or less successful crossings occur*. This is a way to uncover the *hermeneutic potential* of those very instances of seeming untranslatability that may have been previously used to reinforce a sense of incommunicability and disengagement from a commitment to a more global and democratic approach to the production and circulation of knowledge.

Translational Encounters

While working on *Translating Maternal Violence* I found in Sakai an imaginative and optimistic intellectual companion who, even when anticipating that our attempt to establish a transnational dialogue will be hindered by a history that produced the dichotomy of "the West" and "the Rest" according to a schema of co-figuration, suggests that we can still find ways not to lock ourselves into the same dualistic and mutually

---

[25] This is not to say that there are no such things as untranslatables, but that any such discussion will have to take account of the fact that "the untranslatable, or what appears to resist translation, cannot exist prior to the enunciation of translation" and, therefore, it is already internal to that moment of encounter with alterity that unfolds through translation (Sakai 2009: 177). "[T]he incommensurable and excessive," Sakai claimed on a different occasion, "cannot be apprehended outside the contexts of contact" (Sakai 2001: 800).

exclusive positionalities (Sakai 2005: 192). In fact, "we may be able to invent a number of strategies whereby to avoid reproducing such a discriminatory gesture as that of the exclusionary constitution of the West" (Sakai 2001: 811). In both its form and content *Translating Maternal Violence* explores some of those strategies. The book explicitly avoids rehearsing the culturalist argument that would emphasize difference and separation. Instead, it privileges the notion of *translation* as a powerful method to decentre and provincialize the West as the privileged origin of (feminist) theorizations of the maternal (Chakrabarty 2000). In the process, it insists on the ethical dimension that pertains to translating practices and foregrounds the Japanese case study as the promising site of an encounter that is generative of new theoretical and dialogic possibilities.

Since Susan Bassnett's (1998) landmark intervention that called attention to a "translation turn in cultural studies," there has been a bourgeoning focus on translation and translation processes in the humanities. This has stimulated the broadening of the horizon of translation and moved the concept beyond its original textual and linguistic dimensions towards more metaphorical uses.[26] However, an expanded but purely metaphorical understanding of translation risks diluting its methodological efficacy as an analytical tool (Bachmann-Medic 2009: 2). "If everything becomes translation," cautions Dilek Dizdar (2009: 90), then translation is unwittingly reduced to a fashionable buzzword arbitrarily employed to describe an ever-expanding range of processes while losing a great deal of the concept's explanatory power and intellectual complexity. This inflationary use of translation, she continues, often opposes a supposedly creative, critical potential of translation metaphors to a "flat" idea of "interlingual translation" or "translation proper" (Jakobson 1959). Making "the *practicum* of translation" (Apter 2006: 6) into translation studies' proper object would then appear to provide justification for the lack of sustained engagement with the linguistic and textual dimensions of translation in the humanities. Dizdar (2009: 90) advocates instead for the necessity of retaining the tension between "translation proper" and expanded or metaphorical uses of the translation concept, and holds that "precisely

---

[26] For a discussion on cultural translation, see Bhabha (1994), Papastergiadis (2000), Trivedi (2005), Polezzi (2006, 2012) and Bachmann-Medick (2014).

this tension could serve as a productive [...] means for analysing interrelations between different orders of signification." Her suggestion resonates strongly with the intellectual work at the heart *Translating Maternal Violence* where the question of translation is taken up on three distinct but intersecting levels: (1) in its most specific linguistic dimension as the transfer of a message from a source language to a target language (the above-mentioned idea of interlingual translation); (2) in more metaphorical terms as the set of transformations (translations) that maternal filicide undergoes as it moves across media; (3) from a distinct philosophical perspective that calls for an ethics of translational/transnational encounters.

The extent to which cultural representations of motherhood's murderous violence changed as they circulated among news reporting, *ribu*'s political writings and Takahashi's literary imagination will become clear as I develop my argument in the following chapters. Here I would like to spend a few words to reflect on the other two dimensions of how translation work is taken up in this book. It would seem only natural, for example, that the conventional notion of interlingual translation is ever-present in *Translating Maternal Violence* where the content of Japanese cultural texts has been translated from Japanese into English to make it accessible to those who do not know the language of the originals. At the etymological level the words "translation," "traduction," "Übersetzung," "traduzione" all denote the activity of carrying something across: this way of conceptualizing translation has traditionally privileged the "faithful" transposition or transmission of a text's semantic tenor "with as little interference as possible from the constraints of the vehicle" (Johnson 1985: 145). Gayatri Spivak (2012: 256) describes this notion of fidelity as "the stringing together of the most accurate synonyms by the most proximate syntax." It is this historical prioritization of the signified over the signifier that led Barbara Johnson (1985: 145) to conclude that translation "has always been the translation of *meaning*."[27]

---

[27] There is, however, a growing scholarship that calls into question Western understandings of translation via a consideration of non-Western conceptualizations of translation work. See, for example, Paker (2002), Cheung (2005), Tymoczko (2006), Snell-Hornby (2007) and Wakabayashi and Kothari (2009).

Yet, ideas of fidelity and betrayal are far from self-evident. We just need to take notice of the fact that, from a pragmatic point of view, the work of translation requires the decoding of a message from a chain of signifiers given in the source language and the subsequent encoding of *another* corresponding message in another chain of signifiers in the target language. "The *choices* of message and signifying chain," Venuti convincingly argues, "demonstrate the profoundly transformative nature of translation and the active intervention of the translator" (1986: 182, my emphasis). In other words, we are not confronted here with *the same* message in two languages, but with two messages whose semantic and formal proximity ought not to be mistaken for linguistic equivalence (the idea that one message in the source language corresponds to one and one only message in the target language). There is always a slide of meaning in the transition due to the non-superimposable character of the semantic fields in the source and target languages, and one of the tasks of the translator is to limit that slide "by choosing to communicate a specific signified to the exclusion of others" (ibid.). Yet, this newly selected signified "can be no more than an interpretation according to the intelligibilities and interests of the receiving language and culture" (171).[28] So, whereas Spivak (2012: 257, 1993) describes translation as the most intimate act of reading that demands from us that we grasp the author's presuppositions and how they inform his or her use of language, Venuti (1995: 18) emphasizes the violence inherent to the practice of translation, which consists of this forcible work of substitution and transformation. To recognize this unavoidable violence as integral to the work of translation means to leave

---

[28] It seems pertinent at this stage to take some time to reflect, at least in passing, on some of the implications of this account of the translator as an agentic subject who mediates between two languages and cultures. Berman (1992: 5) describes, for example, the psychological ambivalence of the translator who wants to force two things: "to force his own language to adorn itself with strangeness, and to force the other language to trans-port itself into his mother tongue." In light of Venuti's account of how the identification of message and signifying chain in the target language is the outcome of a decision process that speaks to the interventionist and transformative nature of translation, we can understand why Berman urges the translator to engage in "self-scrutinizing operations" that should enable him "to localize the systems of deformation that threaten his practice and operate unconsciously on the level of the linguistic and literary choices—systems that operate simultaneously on the registers of language, of ideology, of literature, and of the translator's mental make-up." (6) Berman likens this constant "keeping in check" of the translator's own conscious and unconscious attitude vis-à-vis the original to a "psychoanalysis of the translator" (ibid.).

behind the dream of the perfect translation without residues rooted in a wish that translation would gain without losing (Derrida 1985; Ricoeur 2006).

Similar reflections are crucial if we do not want to misunderstand the intentions behind *Translating Maternal Violence* as a work of translation. In fact, it would run counter to this book's intellectual purpose to conceive of it simply as an opportunity to introduce previously unknown Japanese materials *as if* they were written in English (in other words, effacing the translator's labour and its epistemic implications) (Venuti 1986). We need instead to take notice of the fact that translation maintains a necessary relationship to damage and betrayal even when it presents itself as the means whereby the original is transmitted and granted an afterlife in the target language: "the original has to be crossed, if not partially mutilated, with the emergence of the translation itself" (Butler 2004: 82).[29] This constitutional failure of translation means that the translator "has to give up in relation to the task of refinding what was there in the original" (de Man 1985: 33), and this is consequential for the ways in which we both navigate cultural representations of maternal filicide in postwar Japan and how that investigation is then received by an English-speaking audience at home.

If translation is bound to fall short of its promises, it becomes all the more important to ask what it means when something *cannot* be carried across and what the implications are when elements of the original do not lend themselves to translation. Is there something to gain from a meta-reflection on forms of untranslatability? How do we deal with the silences and omissions in the source language that sometimes encase a maternal potential for violence in a mantle of opaque, dense unutterability? Whereas Bellos (2012) claims that what cannot be said cannot be

---

[29] In a way that clearly resonates with Venuti's understanding of the violent, transformative and inevitably interventionist character of translation work, Benjiamin adds that "no translation would be possible if in its ultimate essence it strove for likeness to the original. For in its afterlife—which could not be called that if it were not a transformation and a renewal of something living—the original undergoes a change" (2007: 73). The transfer that translation is meant to perform can thus never be total, and we must content ourselves with an asymptotic relation between translation and original whereby "a translation touches the original lightly and only at the infinitely small point of the sense, thereupon pursuing its own course according to the laws of fidelity in the freedom of linguistic flux" (80).

translated, this book explicitly concerns itself with the challenge of *translating silences* and makes an effort to illuminate forms of linguistic erasure by means of a critical approach to the practice of translation. *Translating Maternal Violence* attempts to expose the *symptomatic meaning* of those silences in a way that partially also "undoes" them, thus working towards the explicitly political intent of increasing the discursive possibilities of motherhood's violent potential.[30] In some respect then, we could say with Butler (2004: 83) that "the original becomes perceptible in resisting [translation]." But to become perceptible, she carefully points out, ought not to be confused with becoming restored, the idea of "restitution of meaning" being the untenable fantasy fabricated by traditional Western discourses on translation. Implicitly recalling the asymptotic relationship between translation and original that Benjamin so vividly describes, Butler tells us that the original "becomes perceptible at the moment of contact" (83). And she adds, importantly, that "translation meets the original at the site of resistance" (84).

Let me now turn to a tentative meditation on an ethics of translational/transnational encounters. Writing about the *ethical aim* of translating, Antoine Berman argues that "the essence of translation is to be an opening, a dialogue, a cross-breeding, a decentering. Translation is a 'putting in touch with,' or it is nothing" (1992: 4).[31] His considerations introduce us to a conundrum emblematically summarized by Franz Rosenzweig's famous paradox according to which "to translate [...] is to serve two masters: the foreigner with his [*sic*] work, the reader with his

---

[30] Considered in this light, what I propose may be deemed the most unfaithful practice of translation. And yet, Antoine Berman offers some important insights into the work of translation when he describes it as an instrument that allows something of the original to appear that may not appear in the source language. Translation, he perceptively observes, has the potential to turn the original around and reveal *another side* of it (1992: 7); in so doing it may also contribute to a "potentiation" of the source language (Ricoeur 2006: 8).

[31] In his book *The Experience of the Foreign* Berman offers an important contribution to an understanding of the praxis of translation as the site of transformative dialogic possibilities. There he argues that

> [e]very culture resists translation, even if one has an essential need for it. The very aim of translation—to open up in writing a certain relation with the Other, to fertilize what is one's Own with the mediation of what is Foreign—is diametrically opposed to the ethnocentric structure of every culture, that species of narcissism by which every society wants to be a pure and unadulterated Whole.

[*sic*] desire for appropriation, foreign author, reader dwelling in the same language as the translator" (Ricoeur 2006: 4). If the translator focuses on "bringing the reader to the author" by means of a faithful adherence to the syntax, grammar and phonetic effects of the source language, he/she risks "produc[ing] a text leaning toward the unintelligible" (Berman 1992: 3). If, on the other hand, he/she decides for a conventional adaptation of the foreign work that privileges the criterion of fluency and the ideal of a transparent translation, thus "bringing the author to the reader" (see Venuti 1986, 1991), "he [*sic*] will have satisfied the least demanding part of the public [...] but will have irrevocably betrayed the foreign work as well as [...] the very essence of translation" (Berman 1992: 3). The latter becomes here an example of "bad" translation that Berman describes as "the translation which, generally under the guise of transmissibility, carries out a systematic negation of the strangeness of the foreign work" (5).

In order for translation to function as both the groundwork for and the medium through which a dialogic encounter becomes possible, this foreignness or otherness of the Other ought to be partially preserved. The task of the translator becomes that of engaging with the simultaneous demand of making the foreign sufficiently familiar to the reader so that a common ground of communication might be possible, while also preserving what is unfamiliar in order to force the reader into a process of provincialization of his/her mother tongue and structures of thought. In the process the mother tongue is "invited to think of itself as one language amongst others, ultimately to see itself as foreign" (Ricoeur 2006: 9). In a related vein, Richard Kearney (2006: xvi) suggests that the work of translation carries a double duty: "to expropriate oneself as one appropriates the other." A psychically demanding tension between expropriation and appropriation is necessary because full appropriation would take the form of a reduction of the Other to the Same, the erasure and effacement of its alterity. At the site of contact between cultures, between (feminist) intellectual projects and divergent temporalities, this "swallowing" or "taking in" would have the dire consequence of transforming the Other into a mere projection of the Subject's own scheme of things, thus making an encounter with things not-yet-known hardly possible.[32] Claudia de Lima Costa and Sonia Alvarez (2014: 557) oppose such a "cannibalistic" approach to alterity with a formulation that emphasizes the ethical implications and the demand for linguistic hospitality that should be inherent in any work of translation. "In translation," they contend, "there is a moral obligation to uproot ourselves, to be, even temporarily, homeless so that the other can dwell, albeit provisionally, in our home."

This conceptualization of translation as a process of displacement of the self has considerable potential for contributing to the opening up of a space of dialogic exchange. In this book it is employed as a textual strategy that, in combination with a citational practice that favours (albeit never exclusively) non-Western sources, aims at intervening in the global academic political economy (Cerwonka 2008: 809; Connell 2014, 2015). To think in terms of "deprovincializing through translation" also means being alert to how the *directionality of the translation process* impacts on the production and circulation of feminist knowledge and how new analytical categories travel across geographical and disciplinary borders. And that directionality is affected by what Chow (2007: 570) diagnoses as "the fundamental unevenness among the world status of different languages" which strongly influences which languages are considered worth translating (Vatanabadi 2009; Liu 1999). At the same time, the lasting primacy of English as the language of research foregrounds the responsibility of the translator into English (Spivak 2012).

In order to work towards the creation of a more democratic global epistemic community, we need to question the power relations between "East" and "West" in which context emphasis "tends to be placed on the effects of translating Western terms into non-Western languages, which consequently have to adjust or reform themselves in order to accommodate the Western terms" (Chow 2007: 569). *Translating Maternal Violence* is thus confronted with the controversial task of negotiating the epistemic and political ambiguity of writing and translating from Japanese into English from within English-speaking academia. At the

---

[32] See Sara Ahmed's account of the Western self-referentiality and narcissistic character of Orientalism in a chapter of *Queer Phenomenology* (2006, pp. 109–59) aptly entitled "The Orient and Other Others."

same time, it contests Anglo-European translation privilege and resists the "positivistic recommendation of additional acquisition" of non-Western experiences and theoretical paradigms into an intellectual trajectory whose identity remains solidly anchored in the West (575). With this book I hope to contribute to reducing the discursive hegemony of monolinguality in the production and circulation of feminist and gender theories. My use of translation as both a theoretical framework and a methodological tool ought to be understood as a politically invested choice aimed at temporarily undoing the power relations that contributed to the historical isolation of Japanese feminism from actively intervening in the development of feminist theory in the West. As I investigate the multiple ways in which a maternal potential for violence came to be portrayed and negotiated in 1970s Japan, my goal is also to implicitly put the language of Western theories of the maternal "into symbolic expansion" (Derrida 1985: 190), making it more sensitive to its own silences and erasures.

Archives Matter

This final methodological section is intended to offer a series of considerations about the nature of the cultural archives at the heart of *Translating Maternal Violence* and to give a sense, however partial, of the logic behind their selection. To begin with, my decision to delimit my archival material to the years 1970–1975 was motivated by socio-historical considerations. Sociological investigations explicitly refer, for example, to a numerical increase of episodes of filicide that allegedly characterized that five-year period (Kurisu 1974; Sasaki 1980; Tama 2008). The year 1973 has also been repeatedly identified as a pivotal year marked by at least three major events: the first survey on child abuse and neglect that was carried out by the Ministry of Health and Welfare (and which testified to growing public concerns about such a difficult issue); an attempt to revise the Eugenic Protection Law by removing the article that granted women access to abortion on economic grounds (an attempt that, as I will show in some detail in Chap. 3, triggered what arguably became *ribu*'s most important political struggle); an increase in the number of newspaper articles on filicide, child abandonment and child abuse that was perhaps sparked by the 20th International Congress of Psychology held in Tokyo in August 1972 (Kouno 1995; Tama 2008; Goodman 2002; Shigematsu 2012). Also, while 1970 is often identified as the year of the emergence of the Women's Liberation Movement (*ribu*) in Japan (Akiyama 1993; Buckley 1994; Tanaka 1995; Muto 1997), the most recent *ribu* pamphlet I was able to find that engages with maternal filicide to any significant degree dates back to 1975, thus indirectly confirming a temporal framework that remains, in the end, inevitably arbitrary.

Japanese Newspapers

Chapter 2 is based on a qualitative textual analysis of articles published in the *Asahi shinbun* and the *Yomiuri shinbun*—the newspapers with the widest circulation in Japan—in the years 1970–1973. The *Asahi* and the *Yomiuri* produce morning and evening editions (except for Sundays and national holidays) and they are considered quality newspapers with a less sensationalistic approach than Japanese tabloids, although, if we look at their distribution, they may as well be identified as mass papers (Yamamoto 2012; Hayashi 2000). They are independent newspapers which operate without government interference; they are owned entirely by their employees and they are committed to a principle of "impartiality" (meaning simply that they are not committed to any particular party, although they will still take a position on every major issue) (Lee 1985). They do not differ significantly in their editorials or news coverage, and they have been described as "indistinguishable except in matters of degree and emphasis" (Frank Gibney quoted in Lee 1985: 1–2).[33]

---

[33] Such relative homogeneity has much to do with the news-gathering system in Japan, called Press Club (*kaisha-kurabu*): news organizations send their reporters to the Press Clubs attached to government offices, law courts, political party centres and major economic and industry associations which allocate large rooms for use by the reporters in charge of covering those agencies for their companies. Feldman describes these clubs as the operation rooms where reporters "gather, confirm, organize and write all the news that emanate from a certain location," where they "receive briefings, handouts, press releases and other communications" and where they "interact with their information sources" (1993: 69) (see also Lee 1985: 62–73; De Lange 1998; Hayashi 2000: 154–6). The press clubs shape reporters' relationship with their information sources and determine to a great

The "Home and Family" section in these newspapers assumes a particular relevance for the purpose of my argument. Usually assigned two pages in the morning edition of each newspaper, this is the section that offers wider strata of the population an important space for critical debate (Hayashi 2000: 149). Among the articles usually included in the Home and Family section have been practical tips (recipes, fashion, child care, etc.), social issues concerning domestic life (with a focus on women, family and the home) and columns written by women readers (152). Hayashi argues that the function of this section has been to serve "as a pipeline to connect immediate daily problems in private life to the stage of social and political debate" (2000: 150). It was the Home and Family section that introduced Japanese readers to the struggle of the US-based Women's Liberation Movement in the early 1970s (whereas other sections of the newspapers completely ignored the issue) (152), and it is in this section that we encounter the most explicit discussions on women's changing conditions in postwar Japan, maternal filicide, child abandonment or abuse and women's alleged "loss of motherhood." The news items this chapter relies upon can thus be organized into two major groups. The first group consists of those articles that provide a rather factual description of an accident with limited overt expressions of judgement—although, as we shall see, editorial choices, the employment of a specific vocabulary and the spatial distribution of articles in a single page all offer important insights into the communicative strategies and aims of these news accounts. The second group includes editorials, opinion articles and other pieces from so-called experts, letters from the readers and so on that we mostly find in the Home and Family section of the *Asahi* and the *Yomiuri* and which provide a more articulated understanding of the extent to which maternal filicide had become a widely discussed social issue.

Whereas the overall temporal framework for the research pursued in *Translating Maternal Violence* is circumscribed to the first five years of the 1970s, during the research process for this chapter I found myself further limiting the retrieval of news items to the years 1970–1973. The

---

degree the nature of the information they may have access to, thus explaining the similarity of newspapers' media coverage.

reason for this decision was primarily "economic" as it allowed gathering a number of texts that remained manageable in the time and space available, the recognized significance of the year 1973 attesting to the validity of the choice made. The articles were retrieved through keyword search using two online databases: Kikuzo II Visual for the *Asahi shinbun* and Yomidasu Rekishikan for the *Yomiuri Shinbun*. Yomidasu Rekishikan allows access to only the Tokyo edition of the *Yomiuri shinbun* while Kikuzo II Visual contains the Tokyo and Osaka edition of the *Asahi shinbun*. For reasons of consistency I have opted to search articles printed only in the Tokyo edition of both newspapers.

The category of filicide is neither obvious nor transparent and this becomes a further source of complications when working in a foreign language.[34] For reasons of simplicity this book employs the word "filicide" rather loosely and on the basis of its etymological roots: the action of killing a son or a daughter (from Latin, *filius/filia* + *caedere*). My use of this term simply denotes the killing of a child aged less than 18 by a biological parent or parent substitute.[35] Therefore, during the keyword search I discounted those articles where the victim was over 18, where the culprit was not a parental figure and those that were later discovered to be simple accidents. In a few instances more than one article was available about a single case: on such occasions I resolved to count these items only once.

Given the broad connotations with which I used the term "filicide" I identified a wide set of keywords to cover a broad range of news items: *kogoroshi, akachan-goroshi, yōji-goroshi, nyūji-goroshi* (filicide, infanticide);

---

[34] For example, writing within the parameters set by American legal discourse, Lucy Jane Lang identifies "infanticide" as an umbrella term that includes the three subcategories of neonaticide (the killing of a child within the first 24 hours after its birth), filicide (the killing of a child older than one day) and abuse-related death (Lang 2005). However, the legal definition of "infanticide" in England and Wales (UK) describes the crime as the killing of a child younger than 12 months at the hands of his or her biological *mother* (Brookman and Nolan 2006), while filicide denotes more broadly child homicide by either parent.

[35] To set the bar at 18 years of age remains, admittedly, a rather arbitrary choice: not only the age of majority in Japan is 20, but the category of *kogoroshi* (literally child killing) is sometimes used to describe the killing of a son or daughter independently of their age, to the extent that the killing of a middle-aged disabled son by his senile father can be still categorized as "child killing." However, the occurrence of such cases in my data set was rather insignificant and this made setting the limit to 18 years of age seem a more useful approximation.

Table 1.1 Total number of articles per year

	1970	1971	1972	1973
Asahi shinbun	109	93	118	85
Yomiuri shinbun	99	58	70	91

eiji-goroshi (neonaticide); *eiji-shitai, akachan-shitai* (corpse of a baby) and *shinjū* (double suicide). A cursory reading of the material emerging from this initial search enabled the identification of other relevant terms that were eventually also included in the keyword search. Some of these are *noirōze* (neurosis), *sekkan* (discipline, punishment), *kodomo junan, akachan junan* (children suffering) and *bosei sōshitsu* (loss of motherhood). As I was assembling my archive, whenever I happened to come across an article on filicide which had not already been identified by the keyword search, I decided to include it as part of my data set. Table 1.1 shows the total number of news items per year that these sampling criteria enabled me to identify (the figures do not distinguish among news reports, editorials, commentaries, etc.).

The data set so compiled is not meant to be exhaustive of the totality of cases that occurred across Japan. Not only may some articles have gone easily undetected, but the fact that I considered only the Tokyo editions of the two newspapers under consideration means that geographical generalizations were not possible. I am also aware that the use of keyword search to compile a data set is also likely to exclude potentially useful news item and to engender the possibility that some narratives may go unnoticed. While I attempted to compensate such weakness of my data collection process by progressively widening the range of keywords in light of my findings, I also made a conscious decision to maintain a clear focus on maternal filicide in order to preserve the overall coherence of my research.

Ūman ribu

The textual material produced and circulated by *ribu* in the 1970s represents a rather diverse range of documents which were distributed in mimeographed copies during demonstrations, marches or teach-ins. Many of them were just one page long and hand-written, given away for free on the streets and tube stations; others were typed on coloured paper, organized in booklet form and often sold at conferences and summer camps in order to sponsor new activities or the writing and distribution of new pamphlets. As the movement grew stronger, so grew the number of what goes under the name of *minikomi* (mini-communications). This is an umbrella term that covers information sheets, newsletters, zines, informal magazines and journals that constituted the central nervous system of the movement: they functioned as a means to establish and maintain communication among *ribu* groups and to foster a sense of community, but they also represented an alternative to the *masukomi* (mass communications) where discussions of women's issues were infrequently given space. These *minikomi* materials were often accompanied by illustrations or, more rarely, photographs that added to the message conveyed by the written text and contributed to its affective impact.

It is unclear how much of this material has been lost over the years. In the last few decades, however, the desire on the part of some *ribu* activists to preserve the history of the movement and to make this documentation accessible to a wider audience has led to two major archival projects whose importance can hardly been overestimated. Until recently, the three volumes edited by Mizoguchi Akiyo, Saeki Yōko and Miki Sōko with the title *A History of the Japanese Women's Lib in Documents* (*Shiryō nihon ūman ribu shi*) constituted the main reference point for any researcher interested in the history of *ribu*. Published between 1992 and 1995, the volumes offer an invaluable compilation of materials organized in chronological order (vol.1, 1969–1972; vol.2, 1972–1975; vol.3, 1975–1982) and according to other organizational principles such as specific *ribu* groups, events and newsletters. During the process of compilation, hand-written pamphlets were typed up and printed for the first time. A critique that could be levied at this first archive is that some of the criteria on the basis of which the material was collected and chosen for publication remain unclear. In the preface to the first volume of the collection, for example, the editors simply state that

> [the documents] gathered here have been chosen from those which have casually come into our possession. They cannot be said to cover the totality

of the documents of *ribu*, and we hope that others will be able to supplement [them with new materials]. (Mizoguchi et al. 1992: 7)

This task has been recently accomplished, at least partially, by the Group for the Conservation of Documents of the Ribu Shinjuku Centre (*Ribu Shinjuku sentā shiryō hozon kai*) whose efforts have led to the publication between 2008 and 2009 of the Compilation of Documents of the Ribu Shinjuku Centre (*Ribu Shinjuku sentā shiryō shūsei*). The group was founded in 1983 by nine of the original members of the women-only collective Ribu Shinjuku Centre (a major organizing centre in the heyday of the movement), with the aim of recovering, cataloguing and preserving all the pamphlets, bills, newsletters and *minikomi* that the centre had collected during its five years of existence. The materials are organized in chronological order in three volumes: (1) pamphlets; (2) bills; (3) newsletters. This third and last volume is of particular significance as it reprints all 16 issues of the *minikomi Ribu News—This Way Only* (*Ribu nyūsu—Kono michi hitosuji*), the journal produced by the Ribu Shinjuku Centre. No attempt was made in any of these three volumes to type hand-written documents. In addition, each volume is introduced by a table that provides useful information such as date of publication, number of pages of each document reproduced, dimensions of the original and colour of the paper and the ink, thus giving an idea of the original sensuous materiality of the documents they reproduce. We encounter here a different set of problems, as an excessive and indiscriminate reliance upon this second archive to acquire a sense of the discourses produced by the movement in its totality risks foregrounding the perspectives of those groups active at the Ribu Shinjuku Centre to the detriment of others. Therefore, we may argue that the existence of two separate archives is congenial, as they may be said to complement each other and to downplay their respective weaknesses.

Takahashi Takako's Literature

The stories included in my analysis were all published in the first half of the 1970s. Four of them were published in Takahashi Takako's first collection of short stories *Kanata no mizuoto* (Yonder Sound of Water, 1971 [1978]). They are "Sōjikei" ("Congruent Figures"), "Byōbō" ("Boundlessness"), "Kodomosama" (literally "Honourable Child") and "Kanata no mizuoto" ("Yonder Sound of Water"). In addition to these, the stories "Keshin" ("Incarnation," 1972) and "Natsu no fuchi" ("Summer Abyss," 1973) are also considered. To be accurate, a few of these stories were originally published in the 1960s on the pages of various literary magazines. Yet, it was only in the early 1970s that they were republished in collections with wider market circulation. "Kodomosama," for example, first appeared in 1969 in the pages of the literary journal *Gunzō* and was later included in *Yonder Sound of Water*. A similar case can be made about the story "Incarnation" whose original publication in the magazine *Hakubyō* dates back to as early as 1965. The story was then reprinted in the collection *Hone no shiro* (Castle of Bones, 1972) that, although published almost one year after *Yonder Sound of Water*, contains stories that predate those in that first collection. Other examples of stories republished in *Castle of Bones* and that this chapter briefly touches upon are "Byakuya" ("White Night") and "Me" ("Eyes"), which first appeared in 1966 and 1967, respectively. Takahashi's collections surely had a wider distribution than the literary magazines that first introduced them to the public, and this, I believe, provides a strong rationale for conceiving of this second appearance as marking a renewed entry of these stories into the discursive arena that *Translating Maternal Violence* aims to investigate.

It is important to acknowledge that such a selection is somewhat arbitrary and is not meant to identify this period as an independent phase in the author's creative development. Rather, it primarily responds to a desire to maintain a sense of homogeneity with the temporal framework that informs my investigation. The fact remains, however, that these are the years when literary depictions of a troubled and troubling maternal figure appear in Takahashi's writing with disconcerting and suggestive persistence. These stories also participated in the literary climate of the period and echoed the broader changes in terms of style and content that characterized the emergence of a new generation of women writers in postwar Japan (I will expand on this in the introduction to Chap. 5). However, my choice of focusing upon a single writer ought not to be understood as suggesting Takahashi as representative of such revival of women's writing. In fact, mine has been, rather, a strategic choice that allowed for close readings of both her fictional and non-fictional works which, in turn, make it possible to discern a commonality of images and vocabulary between Takahashi's oeuvre and *ribu*'s discursive interventions.

There is no indication, however, that by the time these stories were made accessible to a wider audience Takahashi had been influenced by the increasing political, social or media concerns around filicidal mothers. Some of these stories were originally written before *ribu* developed a specific rhetoric around mothers who kill and this mitigates against speaking in terms of the movement's direct influence upon Takahashi's creative process. Furthermore, cases of filicide had already been reported by the media in the late 1960s and they were clearly not an unheard-of occurrence (Tama 2008). And yet, it is still striking that, even though there's no evidence to suggest Takahashi's conscious or programmatic attempt to intervene in the ongoing discursive construction of maternal filicide in late postwar Japan, all stories in her 1971 collection *Yonder Sound of Water* display a mesmerizing variety of representations of maternal animosity.

2

Filicide in the Media: News Coverage of Mothers Who Kill in 1970s Japan

In the early 1970s media coverage of mothers who killed their children saw such a dramatic increase in Japan that maternal filicide acquired, within media representations in particular, the dimension of a social phenomenon. As we shall see, lack of reliable statistics makes it difficult to determine whether this reflected an actual increase in the number of episodes of violence and abuse or, rather, the overrepresentation of such cases was merely the result of renewed interest in the phenomenon on the part of the media. What is indisputable, however, is the hypervisibility these episodes acquired in the public discourse of the time. Expressions such as "the era of the loss of motherhood" (*bosei sōshitsu jidai*) or "an era of children's suffering" (*akachan junan jidai*) made the headlines of many a newspaper and powerfully conveyed the sense of alarm that news reporting intended to solicit in its readership. This chapter offers an analysis of how mothers who killed their children came to be portrayed by two of the major Japanese newspapers, namely, the *Asahi shinbun* and the *Yomiuri shinbun*.[1] My purpose here is not so much to provide a factual account of the reality of maternal filicide in late postwar Japan, but to explore the discursive and narrative strategies by means of which filicide was represented as a social phenomenon of historic proportions. Here I identify and interrogate the bias that vitiated press coverage and analyse how news media depicted murderous mothers in ways that reinforced gender stereotypes and secured traditional ideas of maternal propriety. While I foreground the rhetorical and editorial choices made by news media as they dealt with the social trauma engendered by concrete manifestations of maternal violence, my analysis also brings into view the central role that news reporting played in the regulation of an understanding of maternal violence and the appearance of that violence within the public sphere. In particular, my identification of recurrent narratives of the "bad" or "mad" mother—so familiar to a Western audience—is here further complicated by a focus on the linguistic specificities of the two major categories under which cases of maternal filicide were represented: *kogoroshi* (literally child-killing) and *boshi shinjū* (commonly rendered as "mother–child suicide" and which constitutes a subcategory of the umbrella term *oyako shinjū*, parent–child suicide). As I will try to show, a translational approach enables us to expose the strategies of silencing and erasure that operated in the fabric of those very categories to contain or even efface the possibility of thinking maternal violence at the very moment when it

---

[1] Together with the *Mainichi shinbun*, the *Asahi* and the *Yomiuri* are often referred to as "the big three," and until the 1970s they represented the three major Japanese dailies: in 1961, at the time of the television boom in Japan, Edward P. Whittemore (1961: 1) claimed that 37 million newspapers were being sold in Japan each day and that of these the *Asahi*, the *Yomiuri* and the *Mainichi* accounted for 19 million newspapers distributed nationally (i.e. more than half the total number of newspapers published in the country). The figures provided 30 years later by Ofer Feldman (1993: 11) confirmed the continued primacy of the big three, with the *Yomiuri* selling 14.5 million copies, the *Asahi* 12.9 million and the *Mainichi* a more modest 6.3 million. More recently, Kaori Hayashi (2000: 148) identified the *Asahi* and the *Yomiuri* as "by far the two best-selling newspapers" in Japan, with the *Yomiuri* selling daily 10 million copies and the *Asahi* 8 million. Multiple factors such as the extraordinarily high circulation of newspapers in Japan, their capillary distribution at the national level (facilitated by Japan's relatively small surface area) and the nearly perfect literacy rate of the population partially explain the considerable influence of the news press on public opinion, and have historically made Japan "one of the most newspaper-conscious countries in the world" (Whittemore 1961: 1).

seemed to be most insistently spoken about.[2] It also alerts us to the risk that an unreflective recourse to translation may overlook the extent to which the cultural intelligibility (and visibility) of maternal violence can be variously negotiated on the level of the linguistic materiality of the categories employed. This, I contend, may further exacerbate the difficulties inherent to the work of intercultural communication, while also interfering with the possibility that similar moments of confrontation with "the Other" might indeed help us recognize the limits of our own conceptualizations.

Framing the Frame

Despite the myth of professional objectivity and journalists' recurrent claims of reporting transparent, factual accounts of actual occurrences, scholars have called attention to the role played by news media in the social construction of meaning and in the shaping of public knowledge of events, actors and places. A rich and partially overlapping vocabulary has been developed to account for and describe the media's variable control over the selection of what is covered and to explain the structuring power of news reporting.[3] To begin with, mass media performs what has been called an *agenda-setting* function, that is, the capacity to set the salience of a given issue and transfer that salience to the public—in other words, the capacity to influence what people think about (McCombs 2005). In this respect, negativity, that is, "natural or man-made violence, conflict,

---

[2] On a different note, the analysis I offer of Japanese news stories provides access to textual materials that have remained largely unexplored in Anglo-American scholarship in the fields of journalism, media studies and communication studies. As might be expected, a cursory review of scholarship in English on media representations of mothers who kill reveals its fundamental reliance on primary sources in the English language. This has inevitably translated into disproportionate attention being given to British, American or Australian news media to the detriment of sources in other languages. See, for example, Barnett (2005, 2006, 2007, 2013), Coward (1997), Douglas and Michaels (2004), Goc (2003, 2007, 2009, 2013). For an article on media representations of maternal filicide based on non-English sources, see Cavaglion (2008).

[3] A highly debated example of media's capacity to circumscribe the visual and narrative dimensions of what then counts as the knowable "reality" has come to the fore in recent years with the practice of "embedded reporting" where the selective power of the media operates in accordance with state directives on how war and conflict are to be reported. See Butler (2010), Tuosto (2008), Fahmy and Johnson (2007), Paul and Kim (2004).

disaster, or scandal," has been identified as a significant ingredient of what makes an event newsworthy, and has been deemed an important criterion for news selection (Graber quoted in Johnson-Cartee 2005: 126). How an event is narrated has also been recognized as central to the capacity of the media to shape our perception of reality. William Gamson and Andre Modigliani (1989) have coined the term *interpretative packages* to designate the set of symbols and narratives employed by the media in order to provide a privileged interpretative grid and guide the audience in making sense of a social phenomenon (Yamamoto 2012). The notion of *media framing* becomes pivotal here. To frame is to single out specific aspects of a news item and to give them salience. Tucker (1998: 143) describes it as "both a process and an effect in which a common stock of key words, phrases, images, sources, and themes highlights and promotes specific facts, interpretations and judgements." Frames "define problems [...] diagnose causes [...] make moral judgements [...] and suggest remedies" (Entman 1993: 3).[4]

The notion of framing has drawn attention to the process of selection and composition behind the construction of news items, and led scholars to think in terms of *narratives* (Johnson-Cartee 2005; Stephens 2005). In this regard, Barbara Barnett (2013: 2) has variously described journalism as a "story-telling platform" or "the art and practice of telling stories" (Barnett 2005: 13), emphasizing that it is how these stories are constructed that allows for organization and interpretation. News media usually construct frames that mirror cultural themes and narratives within society and which often rely upon well-known tropes and stereotypes (Goc 2008). *Stock stories* and *scripts* that are familiar to the public are used to provide news reports with coherence (Cavaglion 2008), but the retelling of known plots also has the inevitable effect of reinforcing conventional or "common-sense" understandings of news content. Conceptually close to the notion of stock story is the idea of *myth*, understood as a narrative structure that draws on the cultural imaginary shared by a given audience and which evokes interpretative grids that are familiar to the readers. Myths inform, but they

---

[4] For a rich discussion on media framing and its relation to the agenda-setting function of news reporting, see Scheufele and Tewskbury (2007) and the many articles in the special issue of the *Journal of Comnunication* (2007) 57(1).

also reinforce existing ideas, values and beliefs; they relay social norms, confirm them and make them effective. They may serve a comforting purpose "by telling tales that explain baffling or frightening phenomena and provide acceptable answers" (Bird and Dardenne quoted in Barnett 2006: 414; see also Lule 2001). The myth of Medea (what Goc called "the Medea frame") is one such narrative that Western culture frequently employs in news coverage of mothers who kill their children (Barnett 2006; Goc 2008). Stock stories revolving around the opposition between "good" and "bad" mothers (and those that further distinguish between the "bad" and the "mad") constitute another recurring organizational and explanatory device when cases of maternal filicide hit the news (Barnett 2006; Cavaglion 2008).

A considerable portion of news coverage is devoted to reports of deviant behaviours and their individual and social repercussions: these reports "inform[…] us about right and wrong, about the boundaries beyond which one should not venture and about the shapes that the devil can assume" (Cohen 2002: 8). And women who kill, Ann Jones (2009: 39) suggests in her now classic book on female violence, do indeed "test […] society's established boundaries," often becoming the object of obsessive mediatic attention. What shape do these boundaries take, then, when maternal filicide becomes news? It seems particularly useful here to recall an observation Barnett (2005: 24) makes in the context of her analysis of media coverage of the Andrea Yates murder case: "events become news when they shatter the fairy-tale notions we have about love, home and family." On these occasions, she continues, "news coverage has less to do with the rarity of the event of infanticide and more to do with the fact that the event shattered the image of the good mother" (ibid.). The traumatic effects of this shattering surface in the form of confusion, bewilderment and outrage that often characterize media portrayals of mothers who kill, and such affective dimension adds to the cognitive dimension of news reporting. In this respect, Belinda Morrissey (2003) and Lizzie Seal (2010) acknowledge the social trauma engendered by women (mothers, in our case) who kill and who, by doing so, contravene cultural assumptions of feminine (and maternal) propriety. Morrissey (2003: 2) further suggests that media discourses appear "as traumatized by the murders women commit as the society from which they emanate," and she describes the attempts to limit and contain the threat such women pose to the gender order as "desperate measures of discourses in crisis."

How are these attempts at containment carried out? What narratives and stock stories consolidate forms of containment that take root in the public sphere? And what are we to gain from running counter this containment function? We can start by observing that not only does news coverage of cases of maternal filicide draw on the sensational character of what it covers, but it also becomes the occasion to express society's indignation for the (highly gendered) transgression it portrays—indignation that, in turn, reconfirms cultural norms of maternal behaviour. In the process, dominant understandings of what it means to be a woman and a mother are secured and perpetuated. At this most basic level we can already see how news reporting becomes, therefore, instrumental to the regulation and the preservation of gender norms. On a more subtle level, Judith Butler's meditation on framing helps us better appreciate some of the mechanisms whereby the structuring of the visual and discursive field by the media "selectively produc[es] and enforc[es] what counts as reality" (2010: xiii). The selective and regulative power of the media, she argues, participates in a strategy of containment that requires relegating something out of the frame. That which is left out is expunged into a domain of unreality and comes to constitute the frame's ghostly remainder, its constitutive outside, as it were, which is necessary to secure the frame's internal coherence and intelligibility.

Butler's reflections are primarily concerned with media representations of war, but her discussion is equally useful to understand the differential treatment of maternal violence in news reporting of maternal filicide: the frames, narratives and language employed in the portrayal of such cases are indeed consequential in regulating the conditions of appearance of a maternal potential for violence in public discourse and in delimiting the extent to which maternal violence acquires intelligibility within given interpretative grids. And yet, Butler also reminds us that "framing cannot always contain what it seeks to make visible and readable" (ibid.) because the circulability of existing images (here broadly understood as modes of representation) can break free from their original context and "expose [them] to new animating conditions" (xiv). This is the case, as we shall see in the following chapters, of *ribu*'s rhetorical investment in the figure of "the woman who kills her child" (*kogoroshi no onna*) but also of Takahashi's mesmerizing portrayals of maternal murderous desires. But whereas the circulation of alternative images (or the recirculation of existing images in alternative contexts) may rally resistance, expanding the limits of what is visible and sayable, it might also become complicit with forms of erasure and silencing. We shall be confronted with an example of such unintended complicity as we move to consider how *ribu* missed the opportunity to engage with the maternal potential for violence that, although inscribed in episodes of mother–child double-suicide, seemed to remain unrecognized.

To sum up, a general discussion on framing and the reliance of the mass media upon stock stories and familiar narratives alerts us to how news coverage operated in Japan through a differential and selective portrayal of mothers who killed their children whereby the categories of *kogoroshi* (filicide) and *oyako shinjū* (parent–child suicide) constituted privileged modes of representation that gave maternal filicide intelligible form in public discourse—modes of representation that regulated the extent to which maternal violence became recognizable and available for explanation. On the other hand, Butler's distinct take on the subject of framing demands that we pay attention to what absences and erasures structure the field of intelligible representation. "As a result," Butler observes, "we cannot understand the field of representability simply by examining its explicit contents, since it is constituted fundamentally by what is […] maintained outside the frame within which representations appear" (Butler 2010: 73). This constitutive outside thus functions as "the non-thematized background of what is represented and [is] thus part of its absent organizing features" (ibid.). Furthermore, if language is not a transparent medium, it does not simply portray or comment on episodes of maternal filicide. Rather, the linguistic materiality of the categories employed to represent them becomes instrumental in conferring (or denying) cultural intelligibility to that violence. If this is the case, what will appear to be the linguistic erasure of a maternal potential for violence can equally contribute to that domain of unreality and unthinkability that Butler writes about and which provides familiar narratives with coherence. It seems to me that a translational approach to the categories employed in media coverage of cases of maternal filicide helps foregrounding such forms of silencing. It exposes the conditions of appearance of a maternal potential for violence in the public sphere, a public sphere that is constituted in part by what cannot be said and what cannot be shown (Butler 2010). Therefore, in the following pages I will direct my attention not only to those media accounts that attempted to confront and make sense of the challenges that filicide posed to a community's values and beliefs (the explicit content of media coverage), but to the schemas of intelligibility that made maternal violence recognizable in the first place, establishing its admissibility into the domain of representability only at given conditions. Framing the frame, as it were, offers thus the "opportunity to examine underlying systems of coherence and sense-making" (Nakagawa 1993: 146) that foreclosed the possibility of thinking of maternal violence as a human, albeit tragic, potential.

Kogoroshi, oyako shinjū and *boshi shinjū*

The linguistic materiality of the categories employed by media reports to comment on cases of maternal filicide was crucial in establishing schemas of intelligibility that determined the conditions of appearance and modes of recognition of a maternal potential for violence within public discourse. In particular, the categories of *kogoroshi* (filicide, infanticide) and *oyako shinjū* (parent–child suicide) constituted the organizing centres of strikingly different narratives that were consequential in engendering more or less sympathetic social reactions to the crimes reported by the media. A reflection on the linguistic and cultural dimensions that characterize these two categories enables us to ask whether the hypervisibility of maternal filicide in the Japanese media did in fact translate into a greater cultural intelligibility of motherhood's violent potential. And it makes us question whether the greater understanding with which parent–child suicides (and mother–child suicides in particular) appeared to be received among the Japanese population also implies that the violence inscribed in such practice had acquired a greater degree of social acceptability.

In Japanese, the two words *kogoroshi* (子殺し) and *oyako shinjū* (親子心中) are linguistically and conceptually distinct and this difference allowed a systematic and differential treatment of maternal violence where these categories where employed. By which I mean that the killing of a child (together with the parent—mostly the mother—who committed it) was perceived in starkly different ways depending on which category it was assigned to. *Kogoroshi* directly conveyed the idea of killing a child, *ko* (子) meaning "child" and *-goroshi* (殺し) being the noun form of the verb *korosu* (殺す), to kill. The Chinese character (*kanji*) in *korosu* (殺) is the same we find in words such as *jisatsu* (自殺) (suicide, literally killing oneself), *satsugai* (殺害) (murder) or *satsujin* (殺人) (homicide).[5] It can be argued, therefore, that the Japanese word *kogoroshi* carried in its linguistic materiality the semantic traces of an unambiguous violence.[6] As we shall see at a later point in this chapter, the narrative trajectory of that unmistakable violence within media accounts further established its conditions of appearance and informed a privileged schema of intelligibility.

On the other hand, the relation of *oyako shinjū* with violence emerges (or rather fails to emerge) in a different way. As an umbrella term *oyako shinjū* designates a parent–child suicide independently of the gender of the parent, but it can also be variously referred to as *boshi shinjū* (mother–child suicide), *fushi shinjū* (father–child suicide), and *ikka shinjū* (whole-family suicide), where the second term *shinjū* denotes a double-suicide committed out of love. The double-suicidal pact between lovers (*shinjū*) was a form of suicidal behaviour that gained increasing social acceptability and prominence in Japan in the Tokugawa period

---

[5] Chinese characters or *kanji* have an intrinsic meaning or range of meanings and more than one pronunciation according to context and position. In this case we can see that the character 殺 has at least two pronunciations: "*koro*" (as in the verb 殺す *korosu*) and "*satsu*" (as in the words *jisatsu* 自殺 or *satsujin* 殺人).

[6] There are other words in Japanese that may function as synonyms of *kogoroshi*: *akachan-goroshi* (赤ちゃん殺し *akachan* = baby), *yōji-goroshi* (幼児殺し *yōji* = infant), *eiji-goroshi* (嬰児殺し *eiji* = infant, newborn baby) and *eijisatsu* (嬰児殺 neonaticide). I want to contend that, because they emerge in combination with either the noun *-goroshi* or, more broadly, the Chinese character meaning to kill (as in the case of *eijisatsu*), my argument about the explicit articulation of violence that characterizes the term *kogoroshi* could be extended to these other linguistic examples without undergoing significant alterations. As a matter of fact, *kogoroshi* in my discussion is almost representative for such broad group of terms that buy into the same semantic field of violence and killing.

(1600–1867) and was immortalized in the plays of seventeenth-century dramatist Chikamatsu Monzaemon (1653–1725).[7] Traditionally, *shinjū* was understood to be the dramatic expression of an unresolvable tension between *giri* (obligation, duty) and *ninjō* (emotions). The notion of *giri* was rooted in Confucian values of self-restraint and constituted a central norm of behaviour for the samurai class, whereas *ninjō* represented a value system that found its highest expression in literature and theatre and which proclaimed the right to love and passion of the rising merchant class. Respectively, *giri* and *ninjō* represented the demand of social order and the emotional drive of the individual: sometimes in conflict, sometimes in a relation of complementarity, these values existed side by side and satisfied different needs. The conflict between *giri* and *ninjō* often found a dramatic resolution in the double-suicidal pact between lovers. Inspired by real events, plays about lovers' double-suicides (*shinjū-mono*) usually portrayed the couple's love as so strong that, when faced with the social impossibility to live it fully, the two lovers opted out of this existence in the belief that they would be finally reunited in their next life. It was not death that they chose, but love that led to death (Kato 1983; Heine 1994).

If we move away for a moment from the 'historical semantics of the word' (Said 2005: 17) and break up the expression *oyako shinjū* (親子心中) in its constitutive characters, we can observe that its two sets of characters literally mean "parent–child" (親子) and "centre-of-the-heart" (心中), and they appear, thus, to foreground the emotional bond between the persons involved at the same time as they sidestep any reference to the idea of "homicide" (Bryant 1990).[8] Anthropologist Roger Goodman (2002: 138) seems to concur with this reading when he observes that "[n]either in Japanese—nor in English translation—is the word 'murder' ever

---

[7] *Sonezaki shinjū* (Love suicides at Sonezaki) and, most notably, his masterpiece *Shinjū ten no amijima* (Love suicides at Amijima) constitute two of the most famous literary and theatrical examples.

[8] News media sometimes employ the expression *muri shinjū* (literally "forced double-suicide"). However, the use of the word *muri* (forcible, forced) seems to be left to the discretion of the single journalist and its occurrence in my data set remains irregular.

used in what is, in practical terms, the murder of the child by the parent followed by the parent's suicide." From a different angle it also seems significant that, even though *oyako shinjū* is usually rendered in English translation as "parent–child double-suicide" or simply "parent–child suicide," the Japanese original does *not* employ the word for "suicide" at all (*jisatsu* 自殺) that, as we have seen, contains the character meaning "to kill."

Sociologist Yuko Kawanishi (1990: 42) suggested that Western countries may lack the appropriate terminology to identify the phenomenon of parent–child suicide and observed that Western media rarely report murder-suicides. But let us notice here the slide of meaning that Kawanishi (writing in English) inadvertently performs as she moves from the category of "parent–child suicide" to that of "murder-suicide," where an implicit process of cultural translation has the effect of bringing to the surface of the target language the violence inscribed in the deed by means of its unambiguous qualification as "murder" (and only then as "suicide") (Takahashi and Berger 1996). By doing so, the "density of accumulated meaning" (Venuti 1986: 182) that we have begun to recognize in the expression *oyako shinjū* is lost. Of course, this is not to suggest that the practice of parent–child suicide is unknown outside Japan, but to foreground the extent to which the linguistic materiality of the categories employed may indeed have important consequences for how we conceptualize the violent nature of the event in question.[9] On the other hand, a keyword search with the word *shinjū* instantly reveals that this category has widespread circulation in the language of Japanese news media (Table 2.1).[10]

---

[9] My argument ought not to be understood as a way to celebrate the untranslatability of the source language compared to the target language. In fact, the same density of accumulated meaning that we find in words like *shinjū* is likely to mark those expressions in the target language (such as "double-suicide" or "murder-suicide") that are variously employed to translate it. This is what Venuti (1986: 182) describes as "a simultaneous excess of target-language meaning and a loss of source-language meaning, both of which the translator tries to limit by choosing to communicate a specific signified to the exclusion of others." This exposes the ethical responsibility of the translator and his/her linguistic choices, and the importance that his/her intentions remain *visible* throughout the translating process (see also Venuti 1995).

[10] Table 2.1 shows the number of news items per year that employed the category *shinjū* in their headlines (the figures do not yet distinguish between parent–child suicides and suicide pacts between actual lovers).

Table 2.1 Occurrence of the word *shinjū* in the *Asahi shinbun* and *Yomiuri shinbun*

	1970	1971	1972	1973
Asahi shinbun	89	79	71	85
Yomiuri shinbun	100	52	62	77

Goodman tells us that, according to surveys of *oyako shinjū*, 70–80 per cent of those cases appear to be *boshi shinjū*, that is, mother–child suicides (2002: 138). The high recurrence of mother–child suicides in Japan, Kawanishi (1990) suggests, testifies to a mother's profound identification with her child to the extent that she considers it part of her "self." Bryant (1990: 5) also calls attention to the fact that, whereas the practice of *boshi shinjū* may involve two events (i.e. the killing of the child by the mother and the mother's suicide),

> it is conceptualized as one act in which the identity of the child as a victim is collapsed into the identity of the parent as a victim. Conceptually, there has been one death; parent and child are one and the same victim of tragic circumstances. The child is not seen to be victimized *in turn* by his/her victimized [mother]. Only in the case of infanticide[11] is the child seen to be victimized by his/her [mother]. (emphasis in the original)

We have seen that, albeit considered tragic occurrences, mother–child suicides are met with a considerable degree of understanding in Japanese society. Several reasons are often adduced to explain this phenomenon: the absence of a religious tradition that considers suicide a sin (Yamamura 1986: 34); the importance that Buddhism places upon the idea of reincarnation, the promise of a better life in the next life and the overcoming of ego boundaries in order to experience oneness with all of existence (Kawanishi 1990); the priority Japanese society gives to interdependence among people as opposed to individual autonomy (Doi 1981; Lebra 1976); the idealization of the maternal role that obliquely compensates a woman's relatively low social status and which easily induces a mother's overinvestment in a child as the source of her identity (Kawanishi 1990).

---

[11] Bryant does not provide in this instance the Japanese original for "infanticide," but to the extent that her use of the term is consistent throughout her article, here she is clearly referring to *kogoroshi* and to the explicit murderous violence the term conveys.

The cultural idealization of the mother–child relationship emerges in expressions such as *ittaikan* (feeling of oneness) or *isshin dōtai* (literally one heart, same body) that are variously used to emphasize the strength of that relationship, but also to foreground the sense of fusion between the individuals involved and their reciprocal emotional attachment (Tanhan 2014; Lebra 1976). In light of such idealized interdependence a mother's killing of her own child is explained (culturally and psychologically) as a form of "extended suicide" where killing the child is equivalent for the mother to killing herself (Takahashi and Berger 1996: 253).

Furthermore, Japanese studies scholars are all too familiar with the existence in Japan of "a heroic, romantic, aesthetic, and moral aura [that] surrounds death in general, and voluntary death in particular" (Lebra 1976: 190). Suicide has been recognized as a culturally established method of communication in Japanese culture: examples include the historical practice of *hara-kiri* or *seppuku* (ritual disembowelment) to protect one's honour (but sometimes also as a form of imposed penalty), the suicide missions of Kamikaze pilots as expression of patriotism, the romantic designation of mass suicides of soldiers and civilians during World War II through the image of "shattering jewels" (*gyokusai*) (Heine 1994; Di Marco 2013, 2016), a mother's suicide as a means to make amends in the eyes of society for her son's shortcomings or misbehaviours, but also as an instrument to force compliance to parental will through the engendering of guilty conscience (Kawanishi 1990). To this "cultural investment in death" (Lebra 1976: 190) we need to add the fact that, as we shall see in Chap. 4, the high value bestowed upon the biological tie between mother and child explains the small number of daycare facilities and institutions for orphans, the deep-rooted stigma attached to adoption and the fact that an adoptive status may constitute a considerable obstacle for a person's participation in social life (Kawanishi 1990; Bryant 1991). In light of these considerations it seems fair to say that a mother's choice of leaving her child behind may generally be perceived as a demonstration of her *not* being a good mother.

In order to highlight the impact that the category of *boshi shinjū* had in the way maternal filicide was portrayed by news media, Table 2.2 shows the total number of *oyako shinjū* (parent–child suicides) within the data set and further distinguishes between those that were officially recognized as being committed by the mother alone (*boshi shinjū*) as opposed to

Table 2.2 Mother–child suicides and parent–child suicides committed by someone other than the mother alone

	1970		1971		1972		1973	
	Total		Total		Total		Total	
Asahi shinbun	58		49		52		40	
	Mother	Other	Mother	Other	Mother	Other	Mother	Other
	39	19	31	18	34	18	24	16
	Total		Total		Total		Total	
Yomiuri shinbun	46		28		36		32	
	Mother	Other	Mother	Other	Mother	Other	Mother	Other
	35	11	13	15	24	12	20	12

those that either were committed by the father or saw the complicity of both parents or else where the culprit was not openly identified.

Table 2.2 suggests that the category of mother–child suicide was deeply engrained in the Japanese cultural imaginary or, at least, in the way this imaginary was reflected in news narratives. Yet it seems to me that, although the notion of *boshi shinjū* conferred a degree of cultural intelligibility to mother–child suicides, it also engendered a series of possible contradictions when it came to providing discursive representations of a mother's potential for violence and murderous intent. This issue will be further unpacked in my analysis of the narrative strategies in which the category *boshi shinjū* was employed. By now, however, we can already appreciate the extent to which the use of this category made it possible to subsume a mother's killing of her child and her own suicide under the romanticized notion of a double-suicide committed out of love despite the fact that the child could hardly be described as consenting to his or her own death. This rhetorical move collapsed the identity of the child with that of the mother and erased, as it were, the child's status as a victim in his/her own right. By foregrounding the emotional bond between mother and child and sidestepping any overt reference to the violence the mother perpetrated against her child, the category of *boshi shinjū* actively hindered the intelligible articulation of a maternal potential for violence. In other words, maternal violence was effaced under the dramatic expression of (maternal) love that emerged "at the centre of the heart" (*shinjū*). It does not seem a coincidence that it was under these conditions of erasure—where both a mother's violence and the child-as-victim disappeared—that maternal filicide acquired a considerable degree of social acceptability and understanding.

Filicide in the Media

In what follows I offer a qualitative textual analysis of media representations of maternal filicide in early 1970s Japan. Although the nature of my data set does not allow for broad generalizations about the incidence of maternal filicide vis-à-vis paternal filicide, it is possible to observe that mothers who killed or were complicit in the killing of their children occupy centre stage in the total number of cases portrayed in the news and this suggests a high degree of visibility of such cases in the public eye. Certainly, the number of cases in which fathers were involved in the killing of their children can hardly be ignored, but this stands in stark contrast to the biased intensity with which filicidal mothers became the object of scorching social critiques whereas paternal responsibility was only rarely acknowledged.[12] The analysis of my data set is organized in two parts. I first build on the work of sociologist Tama Yasuko (2008) to investigate the textual, rhetorical and narrative *amplification strategies* by means of which Japanese newspapers portrayed filicide as an alarming social phenomenon.[13] The

---

[12] A considerable number of news items in my data set offer only short, bare accounts of the circumstances surrounding the accidents and simply provide concise answers to the five Ws of news reporting: Who? What? When? Where? Why? Because of their factual nature these articles do not offer major insights into the social perception of mothers who kill their children. They, however, provide important information about the visibility of this kind of occurrences and about the identity of the culprit: in 70 per cent of the total number of cases the mother was singled out as the culprit, whereas in 23 per cent of cases the father was, while another 5 per cent of news items identified or suggested the complicity of both parents.

[13] These amplification strategies were originally identified in Tama's (2008) study of media coverage of filicide in 1973 in Japan (originally published in 2001 with the title *Boseiai to iu seido—kogoroshi to chūzetsu no poritikusu* [The Institution of Maternal Love: The Politics of Infanticide and Abortion]). Here I draw on her insights and apply them to a data set that is both broader (in terms of years covered) and different in nature from the one she relied upon, but which seems to equally confirm her findings. Tama's data set included articles published in 1973 in the *Asahi shinbun* and *Mainichi shinbun* and comprised news items on *both* filicide and child abandonment. This enabled her to elaborate on the changing conceptions of motherhood, parent–child relationship and family. My data set remains, on the other hand, primarily focused on media coverage of cases of filicide.

second part of my investigation explores how mothers who killed their children came to be represented in the news media as either "bad" or "mad." While such narratives are well-known to Western audiences, the role that categories like *kogoroshi* and *boshi shinjū* played as major organizing principles and guarantors of these narratives' internal coherence further complicated their rhetorical impact and contributed to their capacity to regulate the conditions of appearance of a maternal potential for violence in public discourse.

Media representation of maternal murderous violence as a widespread and disturbing social phenomenon seems to indicate that filicide was high in the news agenda of those years. But while such intense media coverage testifies to an increasing public concern for and visibility of parents who killed their children, we should not necessarily take this as symptomatic of an actual increase in the number of parents committing such crimes. In fact, there are no accurate figures available that allow us to ascertain the possibility of such increase: the official statistics released by the police recognized the killing of a child below one year of age as a distinct category (*eijisatsu*, infanticide), but they recorded all other cases of filicide and mother–child suicide under the generic category of "murder" (*satsujin*) (Sasaki 1980: 60–1).[14] Therefore, it could be argued with Tama (2008: 65) that there is no reliable data on the occurrence of filicide on a national scale. In this respect, the importance of media representations of filicide becomes all the more significant once we observe that, in order to compensate for this shortage of reliable statistics, a great number of sociological studies have relied on media coverage to develop an estimate of the actual occurrence of these crimes. However, even if we ignore the geographical limitations that are likely to characterize the material these studies relied upon, the problem remains that media portrayals were usually taken at face value and not subjected to adequate reflection about their nature or content (66).

---

[14] The classification of cases of *boshi shinjū* under the category of "murder" within official criminal statistics suggests yet another way in which maternal violence might have been apprehended differently in a different discursive site, and would certainly add an interesting layer to the narrative I provide in *Translating Maternal Violence*.

Temporal and Geographical Amplification

News media employed a range of strategies that functioned rather unambiguously as amplification devices in the construction of filicide as a phenomenon of frightening proportions. A first set of strategies that had the rhetorical effect of amplifying the perceived magnitude of the phenomenon was the inclusion in the headlines of specific words that highlighted the *repetitive nature* of such accidents. A single case was, thus, linked to previous ones conjuring the idea of a sequence or chain of filicides that was imagined to unfold across time and space. Let us take a look at an indicative range of headlines that employ this rhetoric strategy:

> Even in Aomori (*Aomori de mo*) 3 persons [involved] in a mother–child suicide.[15]
>
> Also in Gunma (*Gunma de mo*), a mother–child suicide.[16]
>
> Once again (*mata*), [child] disciplined with death. Stepmother arrested.[17]
>
> Infanticide again (*mata akachan-goroshi*). Man fled by his wife.[18]
>
> Once again, a cruel mother (*mata , hidoi hahaoya*). She strangled the child to death.[19]
>
> Three people on the Yokohama line too (*Yokohamasen de mo*). It's neurosis. Mother dies and takes the children with her.[20]
>
> Once again (*mata*), mother kills two infants.[21]
>
> Also in Hokkaido (*Hokkaido de mo*) mother [dies and] takes her children with her.[22]
>
> Why? Child-murders happen one after another (*aitsugu*).[23]

---

[15] "Aomori de mo boshi sannin shinjū." *Yomiuri shinbun*, 15 May, 1970, p. 15. Morning ed.
[16] "Gunma de mo boshi shinjū." *Asahi shinbun*, 5 June, 1970, p. 11. Evening ed.
[17] "Mata shi no sekkan." *Asahi shinbun*, 13 September, 1970, p. 22. Morning ed.
[18] "Mata akachan-goroshi." *Yomiuri shinbun*, 28 September, 1970, p. 14. Morning ed.
[19] "Mata, hidoi hahaoya." *Yomiuri shinbun*, 17 November, 1970, p. 13. Morning ed.
[20] "Yokohamasen de mo sanninn. Noirōze. Haha ga michizure." *Asahi shinbun*, 17 November, 1970, p. 22. Morning ed.
[21] "Mata haha ga niji wo korosu." *Asahi shinbun*, 11 February, 1971, p. 18. Morning ed.
[22] "Hokkaidō de mo ko-michizure." *Asahi shinbun*, 5 April, 1971, p. 22. Morning ed.
[23] "Naze? Kodomo-goroshi aitsugu." *Asahi shinbun*, 4 August, 1972, p. 11. Evening ed.

An unmarried mother once again (*mata*) a murder.[24]

Once again (*mata*) a brutal filicide. She hated taking care of her own child. A deranged mother.[25]

Once more (*mata*), a *shinjū* in Irōzaki. Mother and two children.[26]

The headlines listed above clearly show how the recurrent use of words such as *mata* (again; once again), *de mo* (also in; even in; in…too) and *aitsugu* (to happen one after another; to occur in succession) constituted a stylistic device frequently employed by journalists to convey a sense of urgency at the apparent proliferation of cases of filicide.

In order to elicit an alarmed affective response these rhetorical choices were often combined with the synthetic, high-impact listing of recent cases: these enumerations grouped together a disparate range of accidents glossing over their specific backgrounds and circumstances. As the following extracts make plain, the likely effect was a heightened focus on the seeming spreading of parental violence and a parallel erasure of the structural causes that might have led to that violence.

On December 20, in the city of Sakura (Chiba prefecture) two little brothers were strangled to death by their mother. "The husband had run away," "the child cried too much," "had wet himself," "did not study," "wouldn't stop playing wrestling"…This year episodes of filicide have occurred one after another (*aitsuida*) with, indeed, numerous and simple explanations. There was even the case of a newborn baby who was buried on the riverbank with only his head out of the ground (August, Ishikawa). 1970, with its enthusiasm over its unprecedented bonus of three trillions yen, appears to be, however, also a dark year of filicides.[27]

The demonic couple who gave almost nothing to eat to their four-year-old child and caused him to die of exhaustion allegedly because he wouldn't listen to them (Kawasaki, Kanagawa prefecture) and the father who strangled to

---

[24] "Mikon no haha mata satsujin." *Asahi shinbun*, 23 October, 1972, p. 23. Morning ed.
[25] "Mata mugoi waga-kogoroshi. Mendō miru iya. Sakuran no haha." *Yomiuri shinbun*, 26 February, 1973, p. 10. Evening ed.
[26] "Mata 'Irōzaki shinjū'. Boshi sannin." *Yomiuri shinbun*, 16, October, 1973, p. 11. Evening ed.
[27] "Wagako no inochi naze ubau." *Asahi shinbun*, 21 December, 1970, p. 18. Morning ed.

death his sixth child out of concern for the [family's] living conditions (Iwaki, Fukuoka prefecture) were both arrested on [April] 12. The day before, in Matsudo (Chiba prefecture) there had just been the case of a young stepmother who had punished and killed her daughter for wetting herself. Even the police officers in charge with the investigations rack their brains with a gloomy expression at the abnormal psychology of these parents who day after day have committed episodes of a cruelty inconceivable to our common-sense.[28]

In the examples above we can observe once again how cases that had occurred in different geographical locations were purposefully placed in connection with each other with a move that stressed the "common nature" of their violence or their shared tragic outcome (i.e. the death of a child). This was done to the detriment of a sustained consideration of the structural features that might have provided a better understanding of the phenomenon. Each of the quoted passages also presents temporal markers similar to those that I have already identified as a stylistic feature of many headlines, and which conveyed a sense of alarming repetition through time: "filicides have occurred one after another," "day after day…" Sometimes, the dry enumeration of accidents could even become the driving force for a major portion of an article such as in the quotation below:

> Filicide. Even if we put together only the major recent cases…• She detested his mental retardation and gave him nothing but bread and water (Kashiwa, Chiba prefecture, 30 July) • Mother hurled her three-year-old only daughter into the air [because] "she had spitted out drinking water" (Shibuya ward, Tokyo, 3 September) • A father in Matsudo: "The crying was annoying" (20 March) • Punishes her daughter before her entry in preschool: she was fretful when it came to studying (Sakai, Osaka prefecture, 8 September) • Stepmother [kills] two-year-old son [because] "he wet himself" (Atsugi, Kanagawa prefecture, 10 September) • Throws from a train window baby daughter to whom she had given birth in a cinema (Shirakawa, Fukuoka prefecture, 4 September) • Man who married into his wife's family and was told that "he had poor earnings" got drunk, hurled his child across the room and hit him against wardrobe and pillar (Gifu prefecture, 20 September) • Left in the closet for eighteen hours [because] "he cried too much," (Higashimurayama, Tokyo) • Father batters daughter (aged one) in drunken frenzy [because] "she had spilled some

---

[28] "Kore de mo oya ka." *Yomiuri shinbun*, 13 March, 1971, p. 15. Morning ed.

miso soup" (Matsudo, 7 November) • [Mother] ties son at his second year of elementary school to a tree [because] "he wouldn't stop playing wrestling" (Mito, 11 November) • Crawls under the electric *kotatsu*[29] and dies of suffocation while the hostess-mother was on a date (Ikebukuro, Tokyo, 19 November).[30]

The passage above occupies the first half of an article aiming to investigate the possible reasons behind the frequent occurrence of filicide. Whereas the second half of the text outlines (in just a few sentences) the opinion of experts and social critics, the entire first half consists of a catalogue of cases complete with bullet points, places and dates. This has the rhetorical effect of exposing the pressing nature of an issue that is understood to haunt Japanese society, and which demands to be urgently addressed.

Spatial Disposition of News Items

The temporal or geographical amplification of filicide was not limited to headlines or introductory paragraphs, but was also brought about through the organization of articles in the space of a single page. In this respect, the various amplification strategies that we have so far identified ought not to be conceived as operating in a text in singular fashion and to the exclusion of all others. Quite to the contrary, it was often the case that the sense of urgency related to cases of filicide and the worrying proportions this crime was believed to have assumed were conjured up through a combination of different rhetorical modes and stylistic choices. Emblematic is the case of feature articles (*tokushū kiji*) where strategies of amplification are interspersed among lead paragraphs and the headlines of the various news items that the articles group together. The magnifying process by means of which filicide assumed the appearance of a pandemic is here further intensified by the reciprocal reverberation of similar articles published on the same page. Let us take a look at just a few examples. The first feature article I want to consider was published in the *Asahi shinbun* on April 5, 1971, and included three news articles under

---

[29] A *kotatsu* is a knee-high table with an electric foot-warmer installed inside on the top board, which is used with a hanging quilt during winter to retain heat.
[30] "Katei no naka mo ningen fuzai." *Asahi shinbun*, 21 December, 1970, p. 18. Morning ed.

the single headline "Sunday...*Shinjū* and suicides one after another" (*Nichiyō...Shinjū ya jisatsu aitsugu*).³¹ Following this headline, the lead paragraph runs as follows:

> Sunday 4 [April], a wave of four suicide cases occurred in Hokkaido, Kawasaki, in the Adachi ward in Tokyo and in the city of Minamiashigara (Kanagawa prefecture). Six people died. A mother planned to commit suicide and to take her three children with her to follow her husband [in death]; a young manager of a company killed his wife and two children and threw himself in front of a train; a mother suffering from a nervous breakdown induced by child-rearing [*ikuji-noirōze*] covered herself in petroleum and set herself on fire; a middle-aged man driven to a deranged state by the impossibility to work and by marital discord attempted to kill himself through disembowelment [*kappuku jisatsu*]. However unspeakable the circumstances might be, killing oneself together with others is not the only way!³²

We can immediately recognize some of the amplification strategies that we have already encountered in previous examples such as the use in the main headline of the verb *aitsugu* (to happen one after another) and the listing of several cases. The four accidents are grouped together under the umbrella notion of suicide, expressed in the headline by the words *shinjū* (double-suicide) and *jisatsu* (suicide). A closer reading of the single news items reveals that all cases apart from one involve a parent's suicide and the concomitant killing of one or more children (and, in one case, also of the spouse). The various episodes are identified by the following sub-headlines:

> [Man] kills his wife and child and throws himself [in front of a train].³³
>
> Also in Hokkaido, [mother] kills herself and her children (*ko-michizure*).³⁴
>
> Mother kills her child and attempts suicide (*jisatsu*).³⁵
>
> Suicide by disembowelment in Adachi.³⁶

---

³¹ "Nichiyō...Shinjū ya jisatsu aitsugu." *Asahi shinbun*, 5 April, 1971, p. 22. Morning ed.
³² Ibid.
³³ "Saishi-goroshi tobikomu." Ibid.
³⁴ "Hokkaidō de mo ko-michizure." Ibid.
³⁵ "Wagako koroshite / Haha, jisatsu hakaru." Ibid.
³⁶ "Adachi de kappuku hakaru." Ibid.

The headlines are reported here according to the ideal reading order of the articles on the newspaper page (right → left, top → bottom).[37] An interesting characteristic of the feature article under consideration is the fact that the narrative it conveys by gathering a variety of cases under the categories of *shinjū* and suicide spills over, as it were, onto other accidents that were not originally intended to be included in the feature article. More specifically, the last of the four items (the only case that does not involve children) is positioned in such a way as to lead the reader's eyes to two more short accounts, respectively, introduced by the headlines: "Gas poisoning. Child dies. A mother–child suicide?"[38] and "Two drowned children in Tokyo"[39] (this last article covering two cases). Here the three reported accidents (the possible mother–child suicide and the bodies of two small children discovered on separate occasions) are not explicitly included in the feature article, but they, nonetheless, constitute a coda to it: although only the first suggests the possibility that a mother might have killed her child, both of them convey the clear impression that children keep dying in tragic circumstances and thus preserve with a twist the sense of alarm already communicated by the news items included in the feature article.

A second example where the spatial disposition of news items in a feature article has the effect of amplifying the gravity of the phenomenon is an article that was published on September 6, 1973, in the *Asahi shinbun* and which grouped together three articles under the headline "Rushing towards death in the autumn rain."[40] This time the news items are not framed by a lead paragraph that groups together various accidents, but the narrative unfolds through the simple juxtaposition of articles which, once we discount the space devoted to advertisement, occupy most of the page. The articles are identified by the following headlines:

---

[37] Traditionally, Japanese characters are written in columns going from top to bottom and read from right to left. The spatial organization of news items on a newspaper page is devised according to this order.

[38] "Gasu chūdoku / Yōji shinu / Boshi shinjū ka." Ibid.

[39] "Tonai de yōji suishi futari." Ibid.

[40] "Akisame no naka ni shi ni isogu." *Asahi shinbun*, 6 September, 1973, p. 11. Evening ed.

Whole-family suicide [*ikka shinjū*] of an associate professor at Rikkyo University. [The parents] drowned themselves into a river together with their two children.[41]

Another family: it's business failure. They also killed their two children.[42]

Mother and two children. It's [death] by gas.[43]

The circumstances and motivations clearly differ from case to case, but the selection and disposition of the three news items in a broader feature article communicate a sense of shared tragedy. This tragedy is said to affect entire families, but it is the children's drama which constitutes the common thread running across the articles. The first two headlines place the emphasis on the fact that, while it was the parents who faced difficult situations (a scandal in the first case and the failure of the family business in the second), their final resolution to kill themselves cost the life of innocent victims (their children). The use of pictures here functions as an important device that heightens the sense of drama by exposing photographs of the families involved: a family portrait in the first article; four single portraits of mother, father and their two children in the second article. The third article is particularly interesting in this respect as it presents only the photographs of the two child victims of the mother–child suicide. In this case the choice of leaving the mother out and showing instead only the faces of the children may well have been compelled by the limited space available. Nonetheless, the final effect is, once again, an emphasis on the tragic loss of children's lives. If this were not enough, right under the three articles I have analysed so far appears a fourth one about a mother who beat her two-year-old son to the point of causing him fatal brain injuries. The article bears the headline "Mother punishes premature baby to death"[44] and ends with the following sentence: "Shigeru [the child's name] was a premature baby who had finally been able to crawl around." In this way this fourth and final news item brings to a climax the narrative structure encased in the feature article that precedes it, and conjures

---

[41] "Ritsudai jokyōju ikka ga shinjū / Niji wo michizure jusui." Ibid.
[42] "Jigyō shippai no ikka mo / Yahari niji michizure." Ibid.
[43] "Gasu de boshi sannin." Ibid.
[44] "Hahaoya, mijukuji ni shi no sekkan." Ibid.

up once again—this time *explicitly*—the innocence of budding life that had just started moving its first, uncertain steps in the world before it was dramatically and ruthlessly destroyed.

Abstractions

A last, important amplification strategy that I want to highlight here is the creation of a level of abstraction where different categories such as *shinjū*, suicide, infanticide, child abandonment and child abuse can be subsumed into broader categories that communicate a sense of alarm. Once again, headlines are the most immediate example of this rhetorical and narrative strategy:

> The social conditions of children's suffering (*akachan junan*). "Faulty mothers" with no regrets.[45]
>
> An era of children's suffering (*akachan junan jidai*).[46]
>
> Until when [will] children suffer (*akachan junan*)?[47]
>
> Children suffer (*akachan...junan*) again.[48]
>
> Once again children suffer (*akachan...junan*).[49]
>
> The hardships of children (*akachan gonan*).[50]
>
> The era of the loss of motherhood (*bosei sōshitsu jidai*).[51]
>
> The social circumstances of child abandonment and filicide (*kosute kogoroshi no sesō*).[52]
>
> Aaah! Children suffer (*akachan junan*)![53]

---

[45] "Akachan junan no sesō. Kōkai nai 'kekkan hahaoya.'" *Yomiuri shinbun*, 18 August, 1970, p. 13. Morning ed.
[46] "Akachan junan jidai." *Asahi shinbun*, 5 September, 1970, p. 17. Morning ed.
[47] "Akachan junan itsu made." *Asahi shinbun*, 19 September, 1970, p. 22. Morning ed.
[48] "Akachan mata junan." *Asahi shinbun*, 22 September, 1970, p. 11. Evening ed.
[49] "Akachan mata junan." *Yomiuri shinbun*, 11 October, 1970, p. 14. Morning ed.
[50] "Akachan gonan." *Asahi shinbun*, 8 February, 1971, p. 9. Evening ed.
[51] "Bosei sōshitsu jidai." *Yomiuri shinbun*, 22 October, 1972, p. 18. Morning ed.
[52] "Kosute kogoroshi no sesō." *Yomiuri shinbun*, 10 April, 1973, p. 7. Evening ed.
[53] "Aa akachan junan." *Yomiuri shinbun*, 13 July, 1973, p. 23. Morning ed.

Notions such as "the era of the loss of motherhood" and "the era of children's suffering" become, in the rhetoric of the news media, broad categories that allow the organization of a variety of articles under the same rubric: this occurs irrespective of whether or not the selected articles portray parents who kill their children. In these cases the spatial organization of news items on a single page makes it possible for the articles to enter in a relation of co-dependency and to contribute to the creation of unstated new meanings. In this respect, the category of "children's suffering" (*akachan junan*) emerges as a particularly powerful one. The level of abstraction exercised at a rhetorical level by this notion was originally identified by Tama (2008) in her study of media coverage of filicide in 1973, in which context she drew attention to a growing focus on children and childhood in news media. However, as shown by the numerous examples quoted above, this rhetorical strategy had already been in place, to a greater or lesser degree, in previous years. The use of such mechanisms of abstraction made it possible to connect cases of filicide (*kogoroshi*) and parent–child suicide (*oyako shinjū*) to episodes of child abandonment (*kosute, okisari*) or child abuse (*gyakutai*), thus contributing to the impression of a phenomenon of historical proportions that radically questioned images of parents as natural guardians and protectors of their children. The mutual reverberation of such a variety of crimes and accidents created a fertile environment for the emergence of social criticism mostly directed at mothers' alleged egoism and shortcomings.

This is a point to which I will return more extensively in the following section. As an introduction to such an important issue, however, I would like to spend some time on a set of articles that strike me as exemplary of this surreptitious emergence of biased portrayals of mothers. The articles in questions appeared in the *Yomiuri shinbun* on October 30, 1972, and even though they are not organized under a common headline, their distribution on the page is such to create the impression of a feature article, the presence of a lead paragraph confirming that impression. It could be argued, therefore, that the spatial organization of the news items on the page encourages the reader to "connect the dots," so to speak, and see the "bigger picture." The first article of the page (the one of the three to occupy the most space) sets the interpretative lens through which the entire set is likely to be read. The headline and sub-headlines run as follow: "Cold-hearted child-abandonment on the Tōmei Expressway./[The child was] tottering with a nursing bottle in her hands./'A hindrance to the love escape' of the mother."[54] The photograph of a little girl accompanies the text and forcefully conveys the idea of an innocent victim of an awful act. The feeding bottle that she holds in her hand and whose presence in the picture is also pointed at in the caption functions as a reminder of her young age, her necessary dependence on an adult (namely, the mother) and the absence of that adult.

The other two articles in the set report the cases of a mother–child suicide (*boshi shinjū*) and a (maternal) filicide, respectively, under the headlines "Three people [involved] in a *shinjū* at a dormitory for mothers and children"[55] and "[Child] is thrown [around] by his mother and dies."[56] Cutting the composition vertically in two ideal halves is the plea "Daddy! Mommy! Please, don't kill!" (*Papa, mama, korosanaide*) written with a font that clearly distinguishes it from both headlines and sub-headlines. The plea has the double function of separating the news items in two groups (the case of child abandonment on one side of the "divide" and the two accounts of *shinjū* and filicide on the other), while also operating as a rather dramatic introduction to the latter. Placed next to the photograph of the little girl and presented in quotation marks as if it were someone's direct speech, we have the impression that this is, indeed, the child's plea voiced on behalf of all children who are suffering.

The reference to the paternal figure may strike as odd here because none of the reported cases involved a father abandoning, abusing or killing a child. The puzzling mention to a parental figure that may not be explicitly the mother occurs on two more occasions in this set of articles: to begin with, the lead paragraph of the article on child abandonment begins with the sentence "On 29 [October] shocking accidents involving parents and their children (*oyako wo meguru jiken*) happened one after another (*aitsuida*)." Furthermore, at the very bottom of the article on the case of *boshi shinjū* a short paragraph reports the opinion of a professor at the Tokyo Metropolitan University. The paragraph is introduced by the

---

[54] "'Tōmei kōsoku' hijō kosute." *Yomiuri shinbun*, 30 October, 1972, p. 15. Morning ed.
[55] "Boshi-ryō de sannin shinjū." Ibid.
[56] "Haha ni nagerare shinu." Ibid.

small title "Let's rethink the parent–child [relationship]" which, it seems worth noticing, is placed right next to a photograph of the mother and children who committed suicide. It seems to me that what emerges from the spatial disposition of these articles and their rather contradictory rhetorical strategies is a kind of double discourse that, while calling attention to a social problem that is understood to affect both parents in equal measure, conveys the message that the maternal figure is the one who is really falling short of her parental duties. Here we can already begin to observe how, despite the public depiction of filicide as a widespread social phenomenon that saw both mothers and fathers take the life of their children with alarming frequency, mothers became a consistent target for society's indictment and indignation. It is to these biased portrayals of "aberrant" or "failing" motherhood that I now turn.

Parents or Mothers?

The killing of a child by a parent is nothing short of a tragedy. Relatives, neighbours and the whole of society are left with the difficult task of making sense of it and facing its consequences. For society this means coming to terms with the trauma brought about by the shattering of idealized notions of love and family. On these occasions, shock, confusion, rage and indignation are often the immediate affective responses that we find in news media, and which can be understood as symptomatic of society's frustrated attempts to explain an unfathomable, unimaginable explosion of parental violence. As the following headlines from our data set clearly show, in Japan this continued to be true independently of whether the culprit was the child's mother or father:

Is this a parent?![57]

Prison sentence for the "demonic husband and wife."[58]

Why did they rob their children of their lives?[59]

---

[57] "Kore ga oya ka." *Asahi shinbun*, 4 September, 1970, p. 22. Morning ed.
[58] "'Oni-fūfu' ni jikkei hanketsu." *Yomiuri shinbun*, 19 December, 1970, p. 9. Evening ed.
[59] "Wagako no inochi naze ubau?" *Asahi shinbun*, 21 December, 1970, p. 18. Morning ed.

And this would be a parent!?[60]

These cruel parents.[61]

The loss of parental love.[62]

Yet, even though the killing of a child by his father remained a disconcerting occurrence that prompted social outrage and indignation, mothers were, time and again, made the privileged target for social criticism. This biased treatment surfaces, for example, in the way news media portrayed the actors involved in a crime. What this means is that whenever a mother played a role in the killing of a child, it was likely that the father would be just glossed over or simply portrayed in a bewildered and mournful state. This is particularly evident in the numerous cases of mother–child suicide (*boshi shinjū*) whose recurrent narrative structure sees the father coming back from work just to discover the lifeless bodies of his wife and children. As we shall see, these usually laconic reports often mention the mother's nervous breakdown as the primal motivation for her crime, but they never seem to linger on the role that the father and child-rearing arrangements might have played in the onset of said neurosis. On the other hand, when the culprit is the father, the articles are very likely to devote some space to consider the role of the mother in the tragedy. This often translates into the implicit question, where was the mother at the time of the tragedy? Therefore, even when the absence of the maternal figure is not explicitly adduced as *the reason why* the father committed the crime, the mother seems, nonetheless, implicitly indicted for failing to protect the child. Let us take a look at an indicative range of examples:

> Once again a child is killed./Man abandoned by his wife (*tsuma ni nigerareta otoko*) (literally "man whose wife had run away").[63]
>
> Two children involved in a forced *shinjū*/[…]/Husband abandoned by his wife (*tsuma ni nigerareta otto*).[64]

---

[60] "Koredemo oya ka." *Yomiuri shinbun*, 13 March, 1971, p. 15. Morning ed.
[61] "Kono kokuhaku na oyatachi." *Asahi shinbun*, 24 August, 1972, p. 11. Morning ed.
[62] "Oya-gokoro sōshitsu." *Yomiuri shinbun*, 11 June, 1973, p. 11. Evening ed.
[63] "Mata akachan-goroshi." *Yomiuri shinbun*, 28 September, 1970, p. 14. Morning ed.
[64] "Niji to muri shinjū." *Yomiuri shinbun*, 28 May, 1971, p. 11. Evening ed.

[Men] abandoned by their wives (*tsuma ni sarare*): two cases of *shinjū*.⁶⁵

Wife runs away (*tsuma ni nigerare*), he plans father–child suicide (*fushi shinjū*).⁶⁶

Forced *shinjū* [after] wife flees [home] (*tsuma ni sarare*).⁶⁷

Abandoned by his wife (*tsuma ni nigerare*), punishes and murders [his child].⁶⁸

As I translated the headlines above, I also adapted them to the stylistic requirements of Western journalism in order to keep with the telegraphic efficacy of newspaper headlines. I must admit, however, of having indulged in a degree of poetic licence and creativity as I experimented with ways of rendering two very simple Japanese locutions that recur in rather unaltered form in all the examples provided: *tsuma ni nigerare(ta)* and *tsuma ni sarare(ta)*. These two almost formulaic expressions are constituted by the passive form of the verbs *nigeru* and *saru*, verbs that can be variously translated as "to run/go away," "to run off," "to flee," "to leave," "to abandon," and so on. From a grammatical point of view, this form is known in Japanese as *meiwaku no ukemi* or "passive form of inconvenience." The term designates a specific use of the passive form that, on top of indicating that the action was performed by an agent, also adds the connotation that what happened was unpleasant. The passive form of inconvenience is used to express an undesirable feeling, a sense of distress or harm suffered as an indirect consequence of some event or someone else's action. A rather untranslatable and typical example of such usage can be found in the sentence: "*Ame ni furaremashita*" which literally means "It rained [and I suffered some inconvenience because of it]." If the reason of the inconvenience is, say, that I did not carry an umbrella with me as I did not expect it to rain, the locution could be translated rather loosely as "I got caught in the rain" (notice that in many of these cases the passive form is lost in translation).

---

⁶⁵ "Tsuma ni sarare shinjū ni-ken." *Yomiuri shinbun*, 14 November, 1972, p. 11. Evening ed.
⁶⁶ "Tsuma ni nigerare fushi shinjū hakaru." *Yomiuri shinbun*, 20 February, 1973, p. 11. Evening ed.
⁶⁷ "Tsuma ni sarare muri shinjū." *Asahi shinbun*, 12 June, 1973, p. 11. Evening ed.
⁶⁸ "Tsuma ni nigerare sekkan satsujin." *Yomiuri shinbun*, 28 November, 1973, p. 11. Evening ed.

This brief grammatical detour offers a rather disquieting insight into the ways news media may have portrayed many cases of paternal filicide. The expressions *tsuma ni nigerareta* and *tsuma ni sarare(ta)* both suggest that the wife's (*tsuma*) action of running away or fleeing the conjugal home was a cause of distress for the husband and constituted the prelude to the crime *he* committed. In a sense, it is the husband who is portrayed here as a victim of circumstances as he suffers the unintended consequences of his wife's impulsive departure. As she walks out on him, her action becomes thus consequential for the ensuing explosion of murderous violence. And we may dare to wonder whether she is somehow called accountable for the killing despite her absence or, rather, *because* of it. Not only is her departure described as having dire psychological consequences for her husband, but as she leaves the house, she is also implicitly portrayed as forsaking her parental duties, actively contributing to that unsupervised moment of weakness or cruelty when the sudden explosion of paternal violence occurred.

In a similar vein, a feature article that appeared in the *Asahi shinbun* on September 4, 1970, provides a further example of the rhetorical strategies through which this implicit "mother blaming" was carried out. The article in question groups together two news items under the headline "Is this a parent? They killed their own children":[69] the first item offers an account of a mother who repeatedly abused her three-year-old daughter and eventually beat her to death for simply spilling some water,[70] while the second covers the case of a father who was left alone with a seven-month-old daughter, and who ended up strangling the child because her constant crying made it impossible for him to sleep.[71] It seems worth noticing that the first article occupies the most space because of the two pictures that portray the culprit (the mother) and the building where the tragedy took place (whereas the second article is accompanied by the picture of the father only). The article tells of the constant abuse of the child by the mother and ends with the reported comments of a married woman (*shufu*) from the neighbour-

---

[69] "Kore ga oya ka. Jisshi wo korosu." *Asahi shinbun*, 4 September, 1970, p. 22. Morning ed.
[70] "Haha ga yōjo nageotosu." Ibid.
[71] "Matsudo de wa chichioya ga kōsatsu." Ibid.

hood who describes the mother as a "demon" (*oni*). The child is also said to be the result of a liaison with the bartender of the bar where the mother worked as a hostess, but no further reference is made to the putative father of the victim. On the other hand, the second article reports that the baby often cried and that the father blamed the mother for not taking sufficient care of the children. One day, we are told, perhaps worn out by the continuous reproaches, the mother had gotten angry (*okotta*) and had returned with the eldest daughter to her parents' house. The article describes how the father, left alone with his baby daughter, eventually strangled the child, hid the body for a few days, disposed of it in a cardboard box and lied to the mother about the child's whereabouts once she came back home that same month. The body of the child was later discovered and the father was eventually arrested.

Even though the feature article purports to be about failing parental figures, the heightened focus on the *maternal* figure *in both articles* is striking to say the least. In the first story the mother is explicitly labelled as monstrous by another woman who is likely also a mother. Here an implicit contrast is drawn between the image of a "bad" (i.e. abusive and murderous) mother and a potentially "good" mother (with the term *shufu* designating a stay-at-home mother or a housewife and communicating an impression of ordinary respectability). On the other hand, we cannot fail to perceive the emphasis that the second story places upon the image of a mother who leaves her home and husband and takes with her only one of her children, leaving the daughter who needed her the most in the hands of a murderous father. We clearly see how a sense of implicit responsibility is once again attributed to the absent mother. Not only that, the fact that anger is indicated as her main motivation for leaving further suggests the image of a woman that places her emotions before the well-being of her children, an image that stands in stark contrast to a society that values emotional restraint and glorifies maternal abnegation and self-sacrifice. Furthermore, the difference in font size between the headlines of the two articles, with the first of the two printed in larger characters, establishes a hierarchy between the news items whereby the article on maternal filicide (already in first position according to an ideal reading order) is given further prominence. This contributes to setting a privileged interpretative lens whereby our encounter with the "bad" mother of the first story facilitates the recognition of the implicit shortcomings of the maternal figure in the one that follows.

The "Bad" and the "Mad" Mother

A careful analysis of my data set revealed that those mothers who were portrayed as committing *kogoroshi*—that is, those mothers whose murderous violence emerged undeniable on the linguistic and narrative surface of media accounts—came to be described as the most dangerous transgressors of cultural norms of maternal propriety and femininity. The violence they perpetrated against the young lives they were meant to protect was considered inexcusable and was reported accordingly as a monstrous aberration. Filicidal mothers (what the Japanese women's liberation movement would later call *kogoroshi no haha*) were condemned as cold-hearted, cruel and demonic individuals. In the process they were stripped of their maternal identities and plunged into a realm of social abjection. At the same time, the maternal potential for violence they embodied was repressed in the social subconscious, expunged, as it were, from the realm of cultural intelligibility and made into the very limit against which norms of appropriate maternal behaviour were continually re-established. Labelling a mother who killed her child as "demonic" or "monstrous" had the effect of depicting her as an *exception* to an otherwise widely shared maternal ideal and further secured the illusion that that same ideal had survived unscathed. We have observed one such example in the feature article analysed at the end of the previous section where the action of labelling was carried out by another woman and potential mother.

The rhetorical strategies that made it possible to group together cases as disparate as *boshi shinjū*, filicide, child abuse, runaway mothers and child abandonment were also crucial in establishing the trope of the "demonic mother" in the language of the news media. Below is a list of exemplary headlines where, in an effort to better foreground the mutual resonance of different modes of representation of the maternal, I made the conscious decision not to distinguish cases of filicide from all the others:

Mothers…These insensitive, irresponsible [persons].[72]

Savage mum kicks infant to death.[73]

And this would be a mother!?[74]

"Irresponsible mum" sent to the prosecutor.[75]

A demonic hostess-mum.[76]

Once again, a cruel, murderous mother.[77]

A demonic mother…[78]

By now it seems almost redundant to stress that the social stigma attached to mothers who transgressed cultural norms of maternal and gender propriety took full advantage of the amplification strategies that I have expansively explored. Exemplary is a feature article published in the *Yomiuri shinbun* on November 23, 1970, which groups together two news items under the headline "Heartless mums: two more cases."[79] The headline unambiguously identifies both articles as emblematic of cruel or coldhearted (*hijō*) motherhood. However, a close reading reveals that, while the first account is about a mother who beat her four-year-old daughter to the point of causing her death for internal bleeding in the brain, the second one chronicles the discovery of the corpse of a newborn baby in an empty flat. Despite the fact that there seems to be no sound proof that a mother (rather than, say, a father or another family member) abandoned the child, or that the baby had been suffocated before being abandoned, this second accident is still reported as a case of cruel motherhood. Cases of child abandonment, Tama (2008) has clearly shown, become crucial in media coverage that portrays mothers as monstrous or demonic.

---

[72] "Hahaoya…Kono musekinin, mushinkei." *Asahi shinbun*, 19 November 1970, p. 22. Morning ed.
[73] "Zankoku mama, yōji wo kerikorosu." *Yomiuri shinbun*, 11 April, 1971, p. 15. Morning ed.
[74] "Koredemo haha ka!" *Yomiuri shinbun*, 10 April, 1972, p. 8. Evening ed.
[75] "'Musekinin-mama' sōken."*Asahi shinbun*, 3 June, 1972, p. 8. Evening ed.
[76] "Oni no hosutesu-mama." *Yomiuri shinbun*, 8 September, 1972, p. 15. Morning ed.
[77] "Mugoi haha no satsujin mata." *Asahi shinbun*, 11 October, 1972, p. 23. Morning ed.
[78] "Oni no haha wa…" *Yomiuri shinbun*, 4 April, 1973, p. 11. Evening ed.
[79] "Hijō na mama——mata niken" *Yomiuri Shinbun*, 23 November 1970, p. 15. Morning edition.

Although my analysis is limited to representations of mothers who kill, a single example will suffice to suggest the degree to which the notion of the "bad" mother is intertwined with such cases: on January 11, 1972, the "Camera News" section of the *Yomiuri shinbun* published the photographs of two victims of child abandonment. The headline that accompanied them clearly indicted the culprits with the words "Cruel mothers!" (*mujō no haha yo*).[80] In those pictures the innocence of a smiling child and the painfully contracted face of a baby only a few days old interact to convey the idea of children's suffering that we have already considered, while maternal cruelty is unambiguously associated with that suffering.

In addition to this process of monsterification of a failing maternal figure, Japanese news media also made growing use of stock stories that portrayed mothers who kill as mentally unstable. This mode of representation is perhaps more complex to unpack because the growing public awareness of the psychological strains of motherhood was put into use for two rather opposite purposes: on the one hand, it became a convenient narrative strategy that made it possible to explain away the "abnormality" of maternal violence. On the other hand, it could also be used to call for a better understanding of the circumstances that surrounded cases of filicide that, far too often, were attributed to a callous mind, thus running counter to widespread depictions of murderous mothers as cruel monsters. While denying these mothers a fully human status in ways that are analogous to the "bad" mother trope, the narrative of the "mad" mother often appears to gesture towards an understanding of mothers as themselves victims of circumstances. "Mental instability" functions here as an umbrella term that includes references to notions of nervous breakdown, neurosis induced by child-rearing practices, previous histories of hospitalization and medical conditions like schizophrenia. In this respect, the terms that recur more often in the data set are the words *noirōze* (neurosis, nervous breakdown) and its various incarnations like *noirōze-gimi* (a little neurotic, an onset of neurosis, tending towards a nervous breakdown) and *ikuji-noirōze* (child-rearing neurosis).[81]

---

[80] "Mujō no haha yo" *Yomiuri shinbun*, 11 January, 1972, p. 3. Evening ed.
[81] Child-rearing neurosis has been identified as "a condition that emerged as a problem with the nuclearization of Japanese families from the 1960s, when middle-class mothers (typically full-time housewives) came to take on all responsibility for child-rearing" (Goodman et al. 2012: 117).

Japanese news media seems to communicate a more compassionate attitude towards filicidal mothers who were found to suffer from abnormal states of mind (a degree of sympathy that resonates with Western forms of pathologization of the maternal). We may not be surprised to find that this attitude is most likely to accompany news accounts of cases of *boshi shinjū* (as opposed to *kogoroshi*). In fact, in the articles included in my data set the trope of the cruel mother *never* applies to cases of mother–child suicide, in relation to which no harsh judgements is ever to be found. The majority of news articles about *boshi shinjū* consist of bare accounts of the event and, to a minor degree, of public laments about the tragic loss of innocent lives. However, there is no moral condemnation of mothers as the perpetrators of the violence that did, indeed, cause that loss. As already noticed at the beginning of this chapter, if the irrefutable emergence of violence on the linguistic and rhetorical surface of media accounts of *kogoroshi* was consequential in determining the outraged, harsh reception those cases encountered in public discourse, the erasure of that same violence from the romanticized notion of a double-suicide committed out of love (*shinjū*) was key in inhibiting the perception of such occurrences as manifestations of a maternal potential for violence. In addition to subsuming the tragedy of the child in the tragedy of the mother, the violence that she perpetrated (against herself *and* her child) was in the end not recognized as such, but disappeared even further behind the unfortunate circumstances that urged the mother to take her own life. The narrative of mental illness becomes, therefore, a convenient explanatory device that further consolidates schemas of intelligibility which, in turn, regulate and hinder our epistemological capacity to apprehend maternal violence.

At this point we can recognize a certain tension between the romanticized discourse of *boshi shinjū* that drew on its historical semantics and accumulated cultural meanings and a parallel narrative of pathologization which emphasized the mother's exceptional psychic fragility. Francesca Di Marco (2013) helps us better appreciate this apparent lack of homogeneity in the way news media covered cases of mother–child suicide. In her analysis of the making of modern suicide in early-twentieth-century Japan she calls attention to the "unceasing negotiations" between multiple discourses on suicide that accompanied the emergence of psychiatry in Japan. In an effort "to reconcile the competing views of suicide as an internalized pathology versus suicide as national pride," Di Marco argues, "psychiatrists produced an incongruous and at times contradictory response" which relied on "*inconsistent language* and *disharmonious terms*" while providing heterogeneous readings "that varied from pathologization to criminalization and culturalist romanticism of suicide as a peculiar feature of Japanese society" (2013: 325–6, my italics). Di Marco's argument builds upon an archive that dates back to the 1920s and 1930s. Yet it seems to me that the tensions and discursive negotiations she describes can be found—albeit in modified form—in media coverage of cases of mother–child suicide decades later, when appreciation of the physical, mental and spiritual exhaustion that may accompany the experience of mothering came to supplement (but never override) the cultural idealization of the mother–child symbiotic bond implicitly communicated by images of *boshi shinjū*.

It could also be argued, however, that the narrative of the "mad" mother had the added potential to pave the way to a deeper understanding of the social circumstances and psychological strains that induced mothers to kill. In doing so, this process of pathologization, however marred by its own rhetorical limitations, began to complicate the stigmatizing treatment that mothers who committed *kogoroshi* were subjected to. This is made plain in the following excerpt:

> Cruel filicides continue (*taenai*). Many are the crimes of young mothers. On those occasions criticisms such as "Also motherhood has fallen" or "A distortion induced by the process of nuclearization of the family" are repeatedly proclaimed. However, is this sufficient to explain it all? Voices are rising among psychiatrists according to which "If we look at the cases, [we realize that] many of them are naïve and impulsive actions. More than a cold-blooded and planned killing, pre-existent mental conditions also constitute an issue"[82]

Of course, my intention here is not to privilege one discourse over another, but to show how they all concurred, albeit in different ways, in regulating the conditions of emergence of maternal violence in the field of representability. We have seen how the systematic portrayals of mothers who killed

---

[82] "'Oni no hahaoya' to iu keredo uchiki de noirōze ikkan shinai dōki." *Yomiuri shinbun*, 5 April, 1973, p. 16. Morning ed.

their children as either cruel or mentally unstable (with the accompanying processes of monsterification and pathologization) provided journalists with ready-made narratives that were simple, familiar to the reader and highly adaptable to the specificity of the single case. But they also constituted preferential routes whereby the shattered boundaries between what was and what was not acceptable (i.e. gender-appropriate) behaviour were emphasized and reinstated. Considered from the point of view of its contribution to those schemas of intelligibility whereby a maternal potential for violence acquired (or, rather, failed to acquire) recognizability in public discourse, it seems to me that the labelling of filicidal mothers as neurotic, crazy, ill or the victim of a nervous breakdown has nothing to envy to the rhetorical violence with which mothers who committed *kogoroshi* were branded as inhuman monsters: as a matter of fact, both narratives denied mothers the full state of subject and rendered their voices equally inaudible by emphasizing their alleged abnormality. The maternal potential for violence that their deeds brought to the surface of public consciousness was stubbornly denied and expunged from the realm of cultural intelligibility. In this light we can see how both the callous mother and the mother who goes insane fail to act according to the parameters of the properly human and, thus, their violent actions are rendered unintelligible, constantly obscured by an aura of exceptionality. Yet a curious irony remains because, whereas Japanese news media strategically emphasized the aberrant singularity of these crimes (as a way to cope with the trauma and transgression of gender norms that maternal filicide entails), it also declared that same explosion of parental violence a social phenomenon of alarming proportions whose distinctive lack of exceptionality was, arguably, its most alarming feature.

Coda

Media representations of mothers who kill were entangled with broader social criticism that called attention to the "loss of motherhood" (*bosei sōshitsu*), the collapse of the maternal instinct and the breakdown of the family system that were said to plague modern Japanese society. These issues were raised in editorials, column articles and letters to the editor and created an even wider, alarming context for the images of filicidal mothers that we have encountered thus far. The year 1970 emerged as a particularly fertile year for these kinds of discursive interventions and it is indeed fairly plausible that the social commentary which appeared that year in the media constituted a major trigger for the counter-discourse that the Japanese women's liberation movement began to produce and circulate shortly thereafter.

The public lamentation over the loss of motherhood was often intertwined with references to changes that affected the socio-cultural layout of Japanese society in the postwar era. A clear example of this trend can be found in an editorial of the *Asahi shinbun* dated April 12, 1970, where changes in women's conditions such as the right to vote, free access to higher education, new economic and professional opportunities and a budding sense of an autonomous self are obliquely recognized as a major contributory factor to women's straying from their "maternal vocation."[83] The headline of the editorial says it all: "Empowered women, weak mothers."[84]

Concern about the impact of social changes upon the erosion of women's capacity to harbour maternal love is also expressed in an article published in the *Yomiuri shinbun* on October 10, 1970, with the headline "In a changing world" from which the following excerpt is taken:

> Filicides (*kogoroshi*) continue to happen. A biological mother kills her own child. [...] Maternal love is believed to be, so to speak, the deepest of [all] human emotions and much more than a mere animal instinct: a feeling for life itself. And yet, could it be that even that is now in the process of changing and crumbling down? The progress of civilization and the course of history have brought about changes not only in the way we live, but even in [people's] heart. [...] Life goals have expanded and multiple [forms of] self-affirmation [now] collide against each other. We keep up with the visible changes, but the changes within, those that are invisible to the eye, render people anxious and impatient. People call our times an era of revolutions (*henkaku no jidai*). [But] is this epoch of changes a period of transition toward a new world and new values or is it [rather] the twilight of a civilization—our civilization (*wareware ga ikitekita bunmei*)? No one has the answer to this question.[85]

---

[83] For an extended account of the changes that affected Japanese postwar society and their impact on women, see Chap. 3.
[84] "Tsuyoku natta josei, yowaku natta hahaoya." *Asahi shinbun*, 12 April, 1970, p. 5. Morning ed.
[85] "Kawaru yo no naka." *Yomiuri shinbun*, 10 October, 1970, p. 1. Evening ed.

In his most recent study of women's autobiographies and memoirs, Ronald Loftus (2013) vigorously demonstrates that the postwar years in Japan represented a moment of bright hopes and possibilities for young women who were finally able to shake off the burdens and constraints traditionally associated with their sex. As we shall see in the following chapters, the early 1970s also witnessed the emergence of a new women's movement which questioned the gender organization of modern society and reclaimed for women new forms of subjectivity. Therefore, it seems all the more significant that this same historical juncture is what media accounts denounce as a major cause in women's failure to live up to gender expectations. Not only that, this lamented epochal loss of a maternal appreciation for life—which is traced back to the modern emerging of mutually conflicting forms of (female) self-affirmation—would constitute a threat to the natural order and human civilization.

On September 5, 1970, an article in the family column of the *Asahi shinbun* was accompanied by an illustration that portrayed in direct and crude terms the accusation that news media were consistently making against women. The picture offers the stylized but, nonetheless, shocking image of a woman in the act of "zipping up" her once-pregnant belly as she shows her back, uncaring, to a foetus that is floating lifeless head-down in the water. "The era of children's suffering" (*akachan junan jidai*) marks, once again, the main headline of the article this picture was meant to illustrate, while the sub-headline says: "Mothers who desire the best conditions. At its extreme: terrible cases of abortion and abuse."[86] The article mentions the high occurrence of abortions in Japan and the recent numerical increase of cases of abuse and child abandonment; it denounces women's egoism and accuses them of aiming at only the best ever conditions before adequately performing their maternal role. The very next day on the same newspaper, the article "A genealogy of filicide" was published in the editorial section:

> The problem is that too many parents, especially mothers, go mad far too easily. Moreover, although madness is usually described as the loss of reason, could it possibly be that the maternal madness in recent cases of fili-

---

[86] "Akachan junan jidai." *Asahi shinbun*. 5 September, 1970, p. 17. Morning ed.

cide has its origin in the loss of an instinct? For a long time, we have believed that what made women love children was a maternal instinct. [...] However even that appears to be under question in today's world. Originally, there's no doubt that the killing and abandoning of children were extreme exceptions. But because it now occurs with such frequency, we must reconsider the social conditions of our time. The connection between parent and child that used to be the most fundamental human relationship in society has indeed changed into something that is utterly unreliable.[87]

The rhetorical slide from "parent" to "mother" should not go unnoticed here: whereas the passage begins with a broader reference to parents who seem to be losing their rational control and harm their children, the focus moves rapidly away from the image of a gender-neutral parental figure. Suddenly, it is mothers who become the main focus of criticism and concern. Whereas maternal madness is traced back to a loss of an instinct caused by changed social conditions, no reference whatsoever is made to a "paternal instinct." Accordingly, while fathers are spared cumbersome entanglements with the natural world, mothers and motherhood are deeply located within it, and the social changes of an era are said to have somehow engendered the collapse of a biological, maternal function. In the excerpt above, however, the lamentation for the loss of motherhood becomes the opportunity for a reconsideration of the *parent*–child relationship. The paternal figure is clearly included in this relationship, but the rhetorical strategies of the passage sidestep the very possibility that fatherhood might become an object of contestation or reflection.

In the next two chapters we shall see how a new women's liberation movement known as *ūman ribu* (literally woman lib) emerged in the early 1970s in Japan. In the context of a broad denunciation of the illnesses that were said to affect modern society's gender regime, this movement embarked in a spirited engagement with the phenomenon of maternal filicide. Rallies, teach-ins, conferences and other forms of public speaking and political organizing were held to discuss the phenomenon of mothers who killed their children and to challenge those biased discourses that I

---

[87] "Kogoroshi no keifu." *Asahi shinbun*, 6 September, 1970, p. 5. Morning ed.

have outlined in this chapter. Although the extent to which *ribu* was able to bring about a radical change in the consciousness of an entire society remains unclear, on October 22, 1972, the *Yomiuri shinbun* published an article that appears to have taken notice of those counter-discourses the movement was producing and circulating at the time. The article recognizes almost surreptitiously the entry of a new player into the discursive arena that had been developing around the phenomenon of maternal filicide, and demonstrates that with time the news media acknowledged the existence of alternative understandings of a mother's potential for violence. The article in question appeared under the headline "The era of the loss of motherhood."[88] And even though it takes a critical stance towards such a dramatic and sensational formulation, it also testifies to the extent to which the "loss" or "erosion" of motherhood and the "collapse" of women's maternal instinct had assumed wide currency and explanatory power. The sub-headline announces the article's critical perspective on popular discursive practices of monsterification and stigmatization of violent mothers and argues that "[b]y simply placing the blame on 'demonic mothers' the tragedy is not going to be solved."

A significant change of tone becomes apparent in the way the article provides perceptive insights on the acute discrimination meted out to single mothers in Japanese society. The plight of "unmarried mothers" (*mikon no haha*) represented a major concern for the women's liberation movement, which attempted to raise awareness of the deep-rooted discrimination these women faced in society and of the risks their unbearable living conditions posed for the well-being of their children. What is exceptional in this article is its direct referencing of *ribu*, here identified with the figure of Tanaka Mitsu (major theorist and spokesperson of the movement). What interests me here is to highlight how, by the end of 1972, a space seemed to be opening in the news media where alternative, more nuanced understandings of maternal violence appeared to seep in from external sites of contestation. Certainly, this does not mean a radical sea change in media portrayals of mothers who kill, since both Tama's (2008) and my own research appear to confirm the persistence of biased

---

[88] "Bosei sōshitsu jidai." *Yomiuri shinbun*, 22 October, 1972, p. 18. Morning ed.

portrayals of filicidal mothers. However, it is a clear demonstration of the ongoing interaction between existing discourses, and of the possibility that alternative interpretations of the phenomenon might be not only acknowledged, but reproduced and recirculated through the news media itself. It is to one of these counter-discourses that I will now devote my attention as I introduce the Japanese women's liberation movement and explore its relentless rhetorical engagement with the figure of the mother who kills her child.

3

The Women's Liberation Movement in 1970s Japan

In the previous chapter I highlighted how the rhetorical and narrative strategies employed by news media in the coverage of cases of (maternal) filicide contributed to the overall impression of being confronted with a social phenomenon of dramatic proportions. Alarmed voices lamenting women's progressive estrangement from their maternal vocation (the so-called loss of motherhood) pointed the finger at historical changes that were said to have negatively affected Japanese postwar society—changes that, incidentally, had also brought about significant improvements in women's social status. Early 1970s' Japan was marked—or so it seemed—by the increased visibility of maternal violence. However, I hope I was able to show how the categories of *kogoroshi* and *boshi shinjū* operated as major organizing principles that not only contributed to a differential apprehension of maternal violence in public discourse, but were indeed consequential in regulating (and often hindering) the appearance of that violent potential in the realm of representability. Such "rhetorical [and linguistic] proliferation of denials"—to borrow Butler's (2000: 7) felicitous wording—intertwined with the emergence of stock stories of the "bad" or "mad" mother as privileged explanatory narratives that worked to safely contain such widespread manifestations of violence under a rubric of constantly renewed exceptionality.

It is against this background that Japan witnessed the emergence, in the early 1970s, of a new women's liberation movement that forwarded an unprecedented gender critique of Japanese postwar society. This grass-roots movement, known as *ūman ribu* (woman lib) or simply *ribu* (lib), did not make the pursuing of "gender equality" or the promotion of "women's rights" its primary concern or discursive hallmark. Rather, it aimed at fostering a radical transformation of society, questioning its socio-political and economic organization, and attacking the cultural values and ideology that shaped gender roles and human relations. *Ribu* formulated revolutionary counter-discourses that developed around notions of solidarity with mothers who killed their children and women's very potential for violence. This chapter aims to provide the necessary coordinates to locate *ribu*'s emergence within the local and global socio-political and historical landscape, and introduces some of the movement's distinguishing features. But before embarking on an appraisal of *ribu*'s main traits, a disclaimer is needed: both an in-depth exploration of the historical and social factors that made the movement possible and a comprehensive account of its multiple forms of contestation remain beyond the scope of this chapter. Rather, my more circumscribed and immediate purpose will be to offer a contextualization (however partial) of *ribu*'s discursive intervention about mothers who kill their children, an intervention that will constitute the central concern of my next chapter. In order to do so I have strategically adopted, when relevant, a preferential focus on *ribu*'s multifaceted engagement with the maternal which, as I hope my account will not fail to make clear, is not to be reductively understood as the movement's sole preoccupation.

What's in a Name? *Ribu*'s First Public Appearance

On June 23, 1970, a group of women in their early twenties who called themselves "The Preparatory Committee for a Women's Liberation Movement" appeared at an anti-Security Treaty rally[1] held at Yoyogi Park

---

[1] The Japan-US Security Treaty or ANPO (abbreviation for the Japanese *Nichibei anzen hoshō jōyaku*) was signed at the end of the Allied Occupation in 1951, to become effective in 1952, and

(Tokyo) and attended by 70,000 people, and distributed to women participants a mimeographed handbill consisting of an appeal to launch a women's liberation movement in Japan. The pamphlet exhorted women to organize, to denounce their "internalized female consciousness," to dismantle all forms of gender discrimination and to liberate women from any form of oppression (Muto 1997: 149).[2] However, it is October 21, 1970, that is usually identified as the day when the first *ribu* demonstration took place: in the late afternoon of what is known in Japan as the International Anti-War Action Day a women-only demonstration was held in Ginza, one of the major districts in Tokyo: 200 women wearing helmets took to the streets carrying placards with slogans and phrases such as "What do women mean to men? What do men mean to women?," "Let's denounce our internalized female consciousness!" and "Mother, are you really happy with your marriage?"

This extraordinary event captured the attention of the news media which were, indeed, the first to introduce the term *ūman ribu* in the Japanese idiom. The first newspaper article that used the term *ūman ribu* in reference to Japanese women's activism appeared in the *Asahi shinbun* on October 4, 1970. Its title is emblematic: "*Ūman ribu* lands in men's paradise" (Ūman ribu—dansei tengoku jōriku). The choice of the word *jōriku* ("to land" or "to disembark") alluded in a not-so-subtle way to the activities of the Women's Liberation Movement in the United States, which the article described as eventually "landing" on Japanese soil.[3] In the headline the term "Women's Liberation" appeared in English and

---

placed the United States as the effective arbiter of Japan's defence interests. It established that US military facilities be hosted in and about Japan throughout the postwar period with the double aim of (1) protecting Japan against armed attack from without, since the treaty—and the new Japanese constitution imposed during the Occupation—severely restricted the size and purposes of the Japanese Self-Defence Forces; (2) contributing to the maintenance of international peace and security in the Far East. The treaty came up for revision and renewal in the 1960 and this became the focus of the greatest mass movement in Japanese political history. For an in-depth investigation of the implications of the treaty and the social and political contestations triggered by its renewal, see Hara (1987), Kan (1987), Kersten (1996), Sakurada (1997) and Sasaki-Uemura (2001).

[2] According to Shigematsu (2012: 67) the pamphlet distributed at the rally was "The Declaration of the Liberation of Eros" (*Erosu kaihō sengen*), which was to become "one of the first widely distributed *ribu* manifestos."

[3] "Ūman ribu—dansei tengoku jōriku." *Asahi shinbun* [Tokyo ed.], 4 October, 1970, p. 24. Morning ed.

was accompanied by the Japanese abbreviated transliteration *ūman ribu* (ウーマン•リブ).⁴ These considerations confirm Welker's (2012: 28–9) observation that Ninagawa Masao, the male journalist who is credited with coining this new term, clearly saw both the name and the movement it designated as emanating from the United States.⁵ Ninagawa's reference in his article to a Japanese abridged translation of *Notes from the Second Year: Women's Liberation: Major Writings of the Radical Feminists* (a landmark collection of essays of the American Women's Lib edited by Shulamith Firestone and Anne Koedt) further reinforced and promoted the biased understanding that *ūman ribu* was nothing but a mimicking of Western (i.e. American) models.⁶

Secondary literature (in both English and Japanese) voices shared acknowledgement of the tone of ridicule with which *ribu* activists were frequently depicted in mainstream media outlets.⁷ An often quoted example can be found in Ninagawa's "founding" article where "*ribu*" women⁸ were described as "brave micro-mini-skirted beauties" (Akiyama 1993: 36, 39; Mackie 2003: 156). Given the mocking tone with which news media portrayed the American Women's Liberation Movement

---

[4] The Japanese writing system comprises three scripts: Chinese characters (*kanji*) and two phonetic scripts made up of modified Chinese characters (*hiragana* and *katakana*). *Hiragana* is used to write words without character representation, words that are no longer written in characters and following *kanji* to show conjugation endings. *Katakana* is the simplest and more geometric of the two phonetic scripts and is primarily used to transcribe foreign words and as a mark of emphasis. A correct transliteration of "Women's Lib" would have been *uimenzu ribu*, *ūman ribu* (woman lib) being a somewhat incorrect version that, by omitting the mark of the genitive, simplified English grammar to a minimum. Two other examples of transliterated words that we have already encountered are *feminizumu* (フェミニズム, feminist) and *feminisuto* (フェミニスト, feminist).

[5] Akiyama reproduces at least two more articles from the *Asahi shinbun* that make use of the same linguistic strategy (Akiyama 1993: 42, 49).

[6] This constituted a major criticism that Japanese commentators frequently directed at *ribu* and which is variously acknowledged by Ehara (2012: 106), Akiyama (1993: 52), Fujieda and Fujimura-Fanselow (1995: 159), Ueno (2011: 10) and Shigematsu (2012: xxii). Feminist sociologist Ueno Chizuko (2011:10) dismisses this accusation as rooted in xenophobic stereotypes by means of which conservative forces cast everything that is perceived negatively as foreign and, thus, out of place in Japan.

[7] Matsui (1990), Fujieda and Fujimura-Fanselow (1995), Muto (1997), Ochiai (1997), Ehara (2005, 2012) and Shigematsu (2012).

[8] As Welker (2012: 29, note 6) rightly observes, this usage of the term "*ribu* women" is somewhat anachronistic at such an early stage when women activists had yet to consciously identify themselves with the movement.

and later *ribu*, Japanese women activists expressed an initial resistance to adopting the label *ūman ribu* to identify themselves and their struggle.[9] The term rarely appears in the early documents of the movement where we rather find the Japanese expression *josei kaihō undō* (女性解放運動, literally "women's liberation movement").[10] It was only at a later stage that the term *ūman ribu* came into use among women activists as part of the movement's complex process of self-definition. On the other hand, Ochiai Emiko (1997: 87) argues that, despite the biased representations of *ribu* in the media, women in Japan could still be overwhelmed by a sense of excitement in realizing that other women shared their same anger and frustration (see also Akiyama 1993). Shigematsu (2012: 81) confirms this reading and draws on recent scholarship in Japanese to further emphasize how *ribu* activists strategically negotiated and used media attention to spread their message of woman's liberation. In the end, women activists came to identify themselves as *ribu*, the catchy simplicity of the katakana リブ (*ribu*, lib) being preferred to the complexity of the six-character expression 女性解放運動 (*josei kaihō undō*, women's liberation movement) (Akiyama 1993). As we shall see, the decision to identify with *ribu* also meant to differentiate and distance oneself from those images of women's liberation that had been employed by previous postwar women's groups.

---

[9] The first appearance of the American Women's Lib on the Japanese scene can be traced back to the spring of 1970 when articles began to appear in wide-circulation newspapers. Japanese media coverage was fragmentary and biased in the information it provided, focusing almost exclusively on sensational actions of American activists such as disrupting beauty contests, throwing away and burning bras and holding demonstrations against clubs that barred access to women. On March 28, 1970, an article appeared in the *Asahi shinbun* under the headline "Smash 'man's society!' Reject femininity: with 'no bra' and red stockings." The title of the article made use of a linguistic pun that transformed the name of the feminist radical group founded by Ellen Willis and Shulamith Firestone (Redstockings) into an item of clothing, and turned women activists into curiously dressed creatures, while simultaneously arousing the curiosity of the reader (Akiyama 1993: 36–7).

[10] One such example is provided by the name of the above-mentioned "Preparatory Committee for a Women's Liberation Movement" (*josei kaihō undō junbi kai*).

Ribu's Genealogies

No social movement is born in a void and *ribu* constitutes no exception. Shigematsu (2012) has widely explored the numerous instances of cross-pollination both domestic and international that made it possible for *ribu* to emerge.[11] In this section I will be reading with her as I outline how the movement took shape from the cross-fertilization of existing forms of political mobilization and resistance. For reasons of clarity, the account is divided into three parts addressing the influence on the formation of *ribu* of (1) a previous history of women's struggle in Japan, (2) a rich leftist genealogy and (3) a complex dynamic of identification and dis-identification with Western feminist struggles. Although I am not able here to do justice to Shigematsu's rich and detailed argument, a consideration of her insights remains crucial to an understanding of *ribu*'s socio-political and historical specificities and I encourage the interested reader to delve first-hand into her extensive analysis of the movement.

Japan's Women's Movements

Shigematsu concurs with scholars Matsui (1990) and Muto (1997) in arguing that the birth of *ribu* marked the (*re-*)emergence of a radical feminist movement in Japan after the pioneering role played by the Bluestockings Society (*Seitō-sha*). This was a group gathered around the women's literary journal *Seitō* (Bluestockings) established in 1911 by leading feminist and poet Hiratsuka Raichō (1886–1971). The journal was founded with the aim of advancing female literary and intellectual talents and promoting women's self-awareness. Albeit in theoretical or literary form, its contribution expressed opposition to the family system, challenged the institution of marriage and brought into public discourse

---

[11] Shigematsu's path-breaking monograph *Scream from the Shadow: The Women's Liberation Movement in Japan* (2012) constitutes, to my knowledge, the most extensive and thorough analysis of *ribu* in English language to date and offers a compelling account of its multiple genealogies. Counter to the accusation of *ribu* being a mere Western import, Shigematsu locates the movement's emergence squarely in a domestic history of feminist, social and political struggles. My account in this chapter of *ribu*, its organizational strategies, forms of struggle and philosophical principles owes a profound debt to her landmark text.

taboo topics such as divorce, women's sexual expression, childbearing, birth control, abortion and prostitution. These women's "outrageous" demeanour caused them to become the object of ridicule and to face social retaliation: Vera Mackie (2003: 47) recounts, for example, how they became (in)famous for their visits to the pleasure district in Tokyo and for "transgressing the spatial division between respectable women and the women of the entertainment industry."[12] Shigematsu has called attention to *ribu*'s acknowledgement of this important Japanese legacy and to the movement's numerous references to other female figures such as the first feminist women's historian Takamure Itsue (1894–1964) and the anarchist Kanno Sugako (1881–1911).[13]

Ribu was, on the other hand, extremely critical of postwar women's movement such as the Mothers' Convention (*Hahaoya taikai*) that was held every year since 1955 and which gathered together women who identified with their role as mothers while making the protection of children and the defence of peace their main political and social goals.[14] Other important women's organizations from which *ribu* distanced itself were the Housewives Association (*Shufuren*) and the National Federation of Regional Women's Organization (*Chifuren*). Founded in 1948 and 1952 respectively, these were large national bodies with ties with the postwar government and which became the leading forces behind the consumer protection movement of the 1960s (Robins-Mowry 1983; Buckley 1994; Mackie 2003). The massive base of these movements was symptomatic of Japan's "High Economic Growth Era," that is, the years spanning from around 1955 until the Oil Shock in 1973 and during which the Japanese economy grew at an astonishing rate of 9.3 per cent (Gao 2007).[15] Such

---

[12] There is extensive secondary literature on the *Seitō-sha* and the role it played in the history of feminist struggle in Japan. See, for example, Reich and Fukuda (1976), Robins-Mowry (1983), Sievers (1983), Tomida (2004) and Lowy (2004, 2007).

[13] Shigematsu (2012: 6, 78, 130, 221 note 29); see also Satō (2010: 31).

[14] An understanding of womanhood and motherhood as coextensive found in those years confirmation in the idealization of maternal love and the elaboration of a maternalistic discourse that became central to the promotion of women's participation in peace movements in the postwar (Mackie 2016; Swerdlow 1993).

[15] The construction boom around the 1964 Tokyo Olympics and the building of the *shinkansen* (bullet train) became emblematic of Japan's modernization that was eventually celebrated in Expo '70 in Osaka (Sasaki-Uemura 2007; Allinson 1997).

spectacular economic growth was largely based on steel processing and manufacturing, and was triggered by American military activity in Korea in the 1950s and in Vietnam in the 1960s (Sasaki-Uemura 2007; Mackie 2003; Robins-Mowry 1983). It was also driven by a sustained domestic consumer demand that relied on and fostered the rapid development of a middle-class, urban consumer society to the point that, while in 1960 over 70 per cent of the population thought of themselves as middle class, that figure had reached 90 per cent by the early 1970s (Tipton 2008: 179, 187).

The vast support that benefited earlier postwar women's movements, their reliance on socially accepted feminine roles and their close working relationships with the government stood in stark contrast with *ribu*'s much smaller base (approximating a few thousands of participants) and appeared unacceptable in light of *ribu*'s anti-establishment and anti-imperialist stance (Muto 1997; Shigematsu 2012).

Leftist Influences

This dimension of *ribu* was the result of formative influences from the Left which impressed an indelible mark on the movement's organizing principles and strategies of political contestation. As a matter of fact, many *ribu* activists gained first-hand experience of political struggle both within the ranks of the New Left and, later, as members of the student movement *Zenkyōtō* (shorthand for *Zengaku kyōtō kaigi* or All-Campus Joint Struggle Committee). However, many women involved in the New Left had grown highly critical of the masculine principles that imbued its revolutionary ideals, of its exclusive focus on class struggle at the expense of any consideration of forms of oppression deemed specific to the female sex and of the constant competition between its various sects over who possessed the correct revolutionary theory (competition that, in the end, led to dramatic episodes of inter-and intra-sectarian violence).

The internecine struggles of the New Left became object of harsh critique from *Zenkyōtō*: the student movement's refusal of hierarchies and leader figures and its desire to make the single individual the subject of the movement constituted direct reactions to the top-down structure and blind commitment to ideological orthodoxy that had characterized the New Left (Steinhoff 1984; Marotti 2009). Even though *ribu* activists denounced *Zenkyōtō*'s sexism and criticized its privileging of armed violence against riot police as a measure of one's own commitment to the revolutionary cause, *ribu*'s spontaneous organizing and the confrontational character of its political struggles are clearly indebted to the tactics of the student movement. Another important lesson learnt from *Zenkyōtō* was the emphasis on self-reflexivity: key principles informing the student movement were the ideas of "self-denial" (*jiko hitei*) and "self-criticism" (*jiko hihan*) that constituted theoretical tools through which the self was encouraged to become conscious of its own complicities with the system that it meant to oppose and critique. The practices of self-criticism and self-denial were born out of the awareness that, qua university students, the members of the movement were indeed beneficiaries of the current political and economic system. The aim was to question the self that was benefiting from those conditions and to enable the dismantling of the system that produced that privilege. This would make it necessary to unravel and fight internalized discriminatory attitudes against certain social groups, be it disabled people, *burakumin* (outcasts) or *zainichi* Koreans (Koreans resident in Japan). It is ironic that, despite such a self-reflexive attitude, *Zenkyōtō* remained utterly insensitive to male–female relationships and to forms of gendered discrimination (Kersten 2009; Muto 1997). In this respect, *Zenkyōtō* is often described as having played the role of negative example (*hanmen kyōshi*) in reaction to which *ribu* is said to have emerged (Akiyama 1993: 177). At the same time, the self-reflexivity that characterized the new women's movement and urged *ribu* activists to become conscious of forms of internalized discrimination while acknowledging their complicity with forms of oppression which differentially affected other Asian women is symptomatic of the profound debt that *ribu* owes to the political experience of the student movement (Tanaka [1972] 2010; Onnatachi no ima tou kai 1996; Shigematsu 2012: 33–62).

Finally, the anti-Vietnam war movement *Beheiren* (short for "*Betonamu ni heiwa wo!*" *shimin rengō*, commonly translated as "The Citizens' Movement for Peace in Vietnam") was another strong influence that shaped *ribu*'s organizing principles and strategies of political intervention. Its rejection of hierarchies and its self-reflexive stance mirrored those of *Zenkyōtō*. Under the slogan "the Vietnam within ourselves" the anti-Vietnam war movement promoted awareness among its members of their complicity with what was understood as US–Japan neo-imperialism (Shigematsu 2012: 41). *Beheiren* was an "action-oriented" movement that privileged spontaneous, autonomous forms of activism to such a degree that anyone who desired to stand up against the Vietnam War could call herself *Beheiren* and initiate her own local activism (Tsurumi 1969; Akiyama 1993: 176; Avenell 2010; Shigematsu 2012: 40–2). The movement's innovative nature was evident in its reliance upon new forms of demonstrations such as sit-ins and teach-ins and in its opposition to any logic that could be traced back to a rigidly structured organization, a leader or leading committee. Despite the fact that *Beheiren* was (informally) led by male members, these were some of the traits that were inherited by *ribu* and which became apparent in *ribu*'s numerous teach-ins and summer camps.

The "personalization of politics" that characterized *Beheiren* was also recognizable in *ribu* activists' use of expressions like "*watashi wa ribu*" (I am *ribu*) or "*ribu wo ikiru*" (to live *ribu*) (Akiyama 1993: 182). In her *Notes on a Personal History of Ribu* [*Ribu shishi nōto*] Akiyama (1993: 175–9) recalls that anyone who could think of herself as *ribu* "was" *ribu*, and was thus entitled to organize her own forms of activism without permission or censorship, but in spontaneous ways. This view is somehow contested by Shigematsu's research on the history of the movement. In fact, her investigation of the complex dynamics taking place within one of its most well-known communes (the Ribu Shinjuku Centre in Tokyo) seems to suggest that Akiyama's portrayal might be one that oversimplifies *ribu*'s internal politics and idealizes the movement's democratic openness.[16] Shigematsu's work (2012: 107) does, indeed, shed light upon the complex, dialogic process that characterized the movement's attempts

---

[16] I owe this insight to the perceptive comments an anonymous reviewer offered to an article I submitted for publication at the time I was working on this chapter. On that occasion I was reminded that Akiyama's absence from Japan during the early years of the movement and her never having lived in a commune might have made her unaware of the extent to which there were contentious debates around who were the "authentic" or "true" *ribu* activists. And yet, it was only in 1974 that Akiyama left Japan to live in the Soviet Union (where she remained until 1981).

at self-definition and which she describes as involving "tension, struggle, desire, conflict and, contradiction." This seems true particularly in reference to the hectic and somehow restless life at the Ribu Shinjuku Centre where the charismatic presence of Tanaka Mitsu (major theorist and spokesperson in the movement) was perceived by many as a source of tension and conflicts.[17] On the other hand, we may also wonder whether Akiyama's idiosyncratic understanding of *ribu*'s openness ought to be taken as symptomatic of the degree of spontaneity that the movement inherited from *Beheiren*. It seems to me that while we should ask whether Akiyama's personal circumstances made her less perceptive of broader dynamics within the movement, her account surely testifies to the importance placed upon the single individual as the very foundation of the movement. To dismiss her "personal history" as exceptional and thus not sufficiently "representative" of *ribu*'s internal dynamics would actively impose a sense of homogeneity within the movement—where "homogeneity" designates a condition of widespread internal conflicts over the movement's self-definition—therefore contradicting its very nature and organizing principles.[18]

Western Feminism

From what I have outlined thus far it emerges that the processes that led to the birth of *ribu* were already in motion by the time the American Women's Lib hit the news in Japan. Shigematsu (2012: xxx) remarks that an encounter with other configurations of women's activism overseas

---

[17] While recognizing the pivotal role Tanaka played in shaping the movement in its early years, Shigematsu has also acknowledged that her charisma and vigorous ability to make herself heard at public meetings and within the life at the commune made her a contradictory figure within *ribu*, in that she came to be recognized as the leader of a movement that purported to have no leader. For an extensive investigation of this complex dynamics, see Shigematsu's chapter "*Ribu* and Tanaka Mitsu: The Icon, the Center, and its Contradictions" (Shigematsu 2012: 103–135).

[18] We should, nonetheless, acknowledge the fact that, by the time *ribu* emerged, Akiyama was already in her thirties, married and with a child and this might have placed her at a relative distance from *ribu*'s younger constituency and from its fervent critique of marriage and the family system. In this respect, Akiyama herself has described the WOLF group she co-founded (about which more to follow) as a "middle-aged *ribu*" (*chūnen no ribu*) (Akiyama et al. 1996: 47) in contrast to her perception of *ribu* as a "movement of young women/daughters" (*musume no undō*) in their twenties (Akiyama 1993: 188).

constituted part and parcel of *ribu*'s process of self-definition, but she also describes how the emotional impact of such an encounter, together with the feelings of political identification and transnational solidarity it aroused, never eclipsed *ribu*'s critical distance and the domestic dimension of its complex genealogies. Against those views that dismiss *ribu* as a mere Western import, she suggests that US-based Women's Lib constituted a significant, albeit not exclusive, site of both identification and dis-identification (1).

The 1960s and 1970s saw the translation of several American, European and Australian feminist classics into Japanese. Among them were Margaret Mead's *Male and Female* (1961), Betty Friedan's *The Feminine Mystique* (1965), Shulamith Firestone's *The Dialectic of Sex* (1972), Juliet Mitchell's *Women's Estate* (1973), Kate Millett's *Sexual Politics* (1973), Germaine Greer's *The Female Eunuch* (1976) and Juliet Mitchell's *Psychoanalysis and Feminism* (1977). Simone de Beauvoir's *The Second Sex* had appeared in abridged translation (five volumes) as early as in 1953 and it had been an instant bestseller, "selling out more than twenty printings before the final volume even hit the shelves" (Bullock 2009: 75). By the early 1970s the four volumes that compose de Beauvoir's autobiography were also available in Japanese: *Memories of a Dutiful Daughter* (1961), *The Prime of Life* (1963), *The Force of Circumstance* (1965) and *All Said and Done* (1973) (Bullock 2009: 89) and by the time the French intellectual visited Japan in 1966 she had been widely read and had reached high popularity among Japanese women.

Additionally, partial and derisive as they were, the first newspaper reports of the American Women's Lib played a crucial role in introducing American radical feminism to a Japanese audience and they provided useful information about the circumstances of women's struggles overseas. Akiyama (1993) describes, for example, how, following those first mocking articles, women activists searched hungrily for more and more information about the American Lib. In her words:

> It is often emphasized that Japan's *ribu* emerged from an original Japanese context together with an original way of thinking, and there's no doubt about that. However, the influence of the American Women's Liberation Movement cannot be ignored, in that it constituted the trigger that ignited

the grudge smouldering among women in Japan and put that grudge into words and theories. (52–3)

It remains noteworthy that in the archival material I researched there is a dearth of references to Western feminism (usually limited to the simple mention of feminist classics and names such as Firestone and Millett), and that a thorough theoretical engagement with those very texts and thinkers appears to be absent from *ribu*'s writings. Welker (2012: 28) confirms my findings as he acknowledges that "the bulk of writing in the *ribu* sphere [is] essentially local in origin and focus." On the other hand, he also acutely observes that "translations and summaries of reports, essays, and whole books from English did arguably occupy a significant part of *ribu* discourse," and he suggests that the lack of adequate attention to translation in current studies of the movement can be perhaps understood in light of a reaction against the idea that *ribu* might be a foreign import (ibid).[19]

Therefore, while Akiyama's account of the importance of American radical feminism for the evolution of *ribu* might stem from her "personal history of *ribu*," it surely provides a sound rationale behind the foundation of the *Urufu no kai* (WOLF group) of which she was a founding member.[20] Akiyama's group played an important role in retrieving pamphlets, declarations and reports from the American feminist movement and translating them into Japanese. It was the WOLF group that translated *Notes from the Second Year: Women's Liberation: Major Writings of the Radical Feminists* (1970). This collection of essays was published in Japanese under the title *From Woman to Women: A Report from the American Women's Liberation Movement* [*Onna kara onnatachi e—America*

---

[19] Welker's recent work has been at the forefront of a study of the history of *ribu* that privileges the movement's production of "engaged translations" of pamphlets, leaflets and reports produced by the American Women's Lib. For earlier works that provide useful information on the importance of translation in the emergence of *ribu*, see Matsui (1990: 438), Buckley (1997: 185–98) and Mackie (2003: 152).

[20] The name of the group was a Japanese transliteration of the English "Woolf" from Virginia Woolf: since the Japanese rendering of the name does not distinguish between "Woolf" and "wolf," the members of the group were pleased for the name of the group to be a pun on the name of the writer and the animal. Additionally, even though it was not one of the original intentions behind the naming of the group, *urufu* (WOLF) was later said to also stand for "Women's Liberation Front" (Akiyama 1993: 60–1; Welker 2012: 30).

josei kaihō undo repōto]. Drawing on translation scholar Maria Tymoczko, Welker (2012: 29) describes this text as an "engaged translation," that is, a translated text whose translators had specific political agendas and used translation as a vehicle to achieve them. The translation in question was enclosed between an editor's introduction and a roundtable discussion in which members of the group discussed how they had come into possession of the original in English and the role they hoped to play in connecting the American authors now in translation to their Japanese readers (Akiyama 1993: 56–76). These commentaries to the volume were part of the translators' attempt to produce a text that could be immediately relevant to a Japanese audience. Integral to this interventionist approach was the group's decision to translate, in full or in part, only 16 of the original 34 essays that comprised the English collection (those deemed more meaningful) and to reorganize them in three sections: women's experience (*onna no keiken*), love and sex (*ai to sei*) and women's struggle (*onna no tatakai*).[21]

Akiyama has written about some of the problems the group faced during the translation process such as the rendition of English terminology that did not exist in Japanese. The group discussed various strategies to best render that vocabulary in ways that could also be accessible to Japanese readers. In the end, the main strategy became to give the original (English) word in its phonetic transliteration in *katakana* alongside the Japanese rendering of the term in *kanji*.[22] Among the examples listed by Akiyama are terms such as *josei kaihō shisō* 女性解放思想 and *josei kaihō-ron* 女性解放論 (literally "thought" or "theory of women's liberation") which were both accompanied by the transliteration *feminizumu* (フェミニズム, feminism), *kyūshinteki josei kaihō ronsha* 急進的女性解放論者 (literally "radical advocate of women's liberation") that rendered *radikaru feminisuto* (ラディカル・フェミニスト, radical feminist), and expressions such as *onna no danketsu* 女の団結 and *onna-dōshi no*

---

[21] Among the translated essays were Jo Freeman's "The Bitch Manifesto," Shulamith Firestone's "Love," Pat Mainardi's "The Politics of Housework," Ti Grace Atkinson's "Radical Feminism" and "The Institution of Sexual Intercourse," Anne Koedt's "The Myth of the Vaginal Orgasm," Carol Hanisch's "The Personal is Political," Jennifer Gardner's "False Consciousness," Kate Millett's "Sexual Politics" and the "Redstockings Manifesto."

[22] See note 4.

rentai 女同士の連帯 (literally "women's union" or "solidarity of women comrades") chosen to vehicle the notion of *shisutāhuddo* (シスターフッド, sisterhood) (Akiyama 1993: 59).

These may still have represented pioneering attempts to introduce Western concepts into the Japanese idiom, but their value in the history of *ribu* could be suggested by the fact that the translation of *Notes from the Second Year* saw a total of three editions and sold about 5000 copies. The volume provoked a wide response from readers who wrote dozens of passionate letters craving for more information or attempting to get in touch with like-minded women around the country. Several of those letters were later collected in a booklet and included in the first of the three issues of the zine the WOLF group produced: this constituted a renewed attempt to create a sense of dialogue between readers and translators, but it also reflected a desire to promote the formation of a women's network that could be supportive of the transformation of women's consciousness (Akiyama 1993: 69–74; Welker 2012: 31). Limits of space do not allow me to go more in depth into a consideration of the translation activities of the WOLF group, and here I can only mention the fundamental contribution represented by the group's first translation in 1974 of *Our Bodies, Ourselves*, the classic text on women's health and sexuality originally compiled by the Boston Women's Health Book Collective in 1971. This constitutes just another example of *ribu*'s multifaceted interaction with Western (specifically American) feminism and of the importance of translation as one of the vehicles that made such encounter possible.[23]

---

[23] My considerations of the activities of the WOLF Group is deeply indebted to the insights Welker offers in his "Translating Women's Liberation, Translating Women's Bodies in 1970s–1980s Japan" (2012). I refer the reader to this article for an in-depth study of the first Japanese translation of *Our Bodies, Ourselves*. In her book *The Making of* Our Bodies, Ourselves*: How Feminism Travels Across Border*, Kathy Davis acknowledges the existence of this first Japanese translation of *Our Bodies, Ourselves* (revised in 1988) as well as of an unauthorized version that appeared in 1976 in Taiwan (2007: 53). However, Welker acutely observes how she seems to downplay these two early translations "in her narrative about the global spread of the book, perhaps because it runs against the standard narrative of second-wave feminist discourse spreading from the US to Europe to the rest of the world" (Welker 2012: 31–32, note nr. 23). See also Welker (2015).

Consciousness Transformation, Relationality and Revolutionary Commitment

Ribu was never an organic and homogeneous movement, with a hierarchy among its members, a recognized centre and its periphery, but was constituted instead by a multiplicity of autonomous, small groups that emerged spontaneously and organized their own forms of political contestation. This made it possible for *ribu*'s revolutionary commitment to spill over into multiple struggles on a variety of fronts. Despite early misrepresentations of *ribu* as suffering from anti-intellectualism—one of the main reason attributed to the movement's alleged failure to bring about substantial changes in Japanese society (Matsui 1990)—there has been, over the years, increasing acknowledgement of the movement's theoretical sophistication and of its elaboration of a "woman's logic" as opposed to the logic of productivity (or "male logic") perceived to lie at the core of Japan's postwar economic miracle (Tanaka 1995; Ochiai 1997; Muto 1997).

Ribu's relentless efforts to bring about a dramatic remodelling of society unfolded along what can be described as a threefold movement. To begin with, *ribu* called for a radical "transformation of the consciousness" (*ishiki henkaku*) of each individual who was placed at the centre of the movement's revolutionary project. *Ribu* affirmed that the establishment of a clear and free subjectivity (*shutaisei*) ought to be grounded in an internal revolution which, in turn, constituted the premise for any attempt to change society. This transformation demanded of women to unravel and overcome those psychological structures that had come into being as a consequence of the sedimentation and internalization of societal prescriptions of appropriate femininity through sex-role socialization (Inoue 1980: 197–8).[24] *Ribu* aimed at dissecting concepts and stereotypes

---

[24] Despite the imposed democratization of education in the postwar years (with schools becoming co-ed in the 1960s) and the expanded educational opportunities for women which increased the number of girls graduating from four-year universities, the reality of postwar Japan was that schools remained a two-stream, gender-segregated system where women were still perceived to have the obligation to undertake what was called "women's education" (*joshi kyōiku*). This is exemplified by the fact that in 1969 the Ministry of Education made four courses in the home economics curriculum compulsory for women and that, despite the opposition to this change during the 1970s and Japan's signing of the 1980 Convention to End All Forms of Discrimination against Women, the

3 The Women's Liberation Movement in 1970s Japan

such as "femininity," "feminine qualities," and "woman's happiness" that were subtly enforced upon women, but which were also reproduced by those very women in forms of unconscious complicity. Practices resembling the method of consciousness-raising that had been developed by American feminists were regularly employed at *ribu* meetings and teach-ins in order to lay bare woman's "inner feminine consciousness," that is, to unravel the internalized cultural and psychological assumptions that dictated norms of appropriate femininity.[25]

This inner metamorphosis was, in turn, deemed necessary to promote a more genuine relationality (*kankeisei*) between human beings. This meant new forms of relationship not only between woman and man but also—and importantly for the purpose of my argument in this book—between women and between woman and child. Sit-ins, summer camps and the organization of collectives and other forms of communal living constituted a crucial strategy by means of which both the transformation of the self and the creation of a new relationality were sought.[26] The sharing of personal experience became the basic channel through which *ribu* spread its revolutionary message from woman to woman. Emblematic of this dialogic dimension of the movement is the

---

Ministry retained the home economics requirement for girls until 1989 (Buckley and Mackie 1986: 180; Buckley 1993: 359–65; Mackie 2003: 171 note 48; Loftus 2013: 155).

[25] Feminist writer and activist Yoshitake Teruko (1931–2012) recalls how it was thanks to *ribu*'s emphasis on women's mutual sharing of experiences of oppression that she was finally able to come to terms with her own experience of rape at the hands of the American occupation forces shortly after Japan's defeat in 1945. She stresses how the transformation of her inner feminine consciousness constituted a pivotal moment in her healing process:

> That I became able, in these circumstances, to begin to talk about my rape experience, and to write about it, was due entirely to my encounter with (the activists of) women's lib [sic] because they helped me to be aware of the existence of a feminine consciousness located inside each of us. Why had I lived for a quarter of a century trying to conceal the fact that I was a rape victim? Why had I been constantly plagued by a sense of inferiority? As I continued to probe these questions, it suddenly became quite obvious. It was because I was, in the end, still bound up in a stereotypical image of women that defined women's happiness in terms of getting married, being a good wife, and being a good mother. (Yoshitake 2006; quoted and translated in Loftus 2013: 101)

[26] On August 21–24, 1971, the first *ribu* camp (*gasshuku*) was held in the Nagoya prefecture with the participation of 257 women from all over the country, while a second one was held on August 17–21, 1972, in Hokkaidō. Between these two retreats, the first official *ribu* conference (*ribu taikai*) was organized on May 5, 1972, attracting around 2000 participants.

first *ribu* gathering held on November 14, 1970, in the Shibuya ward in Tokyo. Organized by two *ribu* cells and sponsored by the progressive publisher Aki Shobō with the stated purpose of theorizing the movement, this "Symposium for [Woman's] Liberation" saw the participation of women from all paths of life, from high-school students to women in their 40s, 50s or 60s, and included *ribu* activists, members of pre-existing women's movements, working women, housewives, teachers and career women. Despite the fact that *ribu*'s constituency would be later characterized mostly by college-educated young women, such heterogeneity speaks of the wide appeal of its message. For 7 hours, 200 women or so[27] sat around a moderator in an auditorium whose access had been prohibited to men and painstakingly voiced their personal experiences and the problems they faced as women. In addition to the variety of issues raised, what commentators have regularly picked up is the emotional charge that traversed this and other similar gatherings: resentment, dissatisfaction, but also excitement. A few days later, on November 17, 1970, an article on the *Asahi shinbun* offered the moderator's first-hand account of the symposium under the headline "Let's make woman's [*onna*] lived pain our starting point!"[28] The choice of (re-)living women's painful experiences of discrimination as the shared affective root of *ribu*'s struggle for liberation expressed both the desire to place the individual at the heart of the movement and the belief that only through the dialogical exchange of their experiences of oppression could women bring about a revolution of their consciousness (Aki Shobō 1971; Akiyama 1993: 9; Muto 1997: 155–6; Shigematsu 2012).[29]

---

[27] Muto (1997: 155) argues that there were 500 participants at the symposium, while Tanaka (1995: 343) offers an even higher figure of 700. Shigematsu (2012: 72), on the other hand, reports a much more contained 200. In light of her in-depth analysis of the movement, the wide range of sources she uses and her direct contact with many of *ribu*'s founding members, I have decided here to privilege Shigematsu as the most reliable source.

[28] "'Onna no tsūkaku' wo shuppatsuten ni." *Asahi shinbun*, 17 November, 1970, p. 17. Morning ed. For a detailed consideration of the term *onna* and its political underpinnings in the rhetoric of the movement, see the following section "*Onna* and the liberation of woman's sexuality."

[29] An edited transcript of the debate was published four months later in the first book-length publication of *ribu*: *Protesting Sexual Discrimination: The Contentions of Ūman Ribu* (*Seisabetsu e no kokuhatsu—ūman ribu wa shuchō suru*). Emblematic of the emphasis *ribu* placed upon the individual as the subject of the movement, the volume opened with a section that was aptly entitled "What woman's liberation (*josei kaihō*) means to me." Following the record of the symposium was

The third dimension of *ribu*'s struggle entailed challenging society on a multiplicity of fronts through the spontaneous organizing of small, urban-based groups of anonymous activists. These *ribu* cells took part in both localized, independent actions and concerted campaigns, and promoted political identification and solidarity with those groups facing discrimination or criminalization such as sex workers, unmarried mothers, disabled people, the criminalized women of the United Red Army and mothers who killed their children. Together, the three dimensions I have just outlined ought not to be placed along a linear developmental narrative of feminist struggle that moved from the personal to the social. In fact, they constituted coextensive and continually interacting vectors of a single but, nonetheless, multidimensional revolutionary agenda. While changes in individual consciousness were regarded as a fundamental enabling condition for the creation of a new relationality as the basis of society, *ribu*'s experiments in communal living and sustained interaction between women constituted, in turn, fertile environments where such transformation could be lived through. In addition to this, attentive consideration of the movement's numerous campaigns reveals that the support that *ribu* often articulated for discriminated against or criminalized subjects constituted a distinctive feature of its desire to prioritize human relationality in its approach to political struggle. In this respect, Shigematsu (2012: 150) has aptly coined the phrase "feminist praxis of critical solidarity and radical inclusivity" to identify this aspect of *ribu*'s political engagement whereby forms of solidarity with socially abjected individuals were inflected through a critical consideration of the structural conditions that compelled such individuals into criminalized behaviours in the first place. Integral to this approach was the movement's self-reflexive stance that encouraged modes of identification with those who were regarded as defying the system—and whom society deemed deviant—as "a means to examine the self and locate the other within the self" (152). As the next chapter will make clear, provocative declarations

---

a collection of *ribu* pamphlets and a long section that provided detailed information about the American Women's Liberation Movement. This included an abridged translation of Marlene Dickson's article "The Rise of Women's Liberation" published in the December 1969 issue of *Ramparts Magazine* and of Gloria Steinem's essay "What Would It Be Like if Women Win" which appeared in *Time Magazine* in August 1970.

such as "The woman who kills her child is me! She's you!" (*Kogoroshi onna wa watashi deari, anata da!*) and "We might be next!" (*Asu wa wagami!*) were exemplary of the outcry with which *ribu* challenged society's stigmatization of mothers who killed their children, while simultaneously asserting a profound (and revolutionary) affinity with them.

Onna and the Liberation of Woman's Sexuality

Despite the idiosyncratic ways in which the numerous *ribu* groups that mushroomed in Japan articulated the meaning of their localized struggles, there emerged through a dialogic process traversed by tensions and contradictions few widely shared principles which provided the movement with relative coherence. The idea of "consciousness transformation" (*ishiki henkaku*) was one of them and I have written extensively on it in the previous section. Here I explore the central notion of "liberation of *onna*" (*onna kaihō*).

The movement's adoption of the rather untranslatable term *onna* has been compared to the reclamation of "queer" by LGBT movements (Sayama Sachi, quoted in Shigematsu 2012: xvi). Indeed, *onna* had traditionally been a highly derogatory term that designated "woman" and was imbued "with strong and often negative sexual connotations" (Endo 1995: 30; also quoted in Shigematsu, ibid.). Embedded in notions of female physicality, it was considered taboo and "dirty," conveying the image of a highly sexualized woman. *Ribu* reappropriated this term and made it into the signifier of a new revolutionary subject. Shigematsu has played a crucial role in introducing *onna*'s powerful connotations to a wider audience that might not be fluent in Japanese. Her work has also set a new standard that encourages English-speaking academia to consistently adopt the word *onna* (woman) as key to the movement's language and rhetoric (Shigematsu 2012).[30]

---

[30] Although Shigematsu's detailed analysis of the movement does not include an investigation of the role that engaged translations might have played in the early history of *ribu*, she, nonetheless, strongly emphasizes the importance of "the (racialized) labor of translation as a political practice of intercultural mediation" (2012: xxiv). Not only that, she also calls attention to how an attentive engagement with "troubled translations and the nontranslatable" is crucial in "attend[ing] to the

Onna was employed as a semantically rich alternative to be opposed to those terms that classified woman according to the socially accepted roles of mother, wife, housewife or female worker and which had constituted the identificatory base for previous women's movements and women's form of mobilization in Japan (as in the case of the Mothers' Convention and the Housewives Association). *Ribu* denounced these images as man-made fantasies and argued that, moulded by these socially upheld identities, a woman was doomed to live a fragmented existence, never recognized in her wholeness as *onna*, but always "torn apart from within" and forced to live through the roles that a male-dominated society prescribed for her (Ehara 2012: 110). As we shall see, *ribu* also made an impassioned critique against the institution of the family system: the postwar nuclear family came to be identified as the locus where these "negative identities" were maintained and reproduced together with the unequal power relations they sustained. The expression "negative identities" (*fu no aidentiti*) has been employed by Ehara in reference to the rejection of traditional feminine roles that characterized *ribu*'s inception. However, she has also observed that "recovering from negativity" by means of refusal and opposition could not, in itself, be productive of a distinct political subject. Reclaiming *onna* and striving day by day to create a new revolutionary and political subject through the establishment of alternative forms of relationality signalled, according to Ehara (2012: 102), *ribu*'s shift from being simply an oppositional movement to one that promoted an alternative.

In a powerful move that confounded the distinction between women's widely accepted roles within the family system and the socially abjected figure of the prostitute, *ribu* declared that a housewife and a prostitute were "racoons in the same den," two sides of the same coin. One of the much reprinted manifestos of the movement, Tanaka Mitsu's "Liberation from the Toilet" (*Benjo kara no kaihō*) argued that within men's consciousness *onna* was split into the two oppositional images of "mother" and "toilet": either the expression of maternal tenderness (the maternal ideal so dear to Japanese society) or the vessel for the release of man's

---

imbrications and interpenetration of local, linguistic, transcultural and transnational forces" (2012: xxiv).

sexual desire (implicitly and ironically compared to excrements) (Tanaka 1970: 202).[31] The term "toilet" traced back to the highly derogatory expression "public toilet" which was used to designate comfort women during wartime (Ueno 2011: 4). Ironically, that same expression came into use among the New Left and the students of *Zenkyōtō* to refer to female members who expressed an unconstrained sexuality and who were considered mere sexual objects by their male comrades. Yet, Tanaka's use of the term moved a much broader critique to a long history of masculine appropriation of women's sexuality whereby wives and prostitutes discovered themselves grouped together by their common strategies of survival, that is, selling (qua toilets) their sexual services to men in exchange of economic and/or material security. "Liberation from the Toilet" argued, instead, that *onna* consisted of an organic totality that integrated both the emotional quality of maternal tenderness and a woman's sexual desire.

Women's discriminatory experience within leftist, counter-cultural movements like *Zenkyōtō* had made painfully clear that to acknowledge the independence of woman's sexual desire and to liberate woman's sexuality from her subtle enslavement to the monogamous family system ought not to be conceived as synonymous with a "liberation of one's sexual organs" or with a doctrine of "free sex" (Gurūpu tatakau onna 1970: 212; Shigematsu 2012: 68). Rather, *ribu* understood the liberation of *onna* as coextensive with the liberation of sexuality which, in turn, was deemed constrained by the structure of the monogamous family. For the first time woman's sexuality was placed at the core of women's oppression and the adoption of the term *onna* signalled *ribu* activists' distinctive understanding of their own subjectivity, while simultaneously marking a linguistic and epistemological break from other postwar women's movements (Ehara 2012: 119; Shigematsu 2012: 16–19).

Ribu argued that, because a woman had historically been confined to the role of sexual object and denied the possibility to live as sexual subject, she now suffered from a lack of knowledge about her own body

---

[31] There exist two versions of Tanaka's pamphlet "Liberation from the Toilet": the original was circulated in August 1970, and it was followed only a few months later by a longer, revised version in October 1970. I cite here the original version reproduced in Mizoguchi et al. (1992): 201–7. The revised pamphlet has been reprinted in Tanaka (2010: 333–47). For detailed information about the publishing history of these two pamphlets, see Shigematsu (2012: 205–6, note 81).

which, combined with social and moral frameworks that disqualified her from speaking of anything sexual, worked effectively to keep her in a position of subordination within the family system. This is also patently clear from Ogino Miho's (1994: 81) research on abortion and women's reproductive rights in postwar Japan where she highlights women's "ignorance or fear of their own bodies" and their "embarrassment in talking about matters relating to sex due to strong sexual repression." She points to the fact that it is "taboo for women to act knowledgeable about sexual matters and to give instructions to men" to the point that they may prefer "maintaining a passive stance toward sex and leaving contraception in men's hands to discussing these matters thoroughly with men or assuming responsibility for themselves" (80).

Therefore, the liberation of *onna* required that a great amount of energy be devoted to promoting and disseminating knowledge of the female body. The creation of women-only spaces such as centres, communes, cafés and bookstores enabled *ribu* activists to organize teach-ins, seminars and workshops on subjects such as the female sexual apparatus, sex, venereal diseases, contraception, pregnancy, abortion, birth and other aspects of female corporeality. An important contribution to the promotion of women's reappropriation of their bodies was the first translation in 1974 of *Our Bodies, Ourselves*. The foreword to the Japanese edition states: "[Those] women who have felt their bodies somewhat distant, as something other than themselves, by means of knowing about their bodies and by telling each other about their bodies, will make their bodies their own once again" (quoted in Ehara 2012: 126).[32] Some of these spaces also provided women with professional, legal or medical consultations and constituted a network for the dissemination of information both in the form of face-to-face interactions and through the distribution of pamphlets, newsletters, zines and journals. These *minikomi* (mini-communications) represented an alternative media outlet borne out of *ribu*'s painstaking effort to establish alternative channels of communication that could counter the prescriptions of womanhood and feminine

---

[32] For an extensive consideration of the work behind this first translation, see Akiyama (1993: 154–66) and Welker (2012). For an account of a later translation of *The New Our Bodies, Ourselves*, see Buckley (1997: 185–225).

propriety with which the *masukomi* (mass communications or, put it simply, the mass media) bombarded women. This alternative communication network was characterized by an informal and accessible style and played a crucial role in transmitting information among the numerous *ribu* cells across Japan.[33]

Ribu's Critique of the Family System

In conjunction with *ribu*'s celebration of *onna* as a new political subject and its call for liberation of (female) sexuality, a fervent critique of the postwar nuclear family traversed the movement's rhetoric as another of its distinctive traits. *Ribu* argued that the family existed not as a place for the creation of meaningful human relationships, but as the site where woman's sexuality and desire were subjected to masculine dominance and conceived only in (re-)productive terms. Modern Japanese society was understood to be plagued by a capitalist logic of productivity, often identified as a "male logic" (*otoko no ronri*), which was also described as permeating the family system. Such logic, it was argued, demanded of men that they sacrificed themselves to corporate values for the sake of the country's renewed economic prosperity, while women were rendered intelligible only in their prescribed roles of wives and mothers which, in turn, constituted the sole guarantee of their social existence.

The late postwar period had seen a steady increase, numerically as well as proportionally, of the ratio of nuclear family households to total ordinary (i.e. multigenerational) households. Even though the extended family (*ie*) had not disappeared nor had it been replaced, during the 1960s the number of nuclear families increased to 60 per cent of all households and the new, urban, nuclear family became established at a mass level (Ochiai 2005, 1997; Ueno 1988). An increased number of nuclear units composed solely of husband, wife and unmarried children found their material reflection in the wave of high-density urban architecture, the multiunit, suburban housing complexes known as *danchi* becoming the

---

[33] See also Buckley and Mackie (1986: 180–1), Mackie (1992), Buckley (1993: 352), Buckley (1997: 187), Shigematsu (2012: xxviii, 81, 96).

typical accommodation of late post-World War II families and the epitome of what it meant "to live modern" (Nishikawa 1999; Buckley 1993: 352). Ueno (1988) observes how, in the context of a modern industrial society, the family unit came to be placed at the centre of Japan's economic growth and to be organized according to a rigid gendered division of labour: husbands were expected to act as the breadwinners and to spend most of their time working and socializing with colleagues in the public sphere, whereas wives were increasingly confined at home which, in turn, began to be organized around the schedules of children (and mothers). In this regard, sociologist Yoshizumi Kyoko (1995: 185–6) speaks of the emergence in postwar society of "pseudo-single-mother-families" where the father, though legally present, was too busy to spend much time with his family.

The widespread use of new electric appliances like refrigerators, washing machines and vacuum cleaners was said to liberate housewives from household chores, while popular discourse, advertisement and ideological mystification bombarded them with images of woman's happiness in the nuclear family and middle-class lifestyle (Robins-Mowry 1983; Buckley 1993; Tanaka 1995; Muto 1997; Sasaki-Uemura 2007). Yoda Tomiko (2000: 872–3) points at the increased popularity at this historical juncture of so-called *my-homism* (*mai hōmu shugi*, literally "the ideology of home ownership") that symbolized the "middle-class domesticity and material comfort of privatised family life" and which emphasized the vital importance of domestic life for Japan's economic expansion in the form of increased purchasing of consumer durables. Media campaigns promoted the image of the "professional housewife" (*sengyō shufu*) (Buckley 1993: 352; Vogel 1978), while women's isolation from society and from one another, and their subjugation to the sex-role division of labour that characterized the modern nuclear family came to be disguised as "the happiness of the home" (Ueno 1988: 169; see also Loftus 2013: 154–5). With men pressured to devote themselves fully to the company cause, internalize company values and leave childcare and housework entirely in the hands of their wives, the modernization of the family had also translated into women's more thorough confinement to the domestic sphere: women found themselves trapped in a new form of subjugation reminiscent of the predicament of those who suffered from the "feminine mystique" in Betty Friedan's middle-class America (see also Welker 2012: 33; Yoda 2000: 873).[34]

Regarded as the foundational unit of society and the cornerstone of Japan's postwar economic miracle, the institution of the family was regulated and legally validated by the family registration system (*koseki seido*). This had been in place since 1872 and required that family status events such as birth, marriage, divorce, adoption and death be registered with the government. The family registry was and is still used to determine a person's eligibility to education and income assistance. It serves as certificate of citizenship, for passport issuance and renewal, and it was traditionally required by schools, prospective employers and future parents-in-law to verify the family background of an individual. *Ribu*'s critiques of family registration denounced it for reinforcing a patriarchal model of the family and for reproducing traditional gender norms whereby a wife married into her husband's family, took his name and was registered into his family registry. Taimie L. Bryant (1991) has described in detail the negative impact of family registration on the opportunities of *burakumin* (outcasts) and *zainichi* Koreans (Koreans resident in Japan) for participation in Japanese society and she has widely documented its negative effects on the life of women. As the authoritative source of Japanese nationality, only Japanese can have family registries. However, the demand that a married woman be removed from her family registry in order to be entered into the family registry of her husband could have serious implications for her and her children if the husband was not Japanese. To begin with, "non-Japanese fathers did not have Japanese family registries in which their wives or children could be registered" (Bryant 1991: 131), and because the mother had been expunged upon marriage from her original family registry, her children could not be conferred Japanese citizenship (with all the social consequences that this might have entailed). This placed Japanese women at a disadvantage vis-à-vis Japanese men

---

[34] In this regard, Ueno (1988: 171) has bleakly stated that "[i]ndustralization organized male members of the society as wage labourers but it left women in the private sphere with children, the elderly, the diseased and the handicapped."

who could simply enter their non-Japanese wives on their parents' family registry[35]:

> Because women "followed their husbands" and left their parents' registry upon marriage, Japanese women who married non-Japanese were forced to choose between illegitimacy and Japanese nationality for their children. If a Japanese woman had children before marriage, her children would be illegitimate but they would be Japanese by virtue of her being able to establish her own family registry or remaining on her parents' family registry. If the Japanese woman married before having children, her children would be legitimate but they would not have Japanese citizenship. (ibid.)

As if this were not enough, Bryant (1991: 139) has also observed how the family registration system reinforced the stigma of illegitimacy and adoption which attached not only to the child (whose adoption is recorded on the family registry of the adoptive parents) but also to the biological mother who "must retain the stigmatizing record of the child's birth on her family registry." The extent to which *ribu*'s attacks against the family registration system and the institution of the family it supported were relevant for the movement's solidarity with mothers who killed their children becomes apparent when we consider that, as late as in 1986, 82.2 per cent of victims of infanticide were "non-marital children" (136). In this respect, it is important to acknowledge that, while the spontaneous emergence of *ribu* collectives and other forms of communal living was meant to create suitable conditions for *onna*'s self-discovery, it also represented a major challenge to the institution of the family.[36] In particular, the creation of collectives of women and children aimed at experimenting

---

[35] Until 1985 neither Japanese women nor men could establish a new family registry in case they married a non-Japanese. However, due to the fact that Japanese men were not removed from their parents' family registry upon their marriage, they were in a position to sidestep such a dilemma of illegitimacy/citizenship for their children. This was a legal issue that was specific to Japanese women and that was partially resolved only in 1985 when a revision of the National Law made it possible for either parent to confer Japanese nationality to his or her child (Bryant 1991: 132).

[36] Nishimura (2006: 52–3) differentiates *ribu* collectives into three groups, according to the rationale and aims behind their original formation: those focused on elaborating and practising new modes of childrearing, those that emerged as centres for the organization of *ribu*'s activities and were devoted to the circulation of information and, lastly, those that were simply born out of a desire to experiment with alternative forms of female communal living. Among the numerous women-only collectives that emerged in the 1970s, the Ribu Shinjuku Centre occupied a distinc-

with a lifestyle that was openly critical of the traditional family system and which could allow "unmarried mothers" (*mikon no haha*) to avoid and counter social stigma. Many *ribu* scholars have identified the desire to fight the discrimination meted out to single mothers as an important element of *ribu*'s agenda which prompted many activists to decide to have children out of wedlock, while searching for and experimenting alternative forms of childcare. The Japanese expression *mikon no haha* (未婚の母) that designated single mothers was exemplary of the social pressure for women to marry and have children within the legitimacy of the monogamous family. The word *mikon* (未婚) results from the union of the two characters 未 which means "not yet" and 婚 which means "to marry." The term, thus, framed unmarried mothers in terms of their "marriageability" and their position within the life cycle that society prescribed for women: an unmarried woman was conceived as "a woman who is not yet married, even though she will have to marry sooner or later" (Inoue 1980: 198). Shigematsu (2012: 20) underscores how *ribu*'s sensitivity to the political dimension of language prompted women activists to coin the alternative term *hikon no haha* which literally means "anti-marriage mother" or "negation-of-marriage mother" as a conscious linguistic alternative to the widespread use of "not-yet-married mother."

Given how the modern nuclear family was regarded as fundamental to Japan's rapid modernization and economic expansion, we can begin to appreciate one of the many revolutionary dimensions of *ribu*: as women activists questioned the sex-role division of labour within the family and indicted the family system as a site for the reproduction of unequal power relations and structures of discrimination, they also, as it were, threatened the very foundation of Japan's new material affluence. On the other hand, Ehara (2012: 137) suggests that the most deep-rooted resistance to *ribu* might well have stemmed from its attacks to the "maternal fantasy" that she deems characteristic of Japanese society.[37] It is to this important aspect of *ribu*'s activism that I now turn.

---

tive place in that it played a pivotal role in shaping the contours and priorities of the movement in its formative years (Shigematsu 2012; Nishimura 2006: 57–96; Endō et al. 1996).

[37] For a recent investigation of the emergence of the notion of Japan as a "maternal society" in the 1960s and its consolidation in the 1970s, see Yoda's (2000) insightful article "The Rise and Fall of Maternal Society: Gender, Labor, and Capital in Contemporary Japan."

Dismantling the Myth of Maternal Love

The postwar nuclear family also came under harsh criticism because it represented an important apparatus whereby the prewar and interwar ideology of the "good wife, wise mother" (*ryōsai kenbo*) found novel articulation. Such ideology stemmed from the state-sponsored redefinition of womanhood that originated in the Meiji period (1868–1912) and which promoted a gendered division of labour whereby women were defined as "managers of domestic affairs in the household and nurturers of children" (Uno 1993: 294). Accordingly, women were encouraged to fully inhabit the private sphere and contribute to the nation through complete devotion to the family, efficient house management, care of the old, young and ill, and a responsible upbringing of their children (Nolte and Hastings 1991: 152; Ericson 1996; Uno 1999). Historically, the ideology of the "good wife, wise mother" had been celebrated as pivotal to the establishment of a modern nation-state in nineteenth-century Japan, had been aligned with the country's nationalist and imperialist projects during and between the two world wars,[38] and was now being recovered in altered form to support a vision of the family as essential to Japan's economic miracle in the postwar years.[39] *Ribu*'s repudiation of the "good wife, wise mother" ideal was partially rooted in the movement's anti-establishment and anti-imperialist stance which urged women activists to reject an ideology that for almost a century had framed motherhood as decisive for the prosperity of the nation and, under the pronatalist slogan "bear children and multiply" (*umeyo fuyaseyo*), had supported Japan's war efforts and imperial expansion (Ogino 1994: 71; Mackie 2003: 112–13; Shigematsu 2012: 6–7).[40]

But the ideology of "good wife, wise mother" was also deeply entangled with a cultural sanctification of motherly love and devotion that

---

[38] For an exploration of the ideology and ideal of "good wife, wise mother," see Uno (1991, 1993), Nolte and Hastings (1991), Hara (1995), Borovoy (2005) and Tipton (2009).

[39] Uno (1993: 295) maintains that attempts to prescribe a feminine identity as bound to a woman's role of wife and mother and confined within the boundaries of the domestic sphere continued in various form well into the 1980s.

[40] Wakakuwa (2004) offers a fascinating account of media representations of women's roles during wartime.

defined marriage as woman's happiness, demanded total self-abnegation of mothers and expected them to live for their children. "The trap of the myth of maternal love"—to borrow the title of Ohinata Masami's (2000) important book *Boseiai shinwa no wana*—relied on the idealization of the mother–child bond and on the shared cultural expectation that a mother would sacrifice herself for the greater good of the family, embrace her ingress into motherhood with enthusiasm and naturally establish with her child a relationship saturated with love and devoid of ambivalent feelings (Ohinata 1995; Orpett Long 1996). The myth of maternal love worked by policing the deviant behaviour of women who expressed dissatisfaction, anxiety or fear in relation to their maternal experience, and stigmatized as aberrations those mothers who seemed unable to love their children or, worse, who abused and hurt them (Ohinata 2000: 2; Ehara 2012: 135). We have seen this clearly in Chap. 2, where media coverage has been shown to constitute a significant part of those discursive practices that attempted to "quarantine" mothers who killed their children outside of the realm of cultural intelligibility.

However, whereas *ribu*'s solidarity with mothers who kill might seem, at first sight, to express an unambiguous and utter rejection of the maternal role, it is imperative to realize that *ribu* did not attempt to negate or do away with motherhood altogether (Akiyama 1993; Ueno 2011; Ehara 2012). Rather, it was motherhood as institution (as opposed to mothering as experience) that women activists strenuously questioned (Rich 1979; see also O'Reilly 2004). In addition to this, *ribu* scholars emphasize how the movement took a self-consciously ambivalent stance on motherhood (Ueno 2011: 6) and that "the more they negated [the institution of] motherhood, the more a desire emerged to rescue motherhood into a different form" (Ōgoshi 2005: 134). Ōgoshi also argues that "[t]he ideological radicalism of *ūman ribu* lied in its sanguinary struggle with the problem of motherhood which constituted the utmost aporia in terms of the establishment of female subjectivity" (131). However, this struggle was not grounded in the belief that motherhood and female subjectivity were two mutually exclusive alternatives for women: in fact, to a greater or lesser degree, all *ribu* groups shared the view that the imposition Japanese women faced of having to choose between being a mother or having a strong, independent subjectivity was itself symptomatic of their very oppression in society (Akiyama 1993: 123).

The organization of communes of women and children represented one of *ribu*'s attempts to challenge this enforced either/or. Well-known among them was Tokyo Komu-unu, which opened in Tokyo in August 1972 and whose name was a combination of the word *komyūn* (commune) and the expression *ko umi* (to give birth). Run by the homonymous group, the commune originally comprised three mothers and their children who aimed at forging new forms of relationality between parent and child and "sought to redefine and create new conditions for raising children that rejected the 'sacrificial mother' paradigm that placed all responsibility on the birth mother" (Shigematsu 2012: 20). The commune also functioned as an open, communitarian nursery to which other parents could entrust their children and where the founding members were intermittently joined by other women and men also involved in childcare activities. The group criticized the commonly held belief that giving birth and raising a child was a woman's life purpose and that it was by becoming a mother that she could affirm herself in society. It strongly opposed the social expectation that from birth until the moment when she could depart from her child a mother's energies ought to be devoted exclusively to childrearing within the limits of the domestic sphere (Mizoguchi et al. 1994: 26).[41] Indeed, the commune was created with the fundamental conviction that "[t]he very struggle of *onna* while she gives birth and raises a child is the struggle to choose the tomorrow" (Tokyo Komu-unu 1975: 372). This represents a concise and powerful

---

[41] We cannot fail to notice the reality gap that distinguished the late postwar period in Japan and which emerged from the simultaneous intensification of women's participation in the labour force and the tendency in popular discourse to valorize women in their primary role as mothers. Despite women's increasing access to higher education, scholars have highlighted the consolidation of the (in)famous M-curve in women's employment statistics. According to this typical pattern women worked while single, left their jobs on marrying or on occasion of their first pregnancy and returned to work after the birth of their last child, although this time with a shift from full-time to part-time employment. This pattern combined with the constant wage differential according to gender and with women's limited opportunities for career advancement. Furthermore, women's employment conditions were regulated by the Labour Standards Act whose "protective" provisions secured maternity and menstruation leave and prohibited women from dangerous occupations and excessive overtime or night work, thus suggesting that women were valued mainly in their role as (potential) mothers and not as individuals (Ueno 1988; Buckley 1993; Ochiai 1997; Mackie 2003; Tipton 2008).

articulation of the group's belief that the process of self-transformation and the struggle for the creation of a new revolutionary subject were not incompatible with mothering: the struggle of *onna* could, indeed, unfold alongside the experience of childbirth and child-raising. Tokyo Komu-unu strove to make this convergence possible by questioning cultural assumptions about the mother–child relationship and by affirming the possibility of a maternal experience outside the legitimizing frame of the family system: by referring to the commune as "a family of unmarried mothers" (*mikon no haha no ie*) the members of Tokyo Komu-unu subversively brought into discourse and challenged what current social norms rendered a logical and cultural impossibility (ibid.).

The articulation of new conditions to raise children went hand in hand with a relentless problematization of woman's autonomy (*jiritsu*) as the group made active efforts to promote the right of women with children to participate in a life outside the domestic walls: Tokyo Komu-unu fought for women's right to go shopping, visit museums and even take part in street demonstrations together with their children. By organizing campaigns against the banning of prams from the platforms of the underground and the national railway stations, from department stores and museums, it posed a revolutionary challenge to the social regulations deemed responsible for maintaining a problematic division between public and private space (Tokyo Komu-unu 1974; Akiyama 1993: 185–6; Nishimura 2006: 97–124; Shigematsu 2012: 20). The activism of Tokyo Komu-unu made the *onna*-with-child (*komochi onna*) an important site of social contestation and a specific incarnation of *ribu*'s new revolutionary subject (Akiyama 1993: 186; Mizoguchi et al. 1994: 26).

Ribu and the Eugenic Protection Law Campaign

We can also recognize a certain commitment to rescuing the maternal (rather than rejecting it) in *ribu*'s campaign to safeguard women's access to abortion and to fight against revisions to the Eugenic Protection Law. While this represents an issue that, because of its complexity, warrants an investigation on its own, there are at least two reasons why it is impossible to end this chapter without mentioning it.[42] To begin with, women's strong desire to oppose the proposed amendments to the Eugenic Protection Law triggered a nationwide, coordinated mobilization of *ribu* cells of such dimensions that it simply deserves to be acknowledged. In the second place, some of *ribu*'s discursive interventions involving infanticide and child killing were articulated in the context of these campaigns: although I will devote only minimal attention to the notion of abortion-as-murder or abortion-as-child killing (*kogoroshi*), a certain desire for completeness demands that I briefly consider, at this point of my discussion, such an important aspect of *ribu*'s multifaceted struggle.

Abortion was widely practised in Japan until the Meiji era (1868–1912) which marked the beginning of a rapid period of modernization for the country. In 1880, with the promulgation of the country's first modern penal code, abortion was made a crime for the first time and it has remained a crime since. In June 1948, however, during the Allied Occupation, the Eugenic Protection Law (*Yūsei hogo-hō*) was passed whose Art. 1 stated that the purpose of the law was "to prevent the birth of eugenically inferior offspring" and "to protect maternal health and life" (Norgren 2001: 145). In 1949 economic reasons were added as legitimate grounds for abortion (Art. 14, para. 1, no. 4), and in 1952 another revision was made that simplified administrative access to abortion and eliminated the need for women to appear in front of a Eugenic Protection Board of Examiners, making abortion accessible with the sole recommendation of a certified doctor (Ogino 1994: 72; Norgren 2001: 44–52; Mackie 2003: 166). The continued criminalization of abortion notwithstanding, the "economic reasons" clause constituted a loophole in the law that, in practice, made abortion on demand accessible to Japanese women (even though a eugenic logic, rather than a desire to recognize women's right to self-determination, remained the rationale behind such revisions). Under the new law, the number of induced abortions doubled between 1949 and 1950 and reached over one million (reported) cases per year between

---

[42] Two detailed studies on this topic are Tiana Norgren's *Abortion Before Birth Control: The Politics of Reproduction in Postwar Japan* (2001) and Kato Masae's *Women's Rights? The Politics of Eugenic Abortion in Modern Japan* (2009). See also Tama Yasuko's article "The Logic of Abortion: Japanese Debates on the Legitimacy of Abortion as Seen in Post-World War II Newspapers" (1994).

1955 and 1960. However, due to the tendency among ob-gyns in private practice to underreport the number of performed abortions in order to escape taxation, the actual number is estimated to have been between two and four times higher than the reported rates (Ogino 1994: 72–3; Norgren 2001: 5, 7, 49). By the late 1950s and early 1960s Japan had become internationally (in)famous as an "abortion paradise" (*datai tengoku*) (Norgren 2001: 54). At the same time, a complex interplay of factors such as the experience (and the memory) of the hardships of war, the increase in women's access to higher education (with the consequent rise in age at first marriage) and in their participation in the labour force, and the economic demands to maintain higher living standards all contributed to a dramatic decrease in the Japanese birth rate that dropped to the replacement level by 1960, and didn't show significant changes during the 1970s (Sasaki-Uemura 2007: 317; Allinson 1997; Buckley 1993).[43]

The early 1970s witnessed several attempts by members of the ruling Japanese party (the Liberal Democratic Party, LDP) to restrict access to abortion. In May 1972, with the support of the right-wing, nationalist, anti-abortion religious group Seichō no Ie (The House of Growth), the LDP proposed a bill to revise the Eugenic Protection Law. The revision draft would remove the economic clause and replace it with a mental reason clause that would allow abortion if "the continuation of pregnancy or childbirth [was] likely to seriously harm the mother's mental or physical health [...] and in cases of fetal disease or defect" (quoted in Norgren 2001: 62). In this regard, Shigematsu (2012: 88) makes clear how *ribu* understood this proposed revision "as signifying an ideological shift that would place the blame for abortion on the individual mother instead of improving the societal conditions for giving birth."

It is not my intention to provide here an overview of *ribu*'s campaign against the proposed revisions to the Eugenic Protection Law. What I want to foreground in my discussion is the fact that the argument the movement raised was not grounded in a rejection of motherhood or the identification of women's reproductive capacities as the source of wom-

---

[43] Whereas in the 1970s Japan's fertility rate had reached 2.0, in 1990 it fell to its lowest value of 1.57. Such sensational drop in the birth rate prompted the news media to coin the phrase "1.57 shock" (Ogino 1994: 89).

en's oppression. The issue was not to guarantee women's access to a medical procedure that allowed them to freely terminate a pregnancy at will. In fact, to think along these lines would have meant to fail to challenge the very social conditions that gave woman no other choice but to abort (Ehara 2012). *Ribu*'s intervention to oppose the revisions ought to be understood in the context of the movement's broader demands to radically change the status quo. Kato (2009: 65–83) has made this crystal clear in her analysis of how the alliance that *ribu* formed with the disabled people movement Aoi Shiba no Kai (Green Grass Association) against the revision of the Eugenic Protection Law prompted women activists to question the very rhetoric of rights with which they had originally framed their struggle.[44] Phrases like "Women choose whether to give or not to give birth" (*umu umanai wa onna ga kimeru*) and "Abortion is a woman's right" (*chūzetsu wa onna no kenri*) were soon supplanted by slogans such as "For a society where we can give birth! Where we want to give birth!" (*Umeru shakai wo! Umitai shakai wo!*) and "I want to give birth…but I can't give birth" (*Umitai… demo umenai*). This rhetorical move aimed to emphasize the desire to create a society where women really had the possibility *to choose* whether or not to give birth, and where childbirth and child-raising were no longer a private matter, but a broader social issue. Kato further suggests that what made the alliance between *ribu* and the disabled people movement possible was their sharing of a similar self-image implicitly upheld by society's "logic of productivity" according to which pregnant women, women with children and disabled people (but we could also add the sick and the elderly to the list) were perceived as "deviants" in light of a social norm based on being male, productive and disability free.

This cursory account of *ribu*'s campaign should have made it sufficiently clear that women activists never attempted to do away with motherhood and that, by giving priority to the creation of the very possibility of an alternative, they did place equal weight on both "giving birth" and "not giving birth" (Akiyama 1993: 123). Emblematic of this nuanced

---

[44] Shigematsu has also highlighted how the presence at the Ribu Shinjuku Centre of Yonezu Tomoko—a woman with a disability who developed a close relationship with Tanaka Mitsu—was also fundamental in shifting *ribu*'s politics from a focus on abortion as woman's right to a critique of the state control of reproduction and ableism (2012: 79–81, 90).

understanding of the maternal was the slogan "To give birth is egoism, not to give birth is [also] egoism" (*Umu mo ego, umanu mo ego*) by means of which *ribu* stressed that, while society's common sense considered abortion as a woman's egoistic act, giving birth ought also to be understood as an expression of egoism stemming directly from the unequal gendered organization of society. Some women, *ribu* argued, gave birth just because others did the same or simply to acquire "proper" status in society, to prove their womanhood and justify their existence, while also avoiding being seen as deviant. Some women even used their children as a means of self-realization. The movement denounced the fact that, despite all these manifestations of egoism, giving birth and having children had hardly ever been understood as selfish acts, but they had even become in 1970s Japan a source of societal admiration and recognition (Kato 2009: 72–3). *Ribu* denounced society's myopic vision that conceived only of abortion as an aberration, and pointed at the social expectations that constrained women's experience of motherhood and twisted its profound significance.

Acknowledging *ribu*'s Exclusions

It is important to acknowledge that the movement's discourse on motherhood, its critique of the institution of the family and its urge to make *onna* a new political subject hardly engaged with issues of race, class or age. We can begin making sense of these significant shortcomings by recalling that by the early 1970s 90 per cent of the Japanese population understood themselves to be middle class (Tipton 2008: 187). Furthermore, Shigematsu (2012: xvi) reminds us that most *ribu* members were college-educated young women in their twenties and early thirties who were "predominantly ethnic-majority Japanese largely from the postwar Japanese middle and lower-middle classes" and, thus, "occupied a positionality that was relatively privileged."

As a matter of fact, *ribu*'s profound self-reflexivity prompted its members to question their complicity with forms of sexualized violence that differentially affected other Asian women: the movement denounced the comfort women system, the "colonization of the bodies of Okinawan sex workers by the men of the US military" (Shigematsu 2012: 49) and the sexual exploitation of Korean sex workers in the so-called Kisaeng tourism in South Korea (93–95). However, the movement showed only a limited engagement with the plight of different groups of women within Japan such as *burakumin* (outcasts), *zainichi* Koreans (Koreans resident in Japan) and agricultural workers. Sure enough, a certain disregard of different experiences of oppression can be recognized in *ribu*'s articulation of *onna* as a universalized collective identity, in the movement's critique of the institution of motherhood and in its preoccupation with a maternal potential for violence. This oversight could perhaps be explained by reference to *ribu*'s being a "second-wave"-type movement, although it still remains in a relation of tension with *ribu*'s anti-imperialism, its pan-Asianism and with women activists' openness to confront each other as they walked on the path leading to the transformation of one's own consciousness.[45]

Also, the role of men within the movement remains, to date, deeply underexplored. It is true that *ribu*'s struggle for liberation was not confined to the liberation of women from forms of oppression deemed specific to their sex, but aimed at freeing the whole society from a state of enslavement to a logic of productivity that alienated men in equal measure in their roles of breadwinners and industrious cogwheels within the corporations. However, during the movement's formative years it was crucial for *ribu* to prioritize the creation of those women-only spaces that alone would have allowed women activists to embark on an individual journey of self-transformation. Since there were no instructions, no ready-made new ideals of relationality waiting to be put into practice to bring about the emergence of a new revolutionary subject it was through these experimental attempts of communal living and daily interaction that the movement attempted to envision the very possibility of an alternative. This meant breaking the circuit whereby the masculine gaze was endowed with the power to either dispense or refuse a woman's sense of self-worth. In this respect, women-only spaces became the springboard for a confrontation of *onna* with other *onna*, while they kept at bay the risks harboured by a face-to-face interaction with man (i.e. the reactiva-

---

[45] I am grateful to Sharalyn Orbaugh for this point and careful reminder.

tion of the internalized "feminine consciousness" women were striving to transform).

There were, nonetheless, communes like Tokyo Komu-unu that opened their doors to men's participation and in April 1973 the Ribu Shinjuku Centre began to organize a men's *ribu* (Shigematsu 2012: 224, note 61; Mizoguchi et al. 1995: 395–418). To date, however, there is only one book-length published account of *ribu* as seen through the eyes of those men who took part in the movement (Satō 2010). The original priority *ribu* gave to the transformation of woman's consciousness and the dearth of documentary evidence about men's *ribu* could be deemed partially accountable for the emergence in the following chapter of an image of the movement that fails to engage with or to question the paternal figure.[46]

---

[46] We might also speculate that the gendered division of labour within the modern nuclear family might have made the paternal figure virtually non-existent, thus potentially voiding the chances for *ribu*'s active engagement with it.

4

Contested Meanings: Mothers Who Kill and the Rhetoric of *ūman ribu*

On May 8, 1971, *ribu* cells in Tokyo organized a rally "in solidarity with women who kill their children" (*onna no kogoroshi ni rentai suru shūkai*). Held on the occasion of Mother's Day, this demonstration saw the participation of around 100 people, with women and children marching in the rain with marguerites in their hands (Sayama and Aida 1972: 4). Numerous demonstrations and meetings were held on that day in support of these criminalized mothers, triggering spontaneous forms of activism across the country such as the call to organize a rally in solidarity with filicidal mothers that was circulated in Hokkaido (Japan's northernmost prefecture) by a *ribu* group called Metropolitan (Shigematsu 2012: 24; Mizoguchi et al. 1992: 149). The brief but vivid description of the participants to the May 8 demonstration appeared in the founding issue of *Ribu nyūsu—kono michi hitosuji* (Ribu News: This Way Only), the main publication of the Ribu Shinjuku Centre and the largest circulating newspaper of the movement (Shigematsu 2012: 154). It was accompanied by an excerpt from a letter of 23-year-old *ribu* activist R.K. where the author referred to a recent case which had been reported in the newspapers of a young mother who had abandoned her newborn baby in a

© The Author(s) 2017
A. Castellini, *Translating Maternal Violence*,
DOI 10.1057/978-1-137-53882-6_4

119

coin-locker and caused its eventual death. The excerpt is worth being quoted at length[1]:

> At that time what arose in my heart was not a feeling of compassion for the poor baby, but for the fear felt by this woman as she faced the fact of the child being born. Although I was myself surprised at the form assumed by my own reactions, I lamented at the same time the misery of the woman who killed her child, of the child who had been killed, and the grotesque [disposition] of those people (including the person who had written that article) who, strong in their "common sense," were throwing words of denunciation against that woman.
>
> I think that may well have been the first encounter (*deai*) where I became conscious that there might be a connection between women who have killed their children (*kodomo o koroshita onnatachi*) and myself. I've never been pregnant nor have I ever had an abortion. Nonetheless, I had the impression—whatever the reason—that her misery overlapped with mine, together with the thought "I'm a woman too" (*watashi mo onna nanda*). I felt as if that thought urged me toward something. I felt that I couldn't live were I not to do something, and that, even though I don't know what's the best thing to do, I must start doing something. (Sayama and Aida 1972: 4)[2]

I take this long passage to be emblematic of the terrain this chapter sets off to investigate as it introduces in a nutshell many aspects of the complex relationship *ribu* established with the phenomenon of maternal filicide. The passage acknowledges the importance of news media both as sources of public information about mothers who kill and as promoters of modes of representation that denounced and stigmatized those mothers.

---

[1] The excerpt was part of a much larger article that reviewed the first year of activism of the movement (the founding issue of *Ribu nyūsu* was circulated in October 1972). Brief descriptions of major landmark events were followed by significant quotes from pamphlets or bills produced for each occasion or by excerpts from personal letters of women who might or might not have been *ribu* members. This editorial style was consequential in furthering a sense of community: not only did it communicate the lively, activist spirit that had become the trademark of the movement, but it also included multiple voices which confirmed the extent to which *ribu*'s struggles for social transformation resonated with a wider audience.

[2] Due to the paucity of academic investigations of this specific dimension of *ribu*'s activism, this chapter draws largely on primary sources in Japanese such as pamphlets, bills and booklets that the movement produced and circulated in the 1970s. Unless otherwise stated, all the translations are mine.

It is against the backdrop of these biased portrayals and as a reaction to the crucial role media framing played in the regulation of cultural understandings of maternal violence that *ribu*'s discursive intervention acquires much of its unsettling and revolutionary potential. Furthermore, although the mother portrayed in the news and the author of the letter from which the excerpt above is taken would seem to occupy positions of radical incommunicability due to the stark contrast between their life experiences, a sense of affinity emerges that is recognized in the overlap of their individual miseries and which is rooted in the shared condition of being a woman (*onna*). However, the moment of epiphany R.K. is recounting for us should not be taken to signal naïve identification: it partakes instead of the movement's relentless emphasis on alternative forms of relationality whereby the meaning of *onna* as a new political subject would tentatively emerge through new forms of human interaction and mutual recognition. The author's "encounter" (*deai*) with the phenomenon of maternal filicide can be thus read as a synecdoche of *ribu*'s own encounter with mothers who kill, an encounter that was meant to be inherently transformative and which inspired a renewed desire for activism and social contestation.[3]

We may recall here the notion of feminist praxis of critical solidarity and radical inclusivity coined by Shigematsu to describe *ribu*'s programmatic solidarity with socially abjected or criminalized individuals. This strategy of political contestation called into question society's "common sense," questioned the unproblematic acceptance of moral categories that define a deed as criminal and urged a critical examination of the structural conditions that induced individuals into their criminalized behaviours (Shigematsu 2012: 150–152). Provocative declarations such as "The woman who kills her child is you…" (*Kogoroshi no onna wa anata da…*) (Ribu Shinjuku Sentā 1973), "The woman who kills her child is me! She's you!" (*Kogoroshi onna wa watashi deari, anata da!*) (Niimi

---

[3] The notion of "encounter" (*deai*) became a buzz-word of *ribu*'s activism and rhetoric. It spoke directly to a critique of modern society that was said to plunge individuals into a state of deep alienation and to establish a system rooted in incommunicability which, in turn, denied the possibility of sincere human relationships between man and woman, woman and woman, woman and child (Shigematsu 2012: 61). See also the section "Deai e no mosaku" [literally "blind search for an encounter"] in Tanaka Mitsu's *Inochi no onnatachi e–Torimidashi ūman ribu ron* ([1972] 2010: 147–172).

1974) or "We might be next!" (*Asu wa wagami!*) (1974) were all exemplary of the movement's determination to assert a revolutionary affinity with filicidal mothers. Through these statements *ribu* claimed that the social conditions driving mothers to kill their children could easily plunge *any woman* into analogous circumstances, thus asserting a sense of shared vulnerability to society's alienating living conditions. But they also implicitly suggested—in line with the movement's pronounced self-reflexivity—women's own complicity with those same conditions.

This was not a superficial, rhetorical move, but an ethical commitment fuelled by a profound desire to relate to these mothers: *ribu* activists wrote them letters, showed up at the public hearing of their trials and visited them in prisons or hospitals.[4] These attempts to connect clearly emphasize the importance that *ribu* placed on relationality as a fundamental condition to promote social change, but also as an indispensable strategy for self-transformation. The words of Yonezu Tomoko, member of the Ribu Shinjuku Centre, strongly convey the spirit with which such enterprise was undertaken:

> Our solidarity was not just expressed in words, we tried to contact these women and communicate with them to understand them. Even though we recognized that killing a child is wrong, we didn't want to place the blame on that one mother, rather, the blame could be placed on me as well, for allowing and perpetuating such a society. Even though there is no way I could feel the extent of the pain these women felt, the meaning of our solidarity included how we wanted to reflect on what these women experienced and what were the conditions that allowed this to happen. (quoted in Shigematsu 2012: 24)

Ribu's engagement with mothers who killed their children and its efforts to create an alternative discursive space that could challenge hegemonic

---

[4] Just to provide an example: in 1975 a case of maternal filicide occurred in Iwatsuki (Saitama prefecture) on which occasion the mother was committed to a period of enforced hospitalization. In a pamphlet that was distributed at that time, *ribu* activists informed their readers that they had been at the hospital, that they had been able to meet the doctor in charge and retrieve important information about her. The authors also refer to a rich correspondence they allegedly exchanged with the mother and that they had eventually been able to see her. The pamphlet ends with reference to a phone call she made to inform them of the date of her discharge from the hospital (Urawa et al. 1975).

understandings of maternal violence remain rather underexplored aspects of the movement's multifaceted struggle for social transformation. Scholarly investigations of the relationship between *ribu* and filicidal mothers have also remained few and far between within secondary literature in Japanese.[5] Shigematsu's analysis (2012: xiii) foregrounds how *ribu* articulated an "alternative feminist epistemology of violence that locate[d] violence […] in the feminine subject." She argues that the movement's "politicization of women's relationship with violence" (ibid.) was carried out through a self-reflexive and self-critical approach to the violence perpetrated by women, an approach that purposefully refused to reject or disavow that violent potential within each and any woman, and which interrogated instead the conditions of violence in the contemporary socio-political landscape (153). Following this trajectory, Shigematsu has been able to shed light upon the movement's support of and rhetorical engagement with the unprecedented outbreak of violence that had the United Red Army (a far left revolutionary sect) and its female leader Nagata Hiroko as its protagonists.[6]

Shigematsu (2012: 207, note 98) should also be credited for calling attention to the significance of the child-killing *onna* (a figure to which I will return shortly) "in the consciousness, writing, and activism of *ribu* women." The priority she confers to *ribu*'s relationship with violence clearly constitutes a vantage point from which to consider the promising revolutionary implications of a maternal potential for violence (see also Castellini 2014). However, her analysis seems to inadvertently downplay the rhetorical complexity with which the image of the child-killing *onna* emerges from the movement's archive. It seems to me that the partiality of Shigematsu's account stems from her prioritizing the formative but contradictory role of Tanaka Mitsu as the charismatic spokesperson of a collective movement that purported to have no leader or hierarchies—a privileged perspective into the movement's history and internal dynamics

---

[5] In this respect, my work owes a particular debt to feminist theorist Ehara Yumiko and her invaluable insights into the relationship between *ribu*'s preoccupation with maternal filicide and its broader challenge to cultural idealizations of the maternal role (see Ehara 2012: 131–7, 158–63).
[6] See the chapter "*Ribu*'s Response to the United Red Army: Feminist Ethics and the Politics of Violence" in Shigematsu (2012: 139–70).

that Shigematsu knew could hinder her capacity to do justice to *ribu*'s plurivocality.

As I read and organized the material for this chapter, I grappled with analogous difficulties and what you are now reading is the result of a process of constant rewriting and reshuffling and of an incessant self-questioning of my own authorial choices. In the end, I have made a conscious effort *not to* prioritize the figure of Tanaka and her philosophy of woman's liberation in my investigation of *ribu*'s engagement with maternal filicide, and I have sometimes consciously downplayed her importance in my desire to "reproduce" the movement's choral voice. Yet, Tanaka's theorization of maternal violence has emerged as so specific to deserve in some instances a consideration distinct from the movement's anonymous plurality. Therefore, it could be argued that *ribu*'s structural tensions and internal contradictions have eventually found their way into my own account and have surreptitiously installed themselves in the fabric of this chapter irrespective of my attempts to contain them. I leave it to the reader to consider whether the final outcome succeeds in expanding Shigematsu's pioneering reflections on *ribu*'s relationship with mothers who kill their children.

Contested Meanings

How did *ribu* understand the act of a mother taking the life of her own child? What role did this understanding play in the movement's broader struggle for social transformation? I have already flagged in Chap. 3 how *ribu* never constituted an organic and homogeneous movement and that to speak of *ribu* in the third person singular is thus misleading as it fuels misperceptions about the nature of the movement and its internal dynamics. As we delve into *ribu*'s archival material, we soon realize that, as a result of the movement's heterogeneity and composite nature, we are not dealing with a singular and monolithic understanding of the phenomenon of mothers who kill, but with a cluster of meanings. Maternal filicide was variously understood as the expression of an uncontainable feminine grudge unleashed upon an oppressive society or as a meaningless tragedy that destroyed the lives of both mother and child and which inflicted a trauma to the entire community, or else, it could be deemed symptomatic of the malfunction of the system and the unbalances that afflicted Japanese society. But it could also be all these things at once. In fact, whereas the logic animating *ribu*'s stance on maternal filicide was not singular, its diverse interpretations were not mutually exclusive either, and they could as well emerge side by side in the same text according to the rhetorical and political effects the authors intended to convey. A number of shared assumptions also concurred to provide such diverse range of interpretations with a degree of coherence: the notion of *onna* as a new political subject; the critique of the family system; the urge to dismantle the myth of maternal love and cultural idealizations of the mother–child bond. In what follows my account of these distinctive dimensions of *ribu*'s discursive intervention builds upon and further expands many of the insights I introduced in the previous chapter.

Kogoroshi no onna: The Child-Killing *onna*

You may recall from Chap. 3 that *ribu* reappropriated the taboo term *onna* (woman) and employed it as a semantically rich alternative to those categories such as wife, mother, housewife and female worker that classified women according to their socially upheld roles and which had constituted until then the identificatory basis for women's forms of political mobilization. The notion of *onna* was not a ready-made, pre-existent ideal, but represented a yet-to-be-shaped revolutionary subject that *ribu* activists strove to articulate in their day-to-day lives and alternative forms of relationality. Here I want to take these considerations forward and reflect on the fact that what we encounter time and again in the archival material of the movement is not the "mother who kills her child" (expression that would be rendered in Japanese as *kogoroshi no haha*) but the more emblematic figure of the *kogoroshi no onna* (子殺しの女). At its most basic, to translate *kogoroshi no onna* as "child-killing mother" would be linguistically inaccurate as no dictionary would ever suggest "mother" as an acceptable equivalent for *onna*.[7] More importantly, how-

---

[7] For a detailed discussion about the semantic historicity of the word *onna* and its later reappraisal by *ribu* activists, see Chap. 3.

ever, it would do a disservice to the movement's linguistic and discursive strategy. In keeping with Shigematsu's (2012) lesson, the more apt translation "child-killing *onna*" foregrounds *ribu*'s specific understanding of filicide as the violent act of an *onna* whose very existence was made impossible by crippling norms of appropriate femininity and the overall gender organization of society.[8] According to *ribu*'s logic a woman was, in her role as mother, a mere projective surface for male fantasies and this meant that "mother" (intended here as that role prescribed by the institution of motherhood) could never be a viable incarnation of *ribu*'s message of woman's liberation. In fact, it was woman-as-*onna* (as opposed to woman-as-mother) who, in a desperate attempt to assert her existence, was understood to lay her hands on her child.

Resorting to a vocabulary that became the hallmark of her rhetorical style, Tanaka Mitsu (2010: 16) conceived of woman-as-mother as a manifestation of "the non-existing *onna*" or "the *onna* who is nowhere" (*doko ni mo inai onna*): an empty figure wrapped up in male desires, needs and demands. Tanaka stressed how exhausting and self-consuming it was for a woman to live refracted in the images produced by men and to constantly (mis-)recognize herself in the gaze of another who was unable to acknowledge her as a full human being. She contrasted this phantasmatic existence with the figure of "the here-existing *onna*" (*koko ni iru onna*, the *onna* who exists here and now) whom she described as traversed by the painful contradictions between man-made idealizations of womanhood and the reality of woman's living conditions and corporeality. It was arguably amidst these contradictions and affective turmoil that a woman's manifestations of violence towards her child were understood to occur. Accordingly, when *ribu* activists asserted their solidarity with filicidal mothers with the slogan "the woman who kills her child (*kogoroshi no onna*) is me!," it was *not* with the woman-as-mother that

---

[8] It goes without saying that "child-killing *onna*" is only a partial translation of the expression *kogoroshi no onna* that purposefully calls attention to the assumed untranslatability that marks the semantic texture of the word *onna*. Whereas "woman who kills her child" or "child-killing woman" could be considered viable translations, they still would not convey the vibrant connotations that exude from the term *onna*. The specific way in which Shigematsu emphasizes the resistant materiality of this word is fuelled by a belief in the "militant semiotic intransigence [often] attached to the untranslatable" (Apter 2008: 587).

they claimed identification with, but with the *onna* that they imagined striving for survival through "an existence saturated with contradictions" (*mujun ni michita sonzai*) (Tanaka 2010: 68).

In addition to this, the word *kogoroshi* (child killing, filicide) in the expression *kogoroshi no onna* needs to be also recognized as a crucial element of *ribu*'s rhetorical grammar. In Chap. 2 we have seen that the categories *kogoroshi* (child killing, filicide) and *boshi shinjū* (mother–child suicide) reflect two profoundly different perceptions of the act of killing a child. On that occasion I called attention to the fact that only the former appears to convey an apprehension of maternal violence that becomes then the object of adamant social indictment as the deed of a monstrous, irresponsible or self-centred woman. *Ribu*'s consistent use of the word *kogoroshi* in its writings about mothers who kill combines with the striking absence of any reference to mother–child suicides. This could be motivated by *ribu*'s overt political effort to counter the stigmatization meted out to those mothers who committed *kogoroshi* (i.e. murder) as opposed to those who tragically took their lives together with the life of their child. However, we could also argue that the emphasis placed on the term *kogoroshi* exposed *ribu*'s desire to conceive of that violence as a concrete possibility that further challenged normative stereotypes of femininity. This represented a manifestation of the movement's "productive politicization of women's relationship with violence—as potentially violent subjects—" that Shigematsu (2012: xiii) identifies as one of *ribu*'s most distinctive features.[9] To sum up, a first important dimension of *ribu*'s engagement with mothers who kill is already apparent in such an epistemic break from previous understandings of maternal filicide and in the movement's critical appraisal of the biased nature of a language through which its political contestations were carried forward.[10]

---

[9] To realize the revolutionary impact of *ribu*'s stance vis-à-vis women's potential for violence, we just need to remind ourselves of the emphasis that the Mother's Convention (*Hahaoya taikai*) placed upon the notion of the pacific and protective nature of women's maternal role.

[10] Having here addressed the rhetorical dimension of *ribu*'s use of the category *kogoroshi no onna*, I will hereafter translate *onna* as "woman" for stylistic reasons, emphasizing its distinctive connotations only when the context requires me to do so.

Ribu's Critique of the Family System and Its Challenge to the Mother–Child Bond

The solidarity and support *ribu* expressed towards mothers who killed their children went hand in hand with a profound challenge to cultural beliefs in the symbiotic and natural character of the mother–child bond. This challenge was inscribed within the movement's broader critique of the family system that I have outlined in the previous chapter: "In a social structure that places total responsibility upon the shoulders of the woman who has given birth," *ribu* asked, "what on earth is a child to a woman?" (Ribu Gasshuku Jikkō I'inkai 1971: 323).[11] It also claimed that in the framework provided by the gender organization of the family a woman was bound to devote all her energies and emotional investment to a child who functioned, in the end, as the sole guarantor of her social value. As a result, a woman was said to live an impoverished and vicarious existence, while the child was reduced to an item endowed with exchange value. The same logic denounced the tacit contract that was deemed to be at the foundation of the institution of the family and which demanded that women secure three meals and a roof over their head in exchange for their reproductive capacities: the birth of a child was understood to be nothing but the validation of that silent agreement. In this respect, the mother–child bond could not be naïvely accepted as the uncomplicated locus of meaningful human relationships. The following extract underlines this point:

> Woman and child: nowadays aren't they doing anything but consuming each other's "life"? They are forced into a double suicidal pact. What happens to the aspiration to "life" of a woman who wants *to live* with her child (where the emphasis is not on "with") and to the aspiration to "life" of the child? (ibid.)

---

[11] The Ribu Gasshuku Jikkō I'inkai (Executive Committee for a *Ribu* Camp) comprised *ribu* cells such as Gurūpu Tatakau Onna (Group Fighting Onna) and Shisō Shūdan Esuīekkusu (Thought Group S.E.X), and was founded in order to organize the first *ribu* summer camp (*gasshuku*) on August 21–24, 1971 (Mizoguchi et al. 1992: 315).

The passage forcefully promotes the identity of *ribu* as a life-affirming movement: the excerpt unfolds around the rhetorical distinction between a desire to strive for truly liveable conditions and a notion of life that, repeatedly given in scare quotes, emphasizes the fiction that shrouds an exploitative and oppressive dynamic with the lure of idealized domestic bliss. The quotation becomes, then, a straightforward denunciation of the fact that mother and child, far from being the two terms of a nurturing relationship, consume each other in parasitical fashion, both portrayed as sacrificial victims of the existent social order. In the context of the movement's critique of the family system the child was also often described as a source of contradictions in the life of a woman: while construed by hegemonic discourse as the mark of her fulfilment qua woman, the child emerged in *ribu*'s rhetoric as what "robbed [*onna*] of the freedom of movement when she wanted to fly higher" (Ribu Shinjuku Sentā 1973: 69) and as the vehicle whereby demands to conform to cultural norms of maternal propriety were implemented. "In giving birth and raising a child there are extremely binding conditions"; "[o]nce a child is born you are bound hand and foot, and [whatever you do] it's a no-win situation" (Kogoroshi: Shiryō 1971: 310); "[m]y child's existence overdetermines my own existence" (Take 1971: 309): these are only a few examples that give the flavour of *ribu*'s questioning of the natural and loving character that was assumed to define a mother's relationship to her child. Exhausted by a gender organization of society that didn't allow her to live as *onna*, a woman was said to be "torn to shreds together with her child" (Gurūpu Tatakau Onna 1971b: 187)[12]:

> When a woman kills her child, it's nothing but a misdirected blow. A violent emotion that hits you all of a sudden and of which you don't understand the reason—that's perhaps an impulse impossible to repress, induced by an existential sense of starvation for one's own being. Such woman

---

[12] There are two versions of the pamphlet "Ondoro ondoro onna ga kodomo wo koroshiteku" from which this quotation is taken: one appears in Ribu Shinjuku Sentā Hozonkai, ed. (2008a) and is collectively attributed to Gurūpu Tatakau Onna, while the other is reprinted in Tanaka (2010) and is attributed to Tanaka herself, who was also one of the founders of the group. Although the content of the two versions is identical, this difference in authorial attribution suggests the extent to which Tanaka's vocabulary and ideas might have profoundly informed the output of an entire *ribu* cell (see Shigematsu 2012). Here I will be referring to the former version.

converges and eventually flings this impulse onto the source of contradiction which is most within her reach. Were she to come to her senses, she would have realized that the child was crying, but this does not happen. (Gurūpu Tatakau Onna 1971c: 188)

Here, the fact that the mother is unable to recognize the pain she inflicts upon her child testifies to an alienating lack of human connection brought about by a suffocating gendered division of labour within the family. To describe the act of killing as a "misdirected blow" indicates that the killing was unintended, that the mother's impulsive explosion of violence had unforeseen murderous consequences, thus implicitly countering those representations that depicted filicide as a despicable act of intentional cruelty. At the same time, and as the following excerpt makes clear, the numerical increase of mothers who kill their children was understood to foreshadow the collapse of the long-lasting myth of motherhood and maternal love, together with a value system that oppressed women by celebrating indiscriminately childbirth and reproduction:

> The frequent occurrence of episodes of maternal filicide is nothing but a declaration of bankrupt stamped in the blood of one's own child on account of a way of living whereby woman bears a child to a man in exchange of a place in the house. (Tanaka 2010: 28)

To call into question the "mother-and-child" relationship meant for *ribu* to dispute the "and" under which a spontaneous and unproblematic relationality was subsumed. This did not require a rejection of motherhood, but a relentless effort to separate "mother" and "child" and to create the enabling conditions for a more constructive and authentic relationality. We have seen in Chap. 3 that such effort to separate mother and child in the public imaginary was in itself a revolutionary endeavour which was integral to the process of transformation of female consciousness fostered by the movement's multifaceted activism (Mizoguchi et al. 1971: 7).

Let me give you another example that further documents *ribu*'s critical stance vis-à-vis motherhood conceived as a monolithic identity that exhausts all that there is to a woman. In the following passage a working mother of a four-year-old child affected by cerebral palsy describes the pain and fatigue of being a parent of a child with a disability. This pamphlet questions once again the cultural norms that expect mothers to be devoid of ambivalent feelings in the love for their children, and it denounces both the social pressure to embody a self-sacrificial maternal ideal and the frustration at being acknowledged by society only as a mother:

> It's hard, isn't it? You can do it because you are his mother, can't you? These kind words forced upon me [the ideal] of maternal love and compelled me to dedicate my whole life to my child as a suffering mother. People say: "Isn't she a gay person! She doesn't look like a woman with a disabled child." As a human being, however, I am a mother, a worker, and I have an individual existence that feels now joys, now worries in these and all my other roles, and I can't keep playing all the time the mother of a disabled child. (K. 1973: 363)

The pamphlet from which this quotation is taken offers the author's description of the way in which four years of difficult parenting had the effect of transforming her frustration in resignation, and how she came to painfully recognize that her life had "started exuding a rotting smell from underneath the hypocritical mask of maternal love," that myth of untainted love that "turn[ed] maternal resignation into a sweet narcotic" (364). While acknowledging that she was lucky enough *not* to have killed her child, she also confesses that in the midst of her exasperation she had a hunch that "at the farthest end of resignation is the killing of one's own child" (ibid.). In K.'s account an instinctual struggle for survival reaches the surface of her consciousness only when she becomes aware of the potential for violence that lurks behind the mask of maternal love. It is only at that point that she recognizes a not-fully-conscious desire to vent her impotent desperation upon the outside world, a world that was made coextensive with her child and his needs. Her narration further suggests that it is only her encounter with *ribu* that enabled her to channel such existential turmoil into a constructive project of social and inner transformation:

> To get back a body and soul that had been living for four years almost exclusively as a mother it was necessary to shout as an act of opposition [to

the system]: "Kill the child!" But that also meant "Kill the mother that is (in) me!" (*Hahaoya to shite no jibun wo korose!*). It was at that point that I encountered *ribu* (*kono toki ribu ni deatta*). (ibid.)

A mother's acceptance of her potential for violence emerges here as the expression of a desperate determination to fight the system and reclaim her life as a fully human being. This tentative reappropriation occurs through the figural destruction of the child and the idealized maternal image as the single defining trait of a woman's identity. It goes without saying that this is not the endorsement of actual violence against children. It means, rather, acknowledging that an effective opposition to man-made idealizations of motherhood requires (demands!) the capacity to bring a maternal potential for violence into discourse with a voice that resists appropriation and erasure within the established narratives of the bad and the mad mother. It is in the command "Kill the child!" *screamed out loud* so that both the world and the mother herself could hear that we recognize a woman's refusal of gender norms and her firm resolution to shatter the myth of motherhood's perfect love. It is not in the act of killing the child but in *the (maternal) voice that publicly declares the possibility of that violence*. Opposition to the system, thus, goes hand in hand with an intervention at the level of the articulability and representability of that violent potential in the realm of discourse. And yet, this brave declaration harbours the danger of self-destruction in that the exhortation to kill the child becomes synonymous with the destruction of woman's maternal identity and with it her public recognition in society. I will return shortly to this idea.

The Child-Killing *onna* Between Revolutionary Agency and Victimhood

As we read through *ribu*'s archive and take stock of the various ways in which filicidal mothers were portrayed, we cannot fail to notice a degree of ambivalence in their representations. Side by side with striking claims of the revolutionary spirit that was believed to traverse episodes of maternal violence, we come across numerous declarations of their utterly tragic nature that would deny such episodes any kind of emancipatory potential. I have already observed that this could be explained with reference to *ribu*'s composite nature. On reflection, however, it seems to me that this ambivalence may well be the inevitable outcome of two potentially irreconcilable approaches undertaken by *ribu* activists in relation to the phenomenon of maternal filicide. On the one hand, the movement's programmatic attempts to overthrow society's gender organization motivated a will to embrace maternal violence as the manifestation of a woman's revolutionary intent; on the other hand, the movement's desire to empathize with the plight of these mothers and to connect with them on a human level may have brought about a more nuanced awareness of the deep insufficiency of the former mode of representation. The result is the emergence of potentially contradictory modalities by means of which a maternal potential for violence was given discursive articulation.

The Child-Killing *onna* as Woman's Grudge Unleashed

A powerful and audacious interpretation of maternal filicide was offered by those voices within *ribu* that seemed to attribute to the mother who killed her child a kind of activist consciousness and a wilful desire to defy the system. The following excerpt is typical of the tone assumed by this interpretative strand:

> [T]hose *onna* who, while returning to their own self and as they stained their hands with blood, have raised objection to "the myth of maternal love" have perpetrated acts of filicide whose number has reached, only this year, almost 400 cases. (Gurūpu Tatakau Onna 1971a: 243)

The passage above seems to suggest that behind episodes of maternal filicide it is possible to recognize the working of a rational agency moving objection to cultural idealizations of motherhood. Maternal child killing becomes here the brutal means whereby *onna* asserts her determination to regain control over her life as a full human being. The temporality of the events remains important though: the killing of the child ought not to be conceived as the consequence of *onna* having finally acquired a meaningful existence in society (which would be tantamount to attributing the historical explosion of maternal violence to *ribu*'s successful campaigns for woman's liberation). Rather, filicide materializes the violent eruption of *onna*'s struggle to search and tentatively articulate her status as a new political and social subject. It is only in this light that such an extreme gesture acquires (always with a degree of ambiguity) the status of conscious objection levied against the system.

Filicidal mothers were often referred to as "members of a support army" for the movement (Gurūpu Tatakau Onna 1971d: 251) and were depicted as a different incarnation of the "energy of woman's grudge (*onnen*, 怨念)" understood to animate *ribu* (Shisō Shūdan Esuīekkusu 1971: 176). Filicide came to be seen as a dramatic modality by means of which a woman's "personal resentment (*shien* 私怨) spread through the darkness of the womb from woman to woman" and testified to the fact that something "that had neither form nor could be expressed in words, but that was clearly breaking a taboo, [was] now starting to erupt" (Gurūpu Tatakau Onna 1971c: 188). The notion of woman's "resentment" as constitutive of the spirit of *ribu* was a recurrent image in the language of the movement, especially for groups such as Shisō Shūdan Esuīekkusu (Thought Group S.E.X) and Gurūpu Tatakau Onna (Group Fighting Onna) that collaborated at the Ribu Shinjuku Centre at close contact with Tanaka's vigorous rhetoric. This is further confirmed in a passage from Yoshitake Teruko's memoirs where her encounter with *ribu* is accompanied by a description of the flag of Gurūpu Tatakau Onna emblazoned with the Japanese character for "resentment" or "grudge" (怨). Yoshitake recalls that ever since the *ribu* demonstration on October 21, 1970, "wherever women went to demonstrate, that flag was always unfurled to flutter in the wind" (quoted in Loftus 2013: 96).

But let me briefly go back to the above quotation from Gurūpu Tatakau Onna and notice that the image of a woman's grudge spreading from woman to woman "through the darkness of the womb" bears, once again, distinctive traces of the rhetorical style that became strongly associated with Tanaka Mitsu. In her book-length treatise on woman's liberation *To Women With Spirit: A Disorderly Theory of Women's Liberation* (*Inochi no onnatachi e—Torimidashi ūman ribu ron*, [1972] 2010) Tanaka "conceived of the womb as the place that carried the grudge [...] of women's historicity and [...] oppression, and this grudge bore possibilities that were both violent and creative" (Shigematsu 2012: 26). The language Tanaka employed suggested a metonymic movement whereby the womb came to stand for the totality of woman's experience in modern society: it harboured both woman's potential to live her life as a full-fledged human being and her existential frustration at the unbearable living conditions which moulded her into a mere instrument for human reproduction. "The revival of the womb," as Shigematsu aptly put it, was integral to the liberation of woman's sex and to *ribu*'s recognition of woman's violent potential as both creative and destructive. This potential for life and death was located in the womb as the mark of woman's sexed specificity and the symbol of her capacity for self-regeneration and self-discovery qua *onna*. Maternal filicide, Tanaka contended, constituted a message stained with the blood of innocent children, unfortunate victims of a wider social drama:

> The child-killing *onna* announces the rehabilitation of woman's grudge (*onnen*) that was just rotting in the empty darkness of the womb and stamps it in the blood of her child. Her scattered life which has come to a dead-end lays bare, amidst insanity and delirium, the lie of the myth of maternal love. [...] The womb, which conceals the source of woman's life, is now awakening. (Tanaka 2010: 62)

The addressee of this revolutionary message was society at large, but also every single woman capable of identifying with the existential exasperation believed to prompt such outpouring of violence, and courageous enough to ask herself: "Isn't the mother who kills her child my own very self?" (Nori 1972: 17). Therefore, it was contended that "[t]he meaning of the silent question raised by the child-killing *onna* [spoke] to all women" (Suga 1971: 311).[13] Some voices from within the movement even claimed

---

[13] In the context of the debates around the proposed amendments to the Eugenic Protection Law, Tanaka vigorously urged to recognize the contiguity of abortion and child killing (*kogoroshi*) along the same continuum of violence that resulted from the unbearable circumstances in which women found themselves to live. While it is not my intention to delve into the nuances of these debates, I want to take the opportunity to flag here, with Shigematsu's help, Tanaka's discourse about the distinctive relationship between abortion and filicide. According to Tanaka's logic, child-killing *onna* were those unfortunate enough to have missed the opportunity to kill an unwanted child

that "in the killing of one's own chid there [was] a sort of self-affirmation" and that it was "a different issue whether or not the mother [who committed it was] aware of this" (Mizoguchi et al. 1971: 8).[14]

Maternal filicide was deemed symptomatic of a broader state of alienation that affected late postwar Japan and which *ribu* aimed to denounce. It was argued that the experience of the filicidal mother exposed the naked reality of human existence in modern society and tore the veil of society's wishful ignorance. The fact that both the soaring phenomenon of filicide and the birth of *ribu* occurred as part of the same historical juncture was taken by Tanaka to signify the actuality of *ribu*'s struggle. The crime of mothers who killed their children was understood to partake of the movement's revolutionary intent and this interpretation led to memorable assertions by Tanaka according to which "*ribu* and the child-killing *onna* are nothing but the two extremities of a branch that share one single root" (2010: 207) and "child-killing *onna* are the ones who have screamed out that the king is naked, and *ribu* is nothing but the collective that attempts to make this into a movement" (198–9).

The Child-Killing *onna* as Unwilling Victim of the System

In her account of child killing as integral to the consciousness of the movement, it seems to me that Shigematsu privileges this specific under-

---

before it was born (Shigematsu 2012: 27). Tanaka denounced both child killing and abortion as the infelicitous outcome of the same structural conditions and gender regime. However, she sidestepped issues of morality and argued that "women should recognize their own inherent capacity for violence in their act of aborting their children" *while* they strove to change society (ibid.). This point is vigorously made in the following excerpt:

> When I choose to have an abortion with my own subjectivity, in the objective situation where I "am made" to have an abortion, I want myself to become aware that I am a murderer. The child dies in reality, and if somebody calls the woman a murderer, then, I dare to declare that a woman who had an abortion is a murderer, and while doing so, I would still choose to have an abortion. Declaring that I am a murderer and staring at a foetus cut into pieces, now, I want to argue against a society that makes women do so, giving society no way to avoid the argument. (Tanaka 1972: 63; tr. in Kato 2009: 266)

[14] Such a claim exposes an important tension between *ribu*'s desire to make the tragic experience of these mothers heard and the risk of co-optation of that experience for the movement's political purposes. I will return to this point at the end of the chapter.

standing of maternal filicide as "evidence of women's violent capacity to revolt against the system" (2012: 24). She also interprets the assertions by Tanaka that I have just quoted to mean that "the abject and violent figure of the child-killing mother was the symbolic subject that prefigured the collective movement of *ribu*" (26). This is the point where I depart from her analysis as I find it problematic in its implicit foregrounding of the mother who kills as an uncomplicated agentic subject and in its suggestion of a linear, progressive temporality whereby *ribu* emerges as the "evolution" of maternal violence into a coherent revolutionary movement. In fact, as Shigematsu herself briefly acknowledges, child killing never acquired a positive light in the rhetoric of the movement and *ribu* never advocated such acts of violence (23). Instead of declaring filicide a *positive* affirmation of the self, the killing of one's own child was often described as a woman's "desperate proof of existence" (*girigiri no sonzai shōmei*) (Shisō Shūdan Esuīekkusu and Tora 1972: 185), the deed of someone caught in a situation where she *had to* kill or she would end up being killed by the unliveable conditions forced upon her by society. Thus, contrary to the images of mothers who kill as determined revolutionary subjects that we have so far encountered, in many of *ribu*'s writings the filicidal mother is depicted as committing the crime *not* as a deliberate gesture against the system, but because she has been "cornered" into an unbearable situation. Let us take a look at a range of passages that unambiguously foreground this dimension of external pressure:

> [W]hy is the cornered woman (*oitsumerareta onna*)—a woman driven into the extreme situation of not knowing whether she will live or be killed—blamed for gripping her child by the throat? [...] We don't blame the "child-killing *onna.*" We can't condemn her (*iya dekinai*). It is what pushed her into that corner that our rage is directed against. (Chūpiren 1972: 247)

> Why did they have to kill their own beloved children? Who is the real culprit who plunged (*oikometa*) them into such a situation where they couldn't help but kill? (Metropolitan 1971: 165)

> [Such a claim] attempts to conceal the social problems (poverty, bad housing conditions, child-rearing as an exclusively female burden, etc.) that cornered (*oikomerareta*) her to the point of killing her own child. (Asu wa wagami 1974: 379)

But that which corners (*oitsumeru*) a human being into a situation on the brink, even more than external, apparent and material factors is perhaps that person's psychological exhaustion as she feels the absence of a way out from the deepest darkness. (K. 1973: 363)

In keeping with this logic, the verb that described the mother's murderous gesture was consistently changed in the writing of *ribu* from the active form *korosu* (to kill) to the causative-passive form *korosaserareru* (to be made to kill) in order to suggest that the killing ought to be understood as somehow perpetrated against the woman's will (Gurūpu Tatakau Onna 1971a: 245, 1971b: 186–7; Chūpiren 1972: 247). This was an important rhetorical move that aimed to stress that the urge to kill was fuelled by external social conditions rather than stemming from a woman's evil nature or mental impairment. This move displaced part of the responsibility for the children's death on to a society that was called to be accountable for the crimes these women perpetrated.

Furthermore, even when *ribu* activists understood maternal filicide as the expression of a mutiny against the system that occurred spontaneously in the life of an overburdened mother, they were also profoundly aware that a woman's killing of her child harboured "nothing but an act of self-denial which turn[ed] into a dead-end" (Gurūpu Tatakau Onna 1971a: 246, 1971b: 187). Therefore, the spontaneous and supposedly "revolutionary" act perpetrated by the child-killing *onna* in opposition to a male-dominated society was understood to emerge in the corrupted or "twisted form" (Ōgawara 1973: 381) of a terrible crime which "[tore] the woman's very existence apart" (Shisō Shūdan Esuīekkusu and Tora 1972: 186). Even Tanaka, who described maternal filicide and *ribu* as partaking of the same energy of woman's grudge and who portrayed maternal filicide as "the extreme act of self-expression of the oppressed" (2010: 62), felt compelled to remark that the mother who kills her child commits an "irrevocable mistake" (193) which makes her complicit with the process of her own destruction. Whereas the killing of the child might assume the illusionary appearance of the only way out from alienating living conditions (the only chance for *onna* to assert her existence), there is no survival in that criminal act. Maternal filicide, far from bringing relief to the mother and making it possible for her to realize her human potential, plunges her in the deepest and darkest waters of social abjection.

Digressing into the Abject

Theorists of abjection in the Anglo-feminist tradition may be inclined to read *ribu*'s emphasis on the "revolutionary potential" or "revolutionary meaning" embodied by the filicidal mother as an attempt to positively embrace her (socially) abject status. In this respect, Imogen Tyler (2009) has observed that "[w]hat makes the 'abject paradigm' particularly compelling for feminist theorists is the promise that 'reading for the abject' […] can challenge and/or displace the disciplinary norms that frame dominant representations of gender" (82).

In her influential work *Powers of Horrors: An Essay on Abjection*, Julia Kristeva (1982) elaborates on the concept of the abject as it pertains to both the psychic and social domains. Broadly speaking, "the abject arises in that gray, in between area of the mixed [and] the ambiguous [that] trespasses and transgresses the barriers between recognizable norms or definitions" (Braidotti 1997: 65). At the level of the psyche, abjection has been described as the process whereby the boundaries of the ego are set and maintained by means of the (reiterated) expulsion of the infant's attachment to the maternal body and the pre-Oedipal mother. The latter represents the all-powerful phallic mother of the pre-Oedipal stage who is perceived as both life- and death-giving, object of the uttermost love and horror (because hers is the power to deny the separation that will pave the way to the child's entry into the Symbolic). In this process, what is abjected and expunged outside the subject also defines the subject and its contours, constantly threatening them from the "non-place" of that constitutive outside.

On the other hand, Kristeva has also described abjection as a process of exclusion that is at work *in culture and the social*. Imogen Tyler (2013) has built upon this important insight in an attempt to articulate a theory of social abjection, and she has argued that "[a]bjection is not just a psychic process but a social experience" which "generates the borders of the individual *and* the social body" (2009: 87, 79). It also seems worth noticing that, for Kristeva, any crime can be considered abject because it draws attention to the fragility of the law and social boundaries (1982: 4) and because of this very exposure the abject, even jettisoned, remains a constant threat to the social (Oliver 1993: 56). But the power of the abject to disrupt the social world, Tyler suggests, is functional to the securing of social norms, including those of gender (2009: 84). Any transgression, she bleakly observes, "functions to reinstate those norms: for example, by providing opportunities for punishment and the enforcement of psychic and social laws" (ibid.).

In light of this consideration, it seems to me that mothers who kill their children may be loosely considered liminal figures that linger at the border between social and psychic abjection. As the perpetrators of a crime they are made the object of a process of exclusion that is carried forward by legal and medical institutions and which expels them (at least provisionally) from the fabric of the social. This exclusion operates at once as a guarantor of the stability of social borders and as reinstatement of the law (here also represented by the norms of gender and maternal propriety). On the other hand, as the concrete materialization of the spectre of the phallic mother who can be dispenser of death as well as life, the mother who kills her child could be said to encounter a more violent, visceral form of exclusion that has its roots in the constitutive need of the subject to preserve his/her own boundaries.[15]

Let me now return to the interpretative possibility with which I opened this section on the abject: Can *ribu*'s representations of filicidal mothers as the embodiment of a revolutionary female resentment be understood as an example of the transgressive potential of the abject? Can we interpret this rhetorical move as the process whereby "the abject woman becomes a subversive trope of female liberation" (Covino 2004: 29)? My answer to this question is negative. The murderous mother was never unproblematically made into an ideal liberatory or revolutionary agent in the language of the movement. *Ribu* was fully aware that the child-killing *onna* could not become a full-fledged political subject in the struggle for women's emancipation: her crime would have never acquired the status of a constructive political claim able to foster social change nor would it ever constitute part of a positive process of creation of a liberated self. Therefore, the revolution "prefigured" by the mother who

---

[15] Whether or not this psychic defence mechanism is a significant contributory factor to society's attempts at containing manifestations of a maternal potential for violence in public discourse remains an intriguing question, albeit not one that I am able to pursue in the context of my current analysis.

kills could be considered somehow ineffective: by killing her own child she lost social recognition and her state of cultural intelligibility and she became a logical impossibility, a locus of disorder and incoherence that had to be circumscribed and regulated in order to contain the threat that her actions represented for the gendered organization of society.

To portray the existential complexities that a filicidal mother embodies, Tanaka borrows an image from the Japanese traditional Noh theatre. She compares the transmuted face of the mother who kills her child to the Hannya mask used to represent a woman who is so consumed by grudge, jealousy and anguish that she has turned into a demon, but with some important traces of humanity left. Her pointed horns, gleaming eyes, golden fang-like teeth, combined with a look of pure resentment and hatred are tempered by the expression of suffering around the eyes and the artfully disarrayed strands of hair, which indicate passionate emotion thrown into disorder. The Hannya mask is often described as dangerous and erotic, but also sorrowful and tormented, displaying the complexity of human emotions. The skilled actor learns to master the way in which shadows play on the surface of the Noh mask and how subtle movements can bring about rapid changes in the emotions its otherwise fixed physical features can express. When the actor looks straight ahead, the mask appears frightening and angry; when tilted slightly down, the face of the demon appears transfigured by a profound sorrow, as if she were crying.[16] "The Hannya mask is the face of a woman who has broken the spell," Tanaka claims, "the face of a woman who knows that the king is naked, a woman who has committed an irrevocable mistake" (2010: 193). This is the woman who has "mistakenly" killed her own child (a woman who *has been made to kill* her child). She becomes the symbol of an outcry that would break the hypocritical spell cast by society's wilful ignorance. But she would also be the one who, committing such an "irrevocable mistake," becomes a demon in the eyes of society, and no longer partakes of the quality of the human. Her social recognition destroyed, she is cast as a monster, a deviant creature who has acted against her (maternal) nature. The mother who kills her child ends up being (socially) nothing, an "exception" that society constantly wishes to discard on the base of

---

[16] For a detailed account of the history of the Hannya mask, see Marvin (2010).

her alleged abnormality. In other words, the abject monstrosity of the Hannya mask may well endow a woman with a supernatural violent potential that could bring chaos and temporarily subvert the carefully policed borders of the social world. In the end, however, it effaces her humanity, cripples her capacity to make her voice heard in intelligible ways (her monstrous incarnation being the result of tormented rage that has already reached a place beyond any sensible communication) and expels her to the margins of the culturally intelligible. The only trace that remains of her former identity is the faint glimmer of suffering behind her demonic and threatening appearance.

A Continuum of Women

So far I have introduced you to *ribu*'s portrayals of mothers who kill as either potential (albeit problematic) revolutionary subjects or sacrificial victims of a system that drives them to violent extremes. Here I want to explore what I have identified as a third strand of interpretations that emphasizes a sense of continuity in the experience of *all* women independent of their individual circumstances. This imagined community of female subjects ran parallel to *ribu*'s search for new forms of relationality and nourished its claims of solidarity with filicidal mothers. The most extensive articulation of this notion can be found in a pamphlet circulated by Gurūpu Tatakau Onna on occasion of the rally in solidarity with mothers who kill their children that was held in Tokyo on May 8, 1971. Given the meaningful title "Love Letter to My Mother" (*Haha e no rabu retā*), this document takes the form of a fictional letter of a daughter to her mother. The latter is portrayed here as split between, on the one hand, her roles of dutiful wife and mother (which evoke ideas of passivity and scarce empowerment) and, on the other, what is described as a strong sense of self that urges her to strive "to create her own light, rather than reflect the light of her husband." The pamphlet argues that "[t]he myth according to which a mother is always a pure, high-minded, noble person has produced [the idea of] 'maternal love'" and claims that a woman whose existence is confirmed by such a value system is a woman who has

4 Contested Meanings: Mothers Who Kill and the Rhetoric... 143

accepted "a self-that-is-not-a-self" (*jibun denai jibun*) (1971a: 242–3). In a society that forces upon women this empty self what kind of fate is in wait for a woman with a strong self?

> A woman with a strong self…A woman who tries to live her own life fully and autonomously [...] [W]hat kind of living space will she be able to craft [for herself] within the established order? Your exasperation…[...] The words with which you used to scold me [or] the strength of that hand that hit me [were filled with] the exasperation of a person who had found herself moulded into "a self-that-is-not-a-self" [...] exasperation at a self that was not living. (241)

Resonating with the image of the *doko ni mo inai onna* (the *onna* who is nowhere) that we have previously encountered, the notion of a "self-that-is-not-a-self" is here traced back to the social imposition of man-made idealizations of womanhood. The mother's frustration at being trapped in the selfless images of maternal abnegation and dutiful wifeliness is described as spilling over onto gestures of daily violence towards her child. Expressions of verbal aggression and physical abuse are understood here less as part of the educational practices aimed at enforcing discipline in a child and more as symptomatic of a mother's existential discomfort. It is at this point that the figure of the filicidal mother is introduced:

> Recently, when I was talking about a woman who killed her own child, I was startled to hear a voice from a woman who did actually have a child saying: "That was a misdirected blow!" But then I reconsider that, in your violence, the feeling of starvation for your being compressed into "a self-that-is-not-a-self," [...] [your starvation] for not being able to live, had caused the explosion of "something" that couldn't be suppressed with the use of reason. And I find myself thinking that on the [ideal] prolongation of your line is the woman who killed her child and that, in my having a strong self and being like you, I myself have a place on that very line. (241)

It is here that we encounter the articulation of a *continuum of women* who appear to suffer to different degrees from the social imposition of feminine and maternal ideals and who behave in ways that are more or less compliant with the cultural norms enforced upon them. At one extreme we recognize the woman who has accepted the "self-that-is-not-a-self" thereby developing a form of false consciousness that induces her to wilfully embrace cultural values such as "to be a wife and a mother is the proof of womanhood," "marriage is woman's happiness," "children are [a woman's] life purpose" (Tanaka 1972: 62). At the other end of the spectrum we find the mother who, consumed by her existential suffering and unable to channel the resentment stemming from a frustrating existence, lays her hands on her child. Somewhere between these two extremes we may envision a woman who harbours or is able to develop a strong self, a woman who has not yet capitulated to society's attempts to mould her into an empty subjectivity and who may or may not awaken to an activist consciousness. We can see here how the depiction of women as having a relation of proximity with the experience of mothers who killed their children was a rhetorical strategy aimed at emphasizing that, far from being an exceptional occurrence and the result of pathology or evil personality, maternal filicide was indeed the expression of a drama that touched all women indiscriminately.

The two female figures at the far ends of this imaginary line could be envisioned as two sides of the same coin. They both surrendered (albeit in different forms) to the existential poverty that afflicts their lives, and they both seem unable to provide intelligible articulation to their existential pain: the former because false consciousness has made her incapable of recognizing such pain, and the latter because the very possibility of verbal articulation has been swept away by a criminal act that forcefully removed her from the realm of cultural intelligibility and into a state of abjection. The image of the continuum of women is further evoked by the following extract from a different pamphlet:

> The woman who kills her child and who, after giving birth just because it's a matter of course that a woman has a baby once she gets married, suddenly focuses her anger and dissatisfaction onto her child [...] appears and disappears (*chirachira miete iru*) on the ideal prolongation line of the rage we feel day by day, but we are unable to express. (Ribu Shinjuku Sentā 1973: 69)

A distinction here is made between affect (the feeling of anger that is portrayed as women's common asset) and the ability to express and channel that affect in forms of meaningful protest and social contestation. While women's grudge—as we have seen—was often heralded as emblematic of the energy that informed *ribu*, in order for the movement to foster social change it was key to give verbal articulation to that violent affective charge. In this respect, filicidal mothers fell short of this capacity to articulate resentment and frustration *in discourse*: even though their drama epitomized the difficult living conditions all women arguably faced, their violence was not sufficient to make them full-fledged participants of the movement. The crucial importance of *ribu*'s discursive intervention can hardly be missed in the following passage:

> We believe that filicide is located at the climax of the circumstances in which all women are placed. And it is to eliminate all this that we raise our voices, make a wide appeal and have set up a "Conference to Think about Filicide" (*kogoroshi o kangaeru kai*) (Urawa et al. 1975: 35).

In the excerpt above we can observe how an emphasis on verbal articulation represented *ribu*'s "constructive alternative" to the explosion of unfathomable violence by the hands of mothers who killed their children. The progression from "voice" to "appeal" to "(critical) thinking" in the passage arguably evokes an implicit contrast between, on the one hand, the *inarticulate* sense of impotent resistance acknowledged as part of these mothers' personal drama and, on the other, the pivotal role attributed to a discursive intervention aimed at expanding the realm of representability and the public understanding of maternal violence it regulated.

Man ribu (Men's Lib) and Filicide

Not enough archival material has emerged to make it possible to generalize about the perspective on maternal filicide held by the men within *ribu*. During my research I came across just two examples of this kind. However, because they share a specific nuance in the stance they take on mothers who kill their children, I believed it important to flag their voices at this stage of my argument, however briefly. Of course, I am deeply aware that the charge of essentialism looms large on the horizon as I separate so neatly pamphlets written by men and women as if the gender of the author signified some intrinsic difference in the perspective he/she expressed. In this respect, I chose to consider in this section only those elements that did seem to suggest such a difference in nuance, while blending their voices with those of other activists whenever I recognized meaningful similarities. From the start the two texts under consideration present themselves as the expression of an unmistakably masculine voice within the movement. In addition to the distinctly male name of the authors, also the titles of the pamphlets are fairly unambiguous in this respect: "Guide to the 'Meeting of Men who Find it Hard to Live'" (*"Ikigurushii otoko no atsumari" annai*) (Ōgawara 1973)[17] and "Men don't get their hands dirty!" (*Otoko wa te o yogosanai!*) (Yamakado 1975).[18] They both emphasize that while cases of fathers who kill their children are equally numerous, it is usually upon mothers that society places its blaming gaze:

> In recent years cases of filicide have been numerous. The one who goes on trial is always a woman. When it comes to man, he's either left unquestioned/ignored or he might be described in such a way as to deserve only sympathy. (Yamakado 1975: 406)

Both Ōgawara and Yamakado critically address the gender division of labour within the family. They call attention to the fact that total responsibility for child-rearing is placed on woman's shoulders and that this confines her within the domestic realm, denying her the chance to participate in the public sphere on par with man. Ōgawara also denounces

---

[17] The title juxtaposes the characters 息 (*iki*, breath) and 生き (*iki*, to live) to render the expression *ikigurushii* (choking, which makes breathing difficult) thus suggesting the extent to which these men flounder in circumstances that make life unliveable.

[18] Ōgawara, at that time in his late 20s and a reporter for a press agency, circulated the pamphlet "Guide to the 'Meeting of Men who Find it Hard to Live'" at a *ribu* meeting. About ten other members answered his call. Yamakado's text appeared, instead, in the first issue of *Otoko no tomo* (Man's Friend), a *minikomi* produced by Tokyo Otoko Idobata Kaigi ("The Well Conference of Tokyo Men" or "Tokyo Men's Gossip"). The expression "*idobata kaigi*" originally indicated women's informal gatherings at the local well and had been later used to signify a gender-specific understanding of (women's) gossip. *Shufu no tomo* (The Housewife's Friend), of which *Otoko no tomo* is likely to have been a "male" adaptation, had been established in 1917 and in the 1970s constituted the most popular monthly women's magazines in Japan (Sakamoto 1999: 178; Mackie 2003: 49).

men's hypocrisy and opportunism as they allow "abortions to exceed one million cases a year" while "consider[ing] that same life as something holy when it comes out of the womb" (1973: 381). For a long time, he argues, pregnancy and abortion have been socially controlled by men, and in the context of this denunciation he juxtaposes the two figures of the filicidal mother and the woman who advocates her right to reproductive control: in the same way in which the latter declares her right to give or not to give birth, the mother who kills her child is described as crying out loud "*onna*'s freedom to raise or not raise a child" (ibid.). Man's calculated ignorance of the life experiences that "force" a woman to kill her child is also likened in Ōgawara's pamphlet to a joke and an unintended form of self-mockery:

> A man who laughs at the child-killing *onna* (*kogoroshi no onna*): doesn't he realize that he's laughing at his own existence of which she is pregnant? It is on him, after birth, that revenge is enacted by the "*onna*" that man's society forces to have an abortion to his own convenience. (ibid.)

The reader will be familiar with the image of the vengeful child-killing *onna* that we have already encountered in the previous pages. Here we may observe that by placing clear emphasis on the word *onna*, the author is openly embracing one of *ribu*'s central tenets, suggesting that the violence of filicide (be it in the form of abortion or the murder of an already born child) is symptomatic of *onna*'s desire to affirm a fully human existence. The new layer that Ōgawara's text adds to this interpretative frame is the suggestion of man's complicity in the tragic murder of the child, silent collusion that is recognized in man's tendency to minimize or ridicule woman's constraining existence. Men make fun of woman's life circumstances at their own risk, the author seems to be warning, because filicide is a threat that looms large on men's very future.

The argument developed by Yamakado is even more direct in its indictment of men's complicity. He claims that those women who are going to kill their children are the same ones "who have no chance to associate with men in their everyday lives and who can't communicate their existential suffering (*ikiru kurushisa*) neither to the people around them nor to their families" (1975: 406). And it is "man's way of living," he concludes, that "pushes woman in the corner" (ibid.). In a style that resembles Ōgawara's argument, Yamakado calls attention to the fact that men try to sidestep the issue of their own responsibility in episodes of filicide, and he adds that those are the same men who often leave after the mother has been incriminated, abandoning her to deal on her own with the material and psychological consequences of her actions:

> Facing the fact that only by killing her own child (*kogoroshi to iu katachi de shika*) has woman (*onna*) made her life plainly visible, let's interrupt the circuit whereby man allows himself to live a peaceful life by leaving that woman. (ibid.)

Against a superficial approach that would reductively consider man as either an accomplice in a woman's murdering of her child or someone that we should sympathize with, Yamakado emphasizes the need to question men's way of living and man–woman relationality. In so doing, he complicates those widespread media accounts that contented themselves with describing the shocked and dramatic reactions of these women's partners and husbands, and denunciates both their wishful ignorance and their recurrent unwillingness to become involved in the social and legal consequences of that violence. He urges to reconsider filicide "from the perspective of men's attitude toward life" which may have destructive consequences for other members in their families. In the current state of affairs where society seems blind to these issues, he suggests, we should not naïvely assume that man's degree of responsibility in cases of filicide is limited just because he didn't get his hands dirty with the child's blood. "Now it's the time!" his leaflet ends, "Let's think, *as men*, about filicide!" (ibid., my italics).

Ribu's Challenge to Media Representations of Mothers Who Kill

Thus far I have been navigating *ribu*'s engagement with mothers who kill their children in what I would call "monological" fashion, that is, as a discourse that was internal to the movement itself. Surely, the nature of the archival material at the heart of this chapter and which consists of leaflets, pamphlets and bills, indicates *ribu*'s unambiguous desire to circulate its perspectives outside of those women's groups that produced them and testifies to the movement's attempts to reach out to a wider audience. Although a broad notion of "society" arguably constituted the implicit addressee of its message, no direct interlocutor emerged from the writings that I have so far introduced. This is clearly not the case for the material I explore in this section where news media are made into a privileged target for *ribu*'s critical intervention.

The "Good" and the "Bad" Mother

Ribu activists contested the treatment these women received in mainstream discourse and vigorously denounced the criminal and/or pathological portrayals of filicidal mothers that media coverage was accused of producing and circulating. The urgency with which *ribu* engaged with media representations of mothers who killed their children stemmed from its profound awareness that it was through the biased portrayals published in the pages of Japanese major newspapers that the phenomenon of (maternal) filicide reached public consciousness: "Recently, articles about filicide have been published almost daily in the newspapers," it is argued in one leaflet (Chūpiren 1972: 247); "[i]t is mostly the case that we get to know about filicide in the newspapers," says another (Sapporo Komu-unu 1974: 24); "[d]ay after day," acknowledges a third one, "articles on 'filicide' or 'abandoned children' are constantly published in the newspapers, and they appear in such a sheer amount that it causes the reaction 'Oh! Again!'" (Sayama et al. 1973: 192). There was also a widespread awareness among *ribu* activists that, even though cases of fathers who killed their children appeared no less frequently in the news, it was mothers who used to become the target of public denunciation and to receive the brunt of the blame (Ōgawara 1973; Sayama et al. 1973).

Without engaging in a methodical analysis of media content like the one I proposed in Chap. 2, *ribu* women clearly demonstrated a perceptive awareness of the affective response media rhetoric aimed at engendering in its readership and they were wary of the kind of public it actively contributed to create.[19] Although *ribu* activists admitted that it could well happen that commentators expressed sympathy for the woman who committed the crime, they also argued that this was "the same as saying nothing about the fact that the man was to blame (*otoko ga warui*) or that the welfare system had proved inefficient" (Sayama et al. 1973: 192). They were critical of how news reports framed episodes of filicide in such a way that made it difficult to grasp "the personal anguish that obviously exist[ed] behind those cases" (Ōgawara 1973: 381). *Ribu* vigorously denounced news media for making a "vicious propaganda" (Tanaka 1973: 31) that portrayed cases of filicide as "extraordinary criminal events by the hands of so-called bad women" (Gurūpu Tatakau Onna 1971a: 243). The following quote is exemplary in the movement's denunciation of media coverage for its pathologization, vilification or monsterification of filicidal mothers:

> The newspapers are always the same. Crime! Something committed by a twisted person who grew up in a damaging environment or by some mentally impaired individual, or else by a pleasure-seeker. (Gurūpu Tatakau Onna 1971b)

Ribu claimed that such an attitude was rooted in an attempt to conceal the social problems behind the crime—what Ayres has suggestively described as "the mother's unspoken injuries" (2004: 58)—and to safely stress its "exceptional" nature. By considering each case in terms of an unrepeatable singularity, no space was allowed for a structural explanation of the phenomenon. The rhetorical strength of these accusations reflected the movement's oppositional spirit. However, it would be naïve to attribute media's biased representations and its skilful structuring of the visual and discursive field to forms of intentional plotting. We should instead read them against media's reliance on stock stories, the sensationalization of violence and drama and the way in which these strategies often work to confirm the status quo and established cultural values via

---

[19] For an informative discussion of how publics come into being in relation to texts and their circulation, see Michael Warner's *Publics and Counterpublics* (2005).

the portrayal of exceptional violent events. This point is clearly stated in the following excerpt:

> The mass-media have a great responsibility because the role they play by emphasizing the "abnormality" of filicide is to provide satisfaction to the average woman and to make filicide something that is understood as the act of an exceptional (*tokubetsu na*) individual. In so doing they plunge women who are [already] cut off [from society] into an even deeper darkness. By blaming only the mother filicide is not going to disappear. (Urawa et al. 1975: 35)

Observe here how media portrayals of maternal filicide are described as having the double effect of singling out the murderous mother—thus exorcizing the threat that her maternal transgression represents for the social fabric—and providing a form of reassurance to those women who, confronted with such extreme, negative example of maternal monstrosity, find confirmation of their performances of maternal propriety. At the same time, such portrayals arguably limit women's ability to articulate those affective experiences that may call into question cultural idealizations of unequivocal maternal bliss.

Even in those cases where negative depictions of filicidal mothers were not obvious, news media were accused of making subtle comparisons between "good" and "bad" mothers, and of hiding their harsh moral indictments behind a veil of sympathy and understanding. This understanding is foregrounded in the following quotation from a leaflet circulated in November 1975 by a collective of women and children called Sapporo Komu-unu.[20] The object of its critique is already clear in its title: "We are enraged at the consensus of men and the mass-media who report the news without paying attention to the social background of filicide":

> [F]rom the beginning of September the *Asahi Shinbun* has serialised a sequence of articles that for eight times reported the headline "The Loss of Motherhood" (*bosei sōshitsu*). Because the articles were published in the home column of the newspaper, the articles right next to them conveyed

---

[20] Sapporo is the largest city on the northern Japanese island of Hokkaido. For an explanation of the name *komu-unu*, see Chap. 3.

the touching image of a woman who was a "mother" and a "wife" taking part and doing her best in some social activity. In the campaign articles (*kyanpēn kiji*) they write that even in the case of a woman killing her child there are many aspects that should deserve our sympathy. Nonetheless, if we look at the newspaper in its entirety, she who kills her child turns out to be a demonic mother (*oni no haha*). (Sapporo Komu-unu 1974: 24)

In ways that resonate with the analysis of media coverage I developed in Chap. 2, the passage above testifies to the *Asahi shinbun*'s employment of editorial strategies that relied on a calculated positioning of articles on filicide to implicitly convey unstated meanings. In this respect, the authors of the pamphlet recognize how even the most sympathetic account was bound to enter into a complex web of relationships with other news items across the newspaper and to be overshadowed by those larger narratives which portrayed mothers who killed as an alarming social phenomenon and a threat to modern civilization. They also argue that the content and the spatial organization of articles in the broader structure of newspapers communicated and shaped "the mood of an era in consonance with [those in] power" (ibid.). This led *ribu* to denounce the dynamic whereby society's dominant masculine values appeared to be mirrored and further reinforced by media's discursive strategies. Reporters, critics and commentators (positions mostly occupied by men) were blamed not only for their insensitivity to the social conditions that framed episodes of maternal filicide, but also for "frowning" judgementally at filicidal mothers while writing about them and making money out of their misfortune (Sayama et al. 1973: 192). Seen in this light, *ribu* women felt that the biased portrayals of mothers who killed their children added insult to injury. The sense of urgency animating *ribu*'s discursive intervention—together with its indignation vis-à-vis the dominant narratives that framed public understanding of maternal filicide—powerfully emerges from the following extract:

> A woman (*onna*) who wanted to live, who wanted to live with all her soul, who wanted desperately to live, has been made to kill her child. This is the same type of filicide that only last year reached nearly 400 cases! (This is the history of woman's darkness) (*onna no yami no rekishi*). The cruel "crime"

of a hysteric or of a woman who seeks only pleasure, you say?! Don't talk nonsense! That was just a misdirected blow! That moment when you can't help feeling hatred for your own beloved child to the point of desiring to kill him…you, who behave as if you were good-nature people! You, intellectuals! Do you understand it?! Marriage is a woman's happiness…A child is a woman's life purpose…Curses! Cursing words that are laid on women! (Gurūpu Tatakau Onna 1971b: 186)

My translation of the first sentence of this passage, although motivated by considerations of stylistic consistency, loses much of the rhetorical impact of the original "*ikitai, ikitai, ikitai onna ga, kodomo wo korosaserarechatta*" where the expression *ikitai* (I want to live) expresses the woman's desire as if it were pronounced in the first person (rather than in the third person of my unhappy translation). A more literal translation would have been "An *onna* [who thought/felt] 'I want to live! I want to live! I want to live!' has been made to kill her child." The naked repetition of *onna*'s desire for a life that can be deemed fully human draws the reader into her subjective experience. Furthermore, the sense of "historicity" embedded in her crime functions as an element that connects her to all women past and present, suggesting the enormous burden of suffering imposed upon women and thus making a transformation of society imperative.[21] The "history of woman's darkness" comes to represent both the tragedy of women's living conditions and the revolutionary potential of a resentment rooted in their corporeality and which constituted an asset shared to a greater or lesser extent by all women. In the following section I focus on *ribu*'s challenge to media coverage of a specific case of filicide, a form of critique that I deem representative of the movement's desire to foreground what the murderous mother had in common with other women as opposed to what allegedly made her stand apart.

---

[21] Once again, we may recognize in this pamphlet produced by Gurūpu Tatakau Onna a rhetorical style à la Tanaka: "the history of woman's darkness" recalls the darkness of the womb that I have already elaborated upon and which was deemed to harbour woman's history of discrimination and frustration.

Contesting the Equation "Maternal Filicide = Mental Instability"

On April 18, 1974, an article appeared in the Tokyo edition of the *Asahi shinbun* about a case of maternal filicide which had occurred in the city of Iwatsuki.[22] It was introduced under the headline "She throws the infant in the incinerator: the husband had told her off that he was noisy." The following day, in the same newspaper, coverage of the case appeared again in a brief article under the title "Mother affected by postpartum psychosis." This time it was reported that there was growing suspicion that the mother might have killed her child in a sudden impulse after her mental condition deteriorated due to a difficult delivery. A psychiatric test, the article informed, was going to be performed. However, *ribu* pamphlets called attention to the fact that an article of a very different tone had been published in the Urawa edition of the *Asahi shinbun*[23] under the headline: "The tragedy of a mother affected by schizophrenia." This article was harshly attacked by *ribu* for its alleged attempt to substitute an issue of mental disorder for the dramatic background to the case.

Ribu's writings reported that the culprit was a mother in a family of four living in a six-tatami (9.18 sq. metres), one-room flat in a terraced house and that the husband worked as a night truck driver. The victim was a baby only a few months old who had been a breech delivery. The first two months had been difficult, we are told: the baby's constant crying, the husband's angry outburst as he tried to sleep during the day in order to work at night and the mother's physical exhaustion (Ribu Shinjuku Sentā 1973; Niimi 1974; Ribu Shinjuku Sentā 1974; Asu wa wagami 1974; Urawa et al. 1975). However, the article in the *Asahi shinbun* built its case on the fact that the woman had not only been hospitalized once on the grounds of mental problems during her school-age years, but she had also been hospitalized once again more recently. The article even used appalling expressions like "people affected by mental disorder on the loose" (*nobanashi no shōgaisha*).

---

[22] Iwatsuki was a city located in Saitama prefecture until it merged in 2005 into the city of Saitama.
[23] As for Iwatsuki, Urawa was a city in Saitama prefecture. It merged into the city of Saitama in 2001.

Such an attitude on the part of the news media was severely criticized by *ribu* activists who accused the newspaper of promoting a conflation of filicidal mothers with people affected by mental disorder and of supporting the view that individuals who were mentally disturbed ought to be isolated on the basis that they could constitute a danger for other members of society (Asu wa wagami 1974). The criticism *ribu* levied against the *Asahi shinbun* followed three main lines of argument. To begin with, it mobilized an attack against the discriminatory attitude that this alleged campaign was deemed to support and which was said to negatively affect disabled people (be their disability physical or mental). Second, it denounced the newspaper for patently discarding as insignificant the circumstances in which the mother had found herself living. Finally, it argued that, by reducing the mother who had committed the crime to an "abnormal" (*ijō na*) or unusual woman, it set her apart from the average woman who did, indeed, face analogous circumstances (Urawa et al. 1975). The following excerpt is emblematic of the movement's critique:

> The *Asahi*'s call to deal by any means possible with "mentally unstable people on the loose" promotes and magnifies a consciousness of discrimination and prejudice toward those people; [consciousness] according to which "a person affected by mental disorder is a dangerous presence that doesn't know what he/she is doing." In so doing, it attempts to conceal the social problems (poverty, bad housing conditions, child-rearing as an exclusively female burden, etc.) that cornered the woman to the point of killing her child. (Asu wa wagami 1974: 379)

The *Asahi shinbun* argued that, because the woman's abnormal mental condition had been identified early in her life, relatives or welfare service should have put the child into custody in an institution. It also lamented that in the case of a mother affected by mental disorder it was not possible, under the current legislation, to separate the child from her on the basis of a medical assessment.[24] *Ribu* contended that similar assertions had the effect of promoting discrimination towards people

---

[24] The cursory outline I provide here of the attitude of the *Asahi* in relation to this case of filicide does not emerge from an analysis of the original newspaper articles in the Urawa edition, but is a reconstruction based upon the accounts embedded in *ribu*'s archival documentation.

with mental impairment and to encourage the idea that such individuals should be quarantined because of the potential danger they constituted. A direct connection was drawn between the attitude the *Asahi shinbun* demonstrated and the "logic of productivity" that the movement deemed endemic in modern society: mentally disturbed people were seen as inconvenient or useless in the eyes of the state and corporations, and they should be isolated in psychiatric wards to avoid undesirable disruption to the smooth functioning of society.

Let us note, at this point, that *ribu* never claimed that this mother was not mentally unstable when the crime had been committed or that she had not been suffering from some mental condition all along. What they emphasized was that this was not the issue. Even when they admitted the possibility that she might have suffered from an abnormal psychic condition, they described her criminal action as something that was just to be expected once her life circumstances were to be taken into consideration. Some of the leaflets that covered the case made exactly this point when they stated in their titles: "The woman who kills her child is you…" (Ribu Shinjuku Sentā 1973) and "We might be next!" (Asu wa wagami 1974). Further textual evidence can be found in numerous passages, some of which are reported below:

> She might indeed have developed a neurosis. […] But nonetheless, it's crystal clear that she was plunged into a neurosis as a result of having reached the limits of an accumulation of dissatisfaction, lack of freedom and rage that couldn't find expression. (Asu wa wagami 1974: 379)

> Irrespective of whether or not she had a history of hospitalization, we can't possibly forgive the article of the *Asahi shinbun* which linked to mental disorder a case of filicide that had occurred in [such] living circumstances where all of us, unsurprisingly, would have developed a neurosis[.] (ibid.)

> We cannot forgive the *Asahi shinbun* […] which, in an attempt to connect filicide and mental impairment in the same equation, takes as exemplary an episode of filicide occurred in normal living circumstances where a woman developed a neurosis independently from her having or not a history of hospitalization! (Ribu Shinjuku Sentā 1973: 69)

From *ribu*'s engagement with media portrayals of mothers who kill it emerges that, in order to create an alternative discursive space where a maternal potential for violence could acquire cultural intelligibility, it was necessary to counter those discourses that constructed murderous mothers as exceptional individuals whose abnormal mental state or wicked personality placed them outside the realm of the human. The Iwatsuki case considered in this section highlights the extent to which *ribu* engaged media coverage of filicidal mothers by means of a close reading of newspaper articles and by taking news media to task for their rhetorical strategies. At the end of Chap. 2 I briefly commented on what seemed to be the seeping of *ribu*'s rhetoric in media discourse. Here I want instead to call attention to the fact that a measure of *ribu*'s power to exert pressure upon and affect dominant discourses on maternal filicide may be recognized in the fact that, as a result of the movement's mobilization, the *Asahi shinbun* is said to have published what *ribu* described as a "statement of regret" (*hanseibun*) or "self-criticism" (*jiko hihan*). In the context of that apology the *Asahi shinbun* acknowledged the discrimination and bias that had informed its previous coverage of the case and eventually emphasized its social background (Urawa et al. 1975: 35; Ribu Shinjuku Sentā 1974: 139). Irrespective of whether or not this episode brought about a long-lasting change in the way mothers who killed came to be perceived in society, it certainly represented a major victory that testified to the power of *ribu* activists to alter the landscape in which discursive representations of maternal filicide were articulated.

The Silent Voice of Mothers Who Kill Their Children

Ribu's sustained engagement with maternal filicide notwithstanding, and despite its desire to connect with mothers who killed their children, we may be struck by the realization that the first-person perspective of these criminalized mothers hardly emerges from *ribu*'s written page. Apart from a single, major example, the voice of these mothers strikes us as somewhat inaudible.[25] In fact, a recurrent expression that described the silent (silenced?) voice of filicidal mothers was "*koe ni naranai koe*" ("a voice that does not produce a sound," "an inaudible voice" or "a voiceless voice").

The Association of Voiceless Voices (*Koe naki koe no kai*) was a group that emerged in the context of the ANPO struggle in 1960 (ANPO being short for *Nichibei anzen hoshō jōyaku*, also known as the Japan-U.S. Security Treaty)[26]: it was "an organization formed to allow people who did not belong to any other organization to participate in the marches and demonstrations" (Yoshitake, quoted in Loftus 2013: 91; see also Sasaki-Uemura 2001: 148–194). The fact that the expression used by *ribu* to describe the voices of filicidal mothers recalled the Association of Voiceless Voices may be taken as symptomatic of *ribu*'s local genealogies of political contestation. In line with some of the portrayals we encountered earlier in this chapter, it may also suggest a highly specific understanding of maternal filicide whereby mothers who killed their children, albeit not members of *ribu*, were seen as joining the struggle for social transformation. On the other hand, "voiceless voices" could also be read as a subtle reference to the difficulty of bringing the experience of these mothers into the realm of cultural intelligibility, of creating a space where their voices could be finally uttered and eventually heard. In this respect, their soundless voice would testify to the silent, individual drama these women experienced and which seems to haunt *ribu*'s rhetoric as the spectre of its own possibility (Castellini 2014).

If the voice of filicidal mothers is actually absent from the discourses that *ribu* produced and circulated, how should we relate to this absence? Should we be reassured by the belief that the movement intended to speak on behalf of mothers who killed their children or that its main goal was to give clear and loud expression to these mothers' silent plight? The following excerpt underlines the difficulties we encounter when we attempt to map out the complex relationship of *ribu* with filicidal mothers. The passage is an excerpt from a letter addressed to one of these mothers that a member of *ribu* wrote after attending the court hearing:

---

[25] The exception is represented by the transcripts of a trial against a mother who killed her three-year-old daughter and which the Ribu Shinjuku Centre published as a booklet in June 1973 (Sayama et al. 1973). It seems reasonable to argue, however, that the legal setting that framed the trial is likely to have imposed numerous restrictions on the defendant's liberty of expression, and we may feel legitimated to wonder whether it is unambiguously her voice that we hear as we read through the records of the trial.

[26] See Chap. 3, note nr. 1.

What did you think of my coming to the hearing with my child? From the start comments such as "a child can't be at this trial!" [...] made coming to the trial with a baby a taboo. Or didn't you notice me at all? Were you irritated and maybe thinking "Better you keep it quiet!"? Or were you hostile and thought: "All of you! You can't possibly understand! What have you come here for?! What have you come to look at?!" [...] I was just all nerves with the judge throwing warning looks (*chūi*) at me and people from the public [showing] disapproval (*hinan*). And I was holding my breath at the echoes of my child's voice [in the room]. What were you thinking [that day] in the tribunal with the voice of a child reverberating [...] through the courtroom? (Take 1971: 308)[27]

The passage offers a visual contrast between the mother standing trial, now childless as a consequence of the killing of her own child, and the young mother with child who silently (and retrospectively) addresses her from the public. The author displays a profound awareness of the potential incommunicability of experiences between herself and this other mother. In Take's account the thoughts in the minds of the judge and members of the audience seem almost easy to grasp when contrasted with the silent opacity of the woman standing trial. The word *chūi* used to describe the judge's behaviour means both "to pay attention/to focus" and "to give a warning," thus evoking the idea of a policing gaze that seems to multiply in the eyes of the other people in the room. In stark contrast to this hostile visual interaction, the filicidal mother emerges as an impenetrable and mute(d) space whose contours are drawn only by the writer's insistent questions; questions that, in the end, will remained unanswered.

The fact that the voice of the criminalized mother is inaudible while the perspectives of the judge and the audience offer themselves to a relatively easy verbal articulation may allegorize the power of dominant discourse to dictate what counts as maternal propriety and to shape the norms against which women-as-mothers are judged within society. According

---

[27] Take (Takeda Miyuki) was a member of the collective Tokyo Komu-unu. The fact that she assisted to the hearing and then wrote this letter is another demonstration of *ribu*'s ambivalent stance towards motherhood, which made it possible even for those women striving to conceive new forms of relationality between women and children to harbour a desire to connect with mothers who killed.

to this allegorical rendering this normative viewpoint operates simultaneously on two levels: on the one hand, it appears to have already silenced the perspective of the filicidal mother who is being judged because of her crime and her transgression vis-à-vis the maternal role; on the other hand, it exerts social pressure on the mother in the audience who is openly violating maternal propriety by bringing her child into the courtroom. Whereas we cannot enter the psychic space of the mother standing trial, the mother in the audience openly expresses her sense of discomfort as she faces society's open disapproval. Yet, instead of taking the passage as the objective portrayal of the reality of social pressure, we may even consider that, because society's chastising looks are introduced in the text through the author's subjective perceptions, the policing gaze might well be a projection of the author's own internalized self-discipline rather than being in a relation of exteriority to her. If this were the case, Take would have become, in Foucauldian fashion, her own disciplinarian as the result of her taking upon herself of cultural norms of maternal propriety.

Arguably, the passage could be said to foreground the social conditions that deny filicidal mothers a full-fledged subjectivity or a speaking position. It gestures towards the recognition of the inevitable distance that separates *ribu* and mothers who kill, and the difficulty of establishing a real dialogue. While the archival material does not bear significant traces of this exchange (which seems to have occurred nonetheless), we need to be alive to the fact that *ribu* did not arbitrarily claim to speak on behalf of these mothers. Nor did it simply fill the mute space these women occupied with its rich rhetoric, thus superimposing its interpretation onto their silent experience. As a matter of fact, Take's letter is a clear example of the movement's openness to an encounter with these women, however difficult that might have been. Whether or not *ribu* succeeded in this intent is bound to remain an open contention.

Conclusions

The aim of this chapter has been to explore *ribu*'s engagement with the "phenomenon" of maternal filicide and to map its tentative articulation of an alternative discourse that could oppose dominant perceptions of

4 Contested Meanings: Mothers Who Kill and the Rhetoric... 161

mothers who killed their children. Such counter-discourse challenged on multiple levels common understandings of the actions of these mothers as both isolated occurrences and the occasional deeds of inhuman, cruel or sick women. Vis-à-vis the tendency in society to offer interpretations of motherhood and maternal filicide that made use of "disempowering language" (Ayres 2004: 57), *ribu* created a new discursive space characterized by a highly political use of language which aimed to articulate in culturally intelligible forms the possibility of a maternal potential for violence.

In consonance with the movement's heterogeneous and fragmented nature this process was neither linear nor organic, and it was not necessarily uniform over time. It remains difficult to evaluate the extent to which the Ribu Shinjuku Centre played a pivotal role in shaping the direction of these discursive interventions because the very nature of the archival documentation this chapter relied upon might have inadvertently foregrounded its perspectives to the detriment of the activities of other centres and groups. As outlined in the Introduction, the three volumes edited by the Ribu Shinjuku Sentā Shiryō Hozon Kai (Association for the Documentary Conservation of the Ribu Shinjuku Centre) (2008a, 2008b, 2008c) contained only materials produced and/or preserved at the Ribu Shinjuku Centre during the years of its activities. And whereas I made a strategic attempt to complement the partiality of this first archive with the more wide-ranging volumes edited by Mizoguchi, Saeki and Miki (1992–1995), the fact remains that the number of pamphlets and leaflets on filicide contained in this second archival collection is proportionally small when compared to those preserved at the Centre. Despite these concerns, the analysis of the material at my disposal has given rise to an internally diverse, heterogeneous discursive landscape where different perspectives on mothers who kill intersected in multiple configurations.

The *minikomi* (mini-communication) network *ribu* developed was pivotal in the creation of an alternative discursive space where new perspectives on mothers who kill could be circulated. It seems pertinent here to recall Sasaki-Uemura's description of the role that *minikomi* played in the context of grass-roots activism: "Internally they fostered dialogue and group participation, but they were also used for public purposes, disseminating information not carried in the mass media and reaching out to groups and individuals facing similar struggles to create loose networks of solidarity" (2001: 143). Furthermore, although we can reasonably expect teach-ins and other collective gatherings organized to discuss maternal filicide to be characterized by passionate discussions among activists, the material on which this chapter was based does not suggest that there were major contentions as to the "true" interpretation of the phenomenon. There are also no instances where archival documents refer back to each other in critical fashion. In this respect, this seems to imply that *ribu* activists were motivated more by a shared desire to prompt social and discursive change, rather than to debate with each other over what constituted the correct interpretation of maternal filicide. Above all, whereas *ribu* remained ambivalent about filicide, its numerous interventions never became a celebration of murder, death or despair, but they were traversed by what we may call a celebration of life, the life that the movement relentlessly reclaimed for all those women (*onna*) who screamed out loud: "I want to live! I want to live! I want to live!"

5

Filicide and Maternal Animosity in Takahashi Takako's Early Fiction

My argument in the previous chapters called attention to those schemas of intelligibility that governed the conditions of appearance of a maternal potential for violence in 1970s Japan. It is indisputable that the proliferation of cultural representations of murderous mothers in the media contributed to their increased visibility in public discourse. Yet, we have also seen how the rhetorical strategies and linguistic politics of media coverage of maternal filicide were crucial to the regulation of public understanding of that violence. This structuring of the field of representability was consequential in determining the extent to which motherhood's violent potential was admitted as reality, thus promoting (or rather hindering) its cultural intelligibility according to existing schemas of conceptualization. In this respect, *ribu* made a programmatic effort to expand the field of representability by means of a counter-discourse that foregrounded the figure of the child-killing *onna* and which demonstrated profound awareness of the political dimension of language. In so doing, the movement worked relentlessly towards the creation of a discursive space that allowed for a more sensitive articulation of maternal violence. However, despite *ribu*'s expressions of solidarity with mothers who killed their

© The Author(s) 2017
A. Castellini, *Translating Maternal Violence*,
DOI 10.1057/978-1-137-53882-6_5

children, the movement's writings are marked by the distinct absence of what could be deemed a maternal voice capable of articulating its own violent inclinations.

In what follows I attempt to make up for that silence by means of an exploration of Japanese women's literature and its imaginary creation of a maternal subject position caught in a tormented effort to bring its own potential for violence into the realm of discourse. I enquire into the possible configurations of maternal violence that the literary medium might have allowed women writers to portray in early 1970s' Japan. More specifically, I take Japanese writer and essayist Takahashi Takako (1932–2013) as a case study and delve into the fictional representations of maternal filicide and maternal aggression that distinguish her early works. The stories analysed in this chapter portray the tortuous journey of self-discovery of mothers and wives who strive to come to terms with the dark, murderous energies that surface from the deepest strata of a self that has been buried under the façade of bourgeois family life. Their female characters struggle to break free from their socially constructed identity and to reformulate a new subjectivity. In the process they challenge social prescriptions of what it means to be a woman and a mother, and eventually shatter cultural ideals of a "feminine" nature. Considered in this light Takahashi's stories are very much in line with the kind of criticism of society that was at the heart of *ribu*'s activism and political contestation. At the same time they offer privileged access to figures of maternal subjectivity that populated the literary imaginary of late postwar Japan and which identified motherhood's violent potential as an important site of critical reflection.

In their relentless search for a more authentic subjectivity unconstrained by cultural prescriptions to become a wife and a mother, in their compulsion to dismantle traditional female identities by undertaking antisocial behaviours that turn them into figures of abjection, in their hostility towards pregnancy, motherhood and family life, Takahashi's heroines are far from unique.[1] Quite to the contrary, they join the ranks of a host of other tormented and tormenting female figures created by the fervid imagination of a new generation of women writers. The 1960s and

---

[1] For a rich exploration of Takahashi's thematic motifs, see Mori (1994, 1996, 2000, 2004) and Bullock (2006, 2010).

1970s saw the emergence on the literary scene of individuals of the calibre of Mori Mari (1903–1987), Setouchi Harumi (1922–), Kōno Taeko (1926–), Saegusa Kazuko (1929–2003), Ōba Minako (1930–2007), Takahashi Takako (1932–2013), Kurahashi Yumiko (1935–2005), Tomioka Taeko (1935–), Kanai Mieko (1947–) and Tsushima Yūko (1947–). The increasing recognition these writers received from a traditionally masculine literary establishment motivated many a critic to speak of an "age of talented women" (*saijo jidai*), of a boom in women's writing or even of a "renaissance" in women's literature in Japan long after the great women writers of the Heian period (794–1185) (Mitsutani 1986; Orbaugh 1996; Jones 2003; Dodane 2006).

In addition to the numerical increase in women writers, scholars point at the disturbing peculiarity of the themes these women explored in their works of fiction: sadomasochism, incest, paedophilia, partner swapping, female and male homosexuality, doppelgänger (doubles), violence and murder, woman's quest for sexual fulfilment, hatred or refusal of the maternal, infanticide, female alienation and loneliness, just to name a few of the most outstanding examples. Commentators also emphasize the stylistic use of fantasy, dreams, utopian worlds, delusions, madness and parody as another feature that distinguishes this revival in women's writing from the realist or autobiographical approaches that characterize their literary predecessors (Orbaugh 1996; Jones 2003). Gretchen Jones (2003: 224) describes this boom in women's literature as "a search for delineating a revised identity more befitting the new age" with women authors portraying female characters as they embark onto a quest for self-discovery that often demands "the outright rejection of social and cultural norms" and a reconsideration of "preconceived notions of femininity and womanhood."

It is tempting to speculate about the possible relationship between, on the one hand, the quantitative and qualitative changes that distinguished the literary production of this new generation of women writers and, on the other, the historical, social and cultural transformations that hit Japan in the aftermath of World War II. The dramatic restructuring of society that followed Japan's defeat opened up for women a world of undreamed-of possibilities as notions of political equality, co-education and equality in the workplace entered their mental landscape regardless of their still inadequate implementation (Orbaugh 1996: 126; Loftus 2013). For women writers this epochal sea-change "represented a significant cultural moment in which they could explore through fiction the various discourses and power relationships of postwar Japan" (Orbaugh 1996: 127, 2002, 2003). In a similar vein Julia C. Bullock (2010: 9) suggests that we read the early works of authors like Kōno Taeko, Takahashi Takako and Kurahashi Yumiko as "philosophies of gender in fictional form." She argues that in the decade preceding the birth of *ribu* as a politically active movement, other women had already "sought to critique and subvert hegemonic discourses of femininity that confined women to the 'traditional' roles of wife and mother" and opened up a path "toward a broader range of permissible expressions of feminine subjectivity" (3).[2]

Nakayama Kazuko (2006: 147) suggests that a measure of this literary intervention into the schemas of representability that framed public understanding of femininity and womanhood can be seen in the "dismantling of the myth of motherhood" that she considers instrumental to the destruction of the male paradigm whereby woman's subjectivity is moulded into man-made fantasies of maternal selflessness and all-encompassing love. Drawing on Adrienne Rich's famous formulation, Fukuko Kobayashi (1999: 135) similarly describes this process as the "killing of motherhood as institution" and argues that the creation of female characters "who counter and oppose the conventional motherly types popular in earlier fiction [...] reflect[s] the authors' deep-seated antipathy toward anything to do with the prevailing assumption of

---

[2] In light of these considerations, the title of Nakayama Kazuko's ([1986] 2006) classic survey of contemporary Japanese women's fiction acquires a distinct tone. In the essay "The Subject of Women's Literature and the Transformation of Its Consciousness" ("Joryū bungaku to sono ishiki henkaku no shudai"), Nakayama refers to the feminist movement and feminist thought of the 1970s, and although she never explicitly mentions *ribu*, her use of the expression *ishiki henkaku* (consciousness transformation) in the title suggestively evokes one of the key philosophical tenets of the newly emergent women's liberation movement in Japan. Whether or not the result of a conscious stylistic choice, the title of her essay seems to portray the new anti-heroines of women's literature in postwar Japan as participating in that broader transformation of female consciousness which constituted one of *ribu*'s most radical political purposes. Nakayama's piece, therefore, anticipates Bullock's intuition in portraying women's writing and feminist praxis of political contestation as partaking of a comparable project of social transformation and expansion of our capacity to imagine gender otherwise. An analogous take on the subject can be found in the edited collection *Ribu to iu "kakumei": gendai no yami wo hiraku* (2003) Kanō Mikiyo (ed.) Tokyo: Inpakuto Shuppankai.

motherhood as women's natural calling" (see also Copeland 1992).[3] Refusal of the maternal and rejection of a female procreative function seep into women's writing in the form of strong assertions of female sexuality as distinct from reproduction.[4] At the same time, authors as diverse as Ōba Minako, Kōno Taeko, Tsushima Yūko and Takahashi Takako challenge the myth of motherhood by indulging in extreme examples of what Rebecca Copeland calls "maternal animosity" (2006: 14). By "[c]reating female characters that kill, maim, or otherwise injure children," Copeland contends, these writers "violently disrupted expectations of an inherent [maternal] 'gentleness'" (ibid.).[5]

The stories by Takahashi that I analyse in this chapter clearly participated in the literary climate of the period and echoed the broader changes in terms of style and content that characterized the emergence of this new generation of women writers. However, my choice of focusing on a single writer is not meant to suggest Takahashi as representative of such revival of women's writing. Rather, my decision could be deemed strategic as it allows for close readings of both Takahashi's fictional and non-fictional works which, in turn, make us alive to the extent to which her literary production resonated with other discourses on maternal filicide and maternal violence that were circulating at the same time in Japan. This approach makes it possible to foreground a distinct (feminist?) political dimension that could be seen to traverse much of women's literature in those years, but whose investigation has often been reduced in the existing scholarship to an exterior similarity in terms of subjects and themes.

---

[3] Ōba Minako represents one such example of "resisting woman writer" (Ericson, 2006: 114): many of her short stories such as "The Three Crabs" ("Sanbiki no kani," 1968), "Ship-Eating Worms" ("Funakui mushi," 1970) and "Dream of Hemlock" ("Tsuga no yume," 1971) and the much famous "The Smile of a Mountain Witch" ("Yamauba no bishō," [1976] 1991) portray mothers and housewives whose subjectivity is unconnected to husbands, children, friends and social surroundings. Ōba goes as far as to make one of the characters in "The Three Crabs" argue that "[i]n the twentieth century, pregnancy is not a symbol of fertility but of sterility and destruction" (1968 [1982]: 97). An earlier, disturbing portrayal of maternal selfishness is provided by acclaimed author Enchi Fumiko (1905–1986) in her probably most representative work *Masks* (*Onnamen*, literally "woman's masks," 1958 [1983]). For an informative analysis of her work in context, see Carpenter (1990) and Ruch (1994).
[4] See Mizuta (1995), Orbaugh (1996, 1999), Mori (1996), Niikuni Wilson (1996) and Hartley (1999).
[5] Kōno's fiction is emblematic in this respect: her female characters embody a unique blend of revulsion towards the maternal, masochistic sexual desires and sadistic fantasies of maternal violence that make stories such as "Ants Swarm" ("Ari takaru," 1964 [1996]) and "Toddler-Hunting" ("Yōjigari," [1961] 1996) exceptionally disturbing readings.

But there are other important reasons why Takahashi's fiction is of particular interest to us. To begin with, the striking proliferation of images of maternal animosity and murderous motherhood that distinguishes her earlier works has no parallel in the literature of other women writers in postwar Japan. Second, as they become the occasion for questioning taken-for-granted assumptions about maternal subjectivity as saturated with love and devoid of ambivalent feelings, Takahashi's stories foreground the repeated failure of existing understandings of motherhood to translate a maternal potential for violence into a realm of cultural intelligibility. Takahashi's mothers struggle to communicate their troubled affective experiences and they grope for words that might allow them to give voice to the darkest shades of their maternal turmoil, if always with only partial success. In this respect, the difficulty of bringing the negative side of maternal ambivalence into the discursive field appears intertwined with a character's inner resistance to embarking on such process of verbalization. The silences, interruptions and gaps that punctuate many of the characters' confessions are thus symptomatic of mechanisms of psychic self-defence, ways to fend off the intolerable shattering of a traditional maternal identity that these women have learned to make their own, but which is bound to collapse when confronted with their violent impulses. And yet, I want to contend that, in their portrayals of conflicts that are internal to the characters' maternal identities, Takahashi's stories offer new words and images that played a significant role in expanding the field of representability and the conditions of appearance of a maternal potential for violence in the public sphere.

After a brief biographical account, what remains of this chapter is organized in three parts: the first section offers a close reading of portions of Takahashi's short stories "Summer Abyss" ("Natsu no fuchi," 1973) and "Incarnation" ("Keshin," 1972). I read these stories, which revolve around mothers coming to terms with the actual death of a very young child, as staging the difficulty of articulating in intelligible forms the negative side of maternal ambivalence. They foreground the psychic defences that emerge from within a (maternal) subject as she struggles to put into words her potential for violence. The gaps and silences that mark these mothers' confessions constitute, as it were, an unmarked delimitation of the field of representability, "a set of contents and perspectives that are never shown, that it becomes impermissible to show" (Butler 2010: 73). For this very reason, however, they also become revealing of the repressed or foreclosed background of what *is* allowed access to the realm of verbal articulation and cultural intelligibility, thus exposing how conscious and unconscious mechanisms appear to impinge upon our capacity to conceive of a maternal potential for violence.

The following section offers an analysis of the story "Boundlessness" ("Byōbō," 1971b) and explores how the death of an unborn baby in real life (as the result of a miscarriage) or in hallucinating, murderous fantasies becomes the opportunity to lay bare woman's alienation within the institution of the family. Reading the profound dread of reproduction and pregnancy and the radical problematization of the mother–child bond that characterize this story against the background of Takahashi's non-fictional essays makes it possible to highlight the extent to which her literary production strongly resonates with *ribu*'s attempts at dismantling idealized notions of maternal love.

In the third and final section I read the stories "Yonder Sound of Water" ("Kanata no mizuoto," 1971a) and "Congruent Figures" ("Sōjikei," 1971b) in light of Takahashi's meditations on the "demonic woman," a figure of female awakening that she envisions in stark opposition to the maternal and which makes woman's violent potential into a liberatory energy against prescriptions of appropriate femininity and the shackles of bourgeois family life. As I will highlight more directly in my conclusive remarks to *Translating Maternal Violence*, the staggering similarity between Takahashi's conceptualizations of the "demonic woman" and *ribu*'s rhetorical investment in the figure of the "child-killing *onna*" is just one of the many instances in which both discourses can be seen to jointly contribute to challenging gender norms and increasing the cultural intelligibility of women's relation with violence.

Takahashi Takako

Born in 1932 in Kyoto, the ancient capital of Japan, Takahashi (née Okamoto) Takako was the only child of a well-to-do family. When she was 16 and she had already spent a few years attending a girls' high school, the series of reforms undertaken under the guide of the Allied Forces of the Occupation made the educational system co-ed. This allowed her to be among the first few young women in 1950 to enrol at the prestigious Kyoto University, where she majored in French and graduated in 1954 with a thesis on Charles Baudelaire. Despite the unforeseen possibilities that co-ed education opened for women of her generation, several of Takahashi essays document with clarity the sense of marvel, discomfort and embarrassment that accompanied the early moments of her adaptation to the new system. And she vividly describes the harsh reality of having to confront male students whose previous curricula had better prepared them for the intellectual challenges of life at Kyoto University.[6]

Shortly after her graduation in 1954, Takahashi married fellow student and future renowned writer Takahashi Kazumi (1931–1971), but she never wanted children. In the essay "Sakka no okusan" [The writer's wife] she provides an account of her ardent idealization of Kazumi's sensitivity and literary talent and the amount of energy she invested in helping him in the early stages of his career. In their 17 years of marriage Takahashi prioritized the economic and practical support she gave Kazumi over her own literary aspirations.[7] But she also acknowledged how Kazumi's intellectual companionship, his artistic aspirations and encouragement of her literary talents, coupled with the concrete help she offered him at the beginning of his career, constituted fundamental and formative influences in her own literary development.[8] Despite her devotion in helping Kazumi become a successful writer, Takahashi was, nonetheless, able to pursue her liter-

---

[6] Takahashi recalls, for example, the many bright male students in the department of French Literature, how they constantly criticized and belittled her and how any woman in such an environment was doomed to lose self-confidence. Her experience at Kyoto University is addressed in numerous essays such as "Takahashi Kazumi to sakka toshite no watashi" [Takahashi Kazumi and my literary career] in *Takahashi Kazumi no omoide* [Memories of Takahashi Kazumi] (1977), "Otoko no naka no tada hitori" [The only one among men] and "Unmei no wakareme" [Fateful departure] in *Tamashii no inu* (1975) and "Danjo kyōgaku" [Coeducation] in *Kioku no kurasa* (1977).

[7] For several years after they married Takahashi undertook odd jobs as secretary, translator, tutor of French and English and tour guide in order to support them both and to help Kazumi devote himself to writing.

[8] Takahashi describes how she used to write the fair copies of Kazumi early pieces, sometimes working on a tight schedule made even more demanding by Kazumi's habit of handing over to her full chapters to be copied on the very morning of the day when they were due to the editor.

ary interests: in 1956, shortly after her marriage, she returned to Kyoto University and pursued, in 1958, a Master's degree in French literature with a thesis on François Mauriac. In 1963 she published a translation of Mauriac's *Thérèse Desqueyroux*, a novel which, as we shall see, exercised a great influence on Takahashi's literary style and choice of themes.

However, life after marriage saw her increasingly dissatisfied: the problem was not her relationship with Kazumi, but the monotony and repetitive boredom of married life, the incessant visits of acquaintances and relatives, the small talks that sociality demanded of her, all of which she felt were like an inferior dimension when compared to the "piercing aesthetic tension" of a life devoted to literature.[9] Furthermore, even after gaining literary recognition, Kazumi shielded her from the public eye as it was common at that time: she rarely accompanied him to public events and whenever he received guests, she was expected to maintain a traditional wifely composure, serving drinks but refraining from taking part in conversations. "Not being allowed to participate," she recalls, "I was always watching. I couldn't do anything but watching. It was such a time for a woman."[10] But when she was alone with Kazumi, she was able to flee the drabness of everyday life. At the same time literature became more and more an escape from the vulgarity of mundane reality (Mori 1994).

In spring 1966 Takahashi developed a serious form of neurosis whose roots the author attributed to the deep-seated male chauvinism that she had long suffered while still living in Kyoto and whose symptoms surfaced intermittently in the years to follow.[11] The oppressive patriarchal environment that characterized life in the ancient Japanese capital is described in the essay "Watashi no naka no kyō-onna" [The Kyoto woman within me] where the traditional Kyoto woman is compared to a snail which coils deeply into her shell and never reveals her innermost self to the outside world. Rigid gender norms are said to condition "women to constantly

---

[9] "Takahashi Kazumi to sakka to shite no watashi," in *Takahashi Kazumi no omoide* (1977a: 93).

[10] "Naze shuen ni naru no ka?" [Why does it turn into a drinking party?] in Takahashi, *Takahashi Kazumi to iu hito* [Remembering Takahashi Kazumi] (1997a: 79). See also "'Hi no utsuwa' jushō zengo" [Before and after the reception of the prize for "Vessel of Sadness"] in Takahashi, *Takahashi Kazumi no omoide* (1977a: 77–84).

[11] "Watashi no noirōze no koto" [Concerning my neurosis] in Takahashi, *Sakai ni ite* [Standing on the border] (1997: 122–29).

suppress their own thought and feelings and maintain a bland, compliant demeanor."[12] Takahashi always found such an environment stifling of her development as a person and a writer. She yearned to leave the Kansai[13] area and move closer to Tokyo, which seemed to promise less suffocating social norms and a more welcoming literary environment for an aspiring woman writer. In 1964 she had affiliated herself to a Tokyo-based literary coterie and started publishing her first stories on its magazine *Hakubyō*. The next year Takahashi and her husband finally moved to Kamakura, with Kazumi accepting a teaching position at Meiji University in Tokyo. But when Kazumi decided in 1967 to move back to Kyoto to work as assistant professor of Chinese literature at Kyoto University, she made the brave and shocking decision of not following him. Not only did she live alone for two years and devote herself to her literary career, with Kazumi joining her only during university holidays, but also in April 1967 she embarked on a solitary journey during which she lived in Paris for several months while travelling around Europe. In her heart their relationship had changed forever: "As I left for Paris in April 1967," she writes, "I felt as if we were divorced. Were it not for Kazumi's death, we'd probably still be that way."[14] In 1969, however, Kazumi's health conditions forced him to return to Kamakura and later that year he was diagnosed with bowel cancer. She nursed him devotedly through the entire course of the disease until his untimely death in May 1971.

Meanwhile, Takahashi's literary career had started to bloom. Since 1969 her stories had begun to appear on the pages of the major literary magazines and in 1971 and 1972 her first two collections were published. In the following years she was awarded some of the most prestigious literary prizes: the Tamura Toshiko Prize in 1973 for *Sora no hate made* [To the end of the sky], the Izumi Kyōka Prize in 1976 for *Yūwakusha* [The temptress], the Womens' Literature Prize in 1977 for *Ronrii ūman* [Lonely woman], the Kawabata Yasunari Prize in 1985 for the story "Kou" [To yearn], the Yomiuri Prize in 1986 for *Ikari no ko* [Child of

---

[12] Maryellen T. Mori, (2004: xi).
[13] The Kansai region includes the prefectures of Kyoto, Osaka, Nara and the surrounding area.
[14] "Shakaiteki atsuryoku unnun no koto" [Social pressure and so forth] in Takahashi (1997b), 130–32.

wrath] and, more recently, the Mainichi Art Prize in 2004 for *Kirei na hito* [Beautiful person].

Takahashi's literary style and choice of themes were deeply informed by her highly developed sensitivity for decadent-aesthetic motifs that she nourished through her study of French literature, her profound interest in surrealism and her predilection for fantastic and visionary narrative modes.[15] She also manifested a profound interest in the concept of the psychic unconscious: in her writings reflections abound to Jungian psychoanalysis, to the pivotal importance of dreams as privileged access routes to repressed desires and to notions of a divided self which couple with literary explorations of the motif of the *doppelgänger* or double. These influences combined with her deep interest in Christianity which she pursued through her passionate reading of writers in the Catholic tradition such as François Mauriac, Julien Green and Endō Shūsaku, talks on Christianity she attended from 1974 and a week she spent at a Carmelite convent in Hokkaidō in June 1975.[16] In August of the same year she converted to Catholicism and was baptized. In 1980 she left Japan and spent almost ten years in France participating in the religious life and contemplative practices of a religious society called "Les Fraternités Monastiques de Jérusalem" [The Monastic Communities of Jerusalem] while studying Christian mystical literature in French. She returned to Japan in 1989.

Takahashi's lifelong spiritual quest is widely reflected in her writing and her works of fiction are elegantly infused with Christian symbolism and themes which became more pronounced since the second half of the 1970s. However, Maryellen T. Mori has importantly observed that "Takahashi's continually evolving understanding of Christianity is highly personal and unorthodox" and that "her interpretation of Christian mythology seems to have broadened to not only transcend sectarian distinction but also blur the marks that would bind it to any particular religious tradition" (Mori 2004: xxvi). Takahashi's early fiction might strike as at odds with her religious inclinations as it often portrays socially alienated female characters who vent their violent impulses and a repressed

---

[15] In her essays she makes wide reference to artists such as Marc Chagall, Giorgio De Chirico, Edvard Munch and Caspar David Friedrich and to authors as varied as Charles Baudelaire, E.T.A. Hoffman, Oscar Wilde and Edgar Allan Poe.

[16] "Karumeru-kai shudōin" [The Carmelite convent] in Takahashi *Kioku no kurasa* [174–8].

ferocious exasperation upon those who appear to embody social ideals of feminine propriety, to uphold society's gender norms or to represent reproduction and motherhood as a woman's natural destiny. Other stories depict female characters pursuing unconventional sexual relations with beautiful, feminine boys, indulging in incestuous desires or performing strange rituals aimed at accessing a higher realm of existence through domination and gender reversal. However, an attentive reading reveals that most of her works are infused, to various degrees, with spiritual undertones and can be understood as "female narratives of awakening."[17]

Takahashi's predilection for a visionary literary style which blurs the distinction between dreams and reality enables her to orchestrate narratives that primarily revolve around the inner landscape of her characters. The use of fantasy is strategically important here, because it makes room for the exploration of desires that are repressed or frustrated by social and cultural prescription. From the very beginning literature became for Takahashi a way to dig deep into the unconscious, to express her innermost desires and impulses and explore, in fictional form, the different selves whose existence was foreclosed by society's prescriptive nature.[18] In the context of a published conversation with fellow writer Ōba Minako, Takahashi has openly spoken of her eventual rebellion against that self that had been shaped in accordance to the traditions and the social norms that informed the environment where she was born and raised: "Rather than rebelling against my parents or against the environment to which my parents belonged, it's more appropriate to say that I rebelled against the self that had been shaped in such an environment."[19]

---

[17] For an extensive investigation of the roles of androgynous boys in such female narratives of awakenings, see Maryellen T. Mori, "The Liminal Male as Liberatory Figure in Japanese Women's Fiction" (2000).

[18] Takahashi has often been identified with the so-called introverted generation (*naikō no sedai*), a cluster of distinguished writers such as Furui Yoshikichi and Mori Makiko whose literature turns away from overt social and political commentary in order to privilege an investigation of postwar Japan's sense of identity crisis and change through an inward gaze and the exploration of its characters' inner or spiritual dimension.

[19] Ōba Minako and Takahashi Takako, "*Taidan–Sei toshite no onna*" [Conversations: Woman as sexual being] (1979: 86).

At the Margins of Discourse: The Dark Side of Maternal Ambivalence

"Summer Abyss" opens with the first-person narrator (who identifies herself simply as *Watashi* [I]) paying visit to the Kido family after the sudden death of their only child Akiyuki. The two-year-old boy fell from a cliff while he was out for a walk with his mother Reiko. When *Watashi* and the now 27-year-old Reiko were attending the same university, they were close friends, but during the last few years *Watashi* did not keep in touch with her. In fact, it has been already two years since the last time they met on the occasion of Akiyuki's birth. *Watashi* hesitates in front of the gates to the mansion: she does not want to meet Reiko. She wouldn't even be there—she admits to herself—were it not for the news of the child's death she read about in the newspaper few days before. The reasons for her reluctance will be made clear in the course of a long flashback that occupies a great portion of the story and to which I will briefly return. For the time being, however, it is this more recent encounter between the two female characters that will constitute the main focus of my considerations.

Reiko's old maid takes the narrator through the silent house to the Japanese-style room where the altar for the deceased has been set up. *Watashi* was expecting to find a broken family crushed under the weight of their loss, but the room is dark and empty. The father is utterly absent from the narration.[20] Her attention lingers on the altar and on what looks like a recently taken picture of Akiyuki:

> It's fair to say that, when I came to pay visit on occasion of [Akiyuki's] birth, I almost didn't see the baby and I knew as good as nothing about Reiko's child. But that rather blurred photograph stirred in me a strange feeling. Pictures of the dead are imbued with the sorrow for the departed ones and they are chosen to convey most vividly an image of them when

---

[20] This is an element that "Summer Abyss" has in common with many of the stories considered in this chapter and which seems to suggest a condition of isolation characterizing the experience of numerous female characters within the institution of the family. As a matter of fact, even on those occasions when a husband is indeed present, the protagonist's deep sense of alienation and radical incommunicability constitutes a leitmotif throughout the narrative.

they were still alive. But the picture in front of my eyes looked as if it were the one most out of focus deliberately chosen from among all those in one's possession, and which had been [further] enlarged in order to make it even more blurred. In other words, it felt like it wasn't imbued with Reiko's grief. (Takahashi 1973a: 98–9)[21]

Placed at the beginning of the narrative this passage gestures from the start towards a certain questioning of socially upheld expectations about maternal love and grief over the loss of one's own child. The contrast of this scene with the description of a similar altar that we encountered in the media coverage of the Kimura case could not be more striking.[22] There, the vivid photographs of Kimura's children, the colourful toys placed next to them as the painful reminder of childhood innocence and the carefully arranged white carnations conveyed—not without a touch of exotic and voyeuristic curiosity on the part of the reporter—a family's composed sorrow. Compared to the affective undertones of that first portrayal, the view *Watashi* describes strikes us as desolate and bleak: instead of communicating the mother's painful need to remember Akiyuki, the photograph that adorns the altar exudes an unsettling carelessness and seems to convey a wishful desire to make the memories of the child irrecoverable by rendering his image unrecognizable.

Watashi finds Reiko sitting on a bench in the garden, almost looking as if she were bathing in the burning sunlight of that summer afternoon. She approaches her unsure of how best to address her. With her straight back shining bright in the scorching sun Reiko gives "an impression rather different from that of a woman walled up in the pain of having just lost a child" (99). In rather cryptic fashion, Reiko informs the narrator that for the last three days she had been sitting in the garden, thinking, and waiting for her visit: "You're the only one who can understand," she adds, "I want you to hear everything" (ibid.). *Watashi*, however, remains hesitant because she has perceived something brazen in the way Reiko

---

[21] "Summer Abyss" first appeared in November 1973 in the pages of the literary journal Bungakukai and was reprinted in February 1974 as part of the collection *The Lost Picture* (*Ushinawareta e*). Page numbers refer to the story's original appearance. Unless otherwise indicated, all translations are mine.

[22] See Introduction, note nr. 6.

has spoken: once helpless and somewhat childish, her voice seems now momentarily tinged with a certain aggressive impudence. For a while, the silence between the two is filled by the sounds of summer. The stage is now set for Reiko's recollection of the tragic events that led to the death of Akiyuki. Hers is also a confession or, at least, it is as a confession (*kokuhaku*) that *Watashi* will understand it. The face-to-face of these two women stages in fictional form a moment of confrontation between a society that, in the figure of the narrator, is increasingly shaken by the realization of Reiko's potential for violence and a young mother who struggles to articulate her possible involvement in the death of her own only child. The passage ends on a silent note that, while creating a sense of tense anticipation, also seems to magnify the distance between Reiko's attempt at verbalization and the world of social norms here temporarily embodied by *Watashi*. The silence that looms large between the two women is also symptomatic of a resistance against the articulation of a maternal potential for violence that both characters seem to share, albeit for different reasons. To fully appreciate the complexity and psychological nuances of Takahashi's narrative style, Reiko's recollection needs to be quoted at length:

> She looked different. Sure, there had been the death of her child. But it wasn't only that. There was something ambiguous about her, something that had never existed in her before.
> "Don't doubt!" said Reiko looking straight at me with a sudden intuition.
> "What on earth should I doubt?" I looked her in the eyes.
> "You know, I was standing with my back to the cliff. And while I was standing like that, Akiyuki fell from the cliff." She spoke fast, as if she was a little out of breath.
> "I can't understand if you don't recount things in a more logical order."
> "I didn't realize anything. It happened while I was admiring the setting sun, giving my back to the cliff" repeated Reiko, with no attempt whatsoever to sound [more] coherent. And, as if she'd finished saying something she absolutely must say, she softened her look, which had been cast straight at me, and looked up instead in a different direction, her eyes now vacuous.

"What cliff?" I asked, while going in my head over the words she had repeated twice. She had placed an unusual emphasis on the fact that she had her back to the cliff. (100)

Let me point out the extent to which the narrator is deeply implicated in the structure of the above passage (and of the overall narrative): it is, indeed, *Watashi* that constitutes the reader's privileged entry point into the story, and it is *her* perception of Reiko and, later, *her* recollection of a time passed that enable us to start making sense of the events in "Summer Abyss." It is through the narrator's observations that we catch a glimpse of the radical change that allegedly occurred in Reiko's inner world and which *Watashi* cannot merely attribute to the trauma the young mother has obviously suffered. Whereas a measure of this change is suggested by the brazen quality of Reiko's voice, it is in fact the narrator who recognizes that tone as "audacious" or "impudent" (*futebuteshii*). Yet, Reiko's countenance in the passage can be hardly described as shameless or bold. Quite to the contrary, she is the one on the defensive, stressing repeatedly that she was unaware of the drama that was unfolding behind her. As a matter of fact, Reiko's effrontery appears wrapped up in a fundamental ambiguity: on the one hand, the story has from the outset prompted us to question her attachment to Akiyuki and to suspect her involvement in his death. In this respect, Reiko might have been perfectly aware of her (filicidal?) desires and her "impudence" would then be the manifestation of a defiant stance à la Medea. On the other hand, her insistent claims of innocence contradict the idea of a conscious rebellion against social norms. Reiko's sudden plea "Don't doubt!" might stand here for "Don't doubt about me as a mother!" "Don't doubt my love for my child!" or even "Don't raise suspicions about my involvement in his death!" The fact that the act of doubting has no direct object has the effect of leaving open all these interpretative possibilities, but it also suggests a certain reticence, a holding back from bringing maternal ambivalence into the discursive field. "Don't doubt!" also stands for Reiko's accurate assumption that she has already been judged, and the fact that it is *Watashi* who "recognizes" an impudent tone in her voice seems to support this reading.

Considered from a different angle, the brazen quality sensed in Reiko's voice could also be symptomatic of something in Reiko's demeanour that society perceives as a threat to the integrity of the maternal ideal. However, Reiko seems utterly unaware that she may represent such a threat. In fact, her passionate claims of innocence suggest that she may have taken upon herself those very social prescriptions of what a mother should be, and that she might be herself troubled by an unexpected crack in the myth of maternal love that her experience—whatever that might be—seems to have exposed. Yet, Reiko's voice occasionally does seem to emerge from within a narrative structure set and directed by the narrator, much like maternal ambivalence could be said to surface from the interstices of discourse.

Reiko continues her recollection, while *Watashi* listens with growing discomfort:

> "You know, I got startled when Akiyuki screamed. I was standing facing west. Apparently Akiyuki was playing on the verge of the cliff."
> "In such a dangerous place?"
> "Dangerous? Still, the soil is dry and looks like a sandpit. It's a suitable playground for a child."
> [...]
> "You see, the grass had grown a little."
> [...]
> "It was like that... Akiyuki had almost fallen from the cliff, but he was clinging at the grass with both hands."
> "Eh? Did you see that?"
> "I saw Akiyuki. Only the face was sticking out from the cliff. He was crying and screaming, and the face was all red and congested."
>
> Reiko said those last words as if she were dropping pebbles on a wooden floor with a hard sound, and she suddenly fell silent as though she had precipitated into herself. I was too being lured into the depths of her silence.
>
> "Why did you fall silent all of a sudden?" Reiko asked, raising her head stiffly.
> "It's you who's gone silent!" I said, confused.
> "It was really just a moment."
> "I see... It's strange though."
> "It was an accident! Accidents happen like that all the time!"
>
> As I felt Reiko's voice growing shrill and nervous, I got up from the bench.

"I was lost in the sunset. The evening sun was sinking red, gushing thick blood."
Reiko's voice reached me there where I stood, like hot vapour.
"Reiko…"
I resolved to speak, despite some hesitation.
"When you were looking at the evening sun, wasn't it after everything was over?"
I had hardly said it that a sickening feeling welled up inside me as if I needed to throw up. I made to leave without even asking. I couldn't stay near Reiko any longer.
"Where are you going? Are you leaving already?"
Reiko stood up and followed me.
"Your story, I have perfectly understood it!" I said while continuing in my steps. (101–2)

One of the most striking features of this passage is the disquieting contrast between Reiko's recollection of the last dramatic moments of her child's life and her aesthetic lingering on the beauty of the sunset. No tears are shed nor does she appear to be struggling emotionally with those painful memories (certainly not in the way we might expect a mother would do). As she recalls Akiyuki's crying and screaming in his desperate attempt not to fall, Reiko falls silent, "precipitating" into herself and projecting that same silence on to the narrator in what could be read as a form of psychic defence. This represents the climax of Reiko's confession where we are confronted with her elliptical admission of being somehow implicated in Akiyuki's tragedy, be it only in the form of a purposeful lack of action. But could this also be the occasion that takes Reiko dangerously close to an awareness of dark emotions lurking in her unconscious? Could this be the moment when a murderous desire harboured in the secret profundity of her maternal identity threatens to surface from the depths of psychic repression? It is telling that this moment is marked by a *loss of speech* (Reiko's silence) and by a fundamental *negation*: her forceful assertions that "It was an accident!" and that "Accidents happen like that all the time!"

This seemingly unconscious resistance to a verbal articulation of motherhood's violent potential (articulation that bears the promise of cultural intelligibility) is redoubled by the extent to which Reiko's confession is traversed by a profound sense of fragmentation and linguistic insufficiency. Her recollection is interrupted by pauses, silences, brief or broken sentences that instead of communicating a coherent, linear message seem to cram around the invisible, dark volume of something unsayable. Reiko's falling into silence suggests the difficulty, if not impossibility, of translating this "something" into intelligible words in the context of a social and cultural milieu that vigorously opposes its very articulation. Emotions and behaviours which may threaten to shatter society's maternal ideal are rendered unintelligible, confined to a place of abjection from where they can be retrieved only at great personal risk. This is not merely the risk of being stripped of one's own maternal identity in the eyes of society but also, perhaps, that of experiencing an even greater loss motivated by the psychic investment a woman might have developed in that very identity. We could submit, then, that Reiko's withdrawal into herself works as a defence against this unbearable threat: tellingly, this psychic retreat is accompanied by the sudden inability to proceed in the articulation of meaning and by her looking away as she searches for the source of that silence *outside of herself*, in the narrator. Her gesture of denial is, however, never complete because her recollection has been pre-emptively framed as a confession, and because both *Watashi* and the reader inevitably find the crescendo of emotional tension in her voice suspicious vis-à-vis her claims of innocence. The beauty of the sunset opens and closes Reiko's memories, the chromatic dominance of shades of red colouring the unfolding of the scene. In the end, the figural juxtaposition of the warm glow of the setting sun with the ominous image of blood soaking the sky appears to betray, if only via unconscious associations, Reiko's active participation or, alternatively, an unspeakable sense of anticipation.

Before we move on to another important scene in the story, let me draw your attention to *Watashi*'s reactions and suggest that it is, indeed, *Watashi* who appears to move the closest to a verbal articulation of motherhood's violent potential, even though her final question is formulated in oblique terms. Such indirect questioning has, nonetheless, the power to produce in the narrator a series of violent, material effects, causing a fit of nausea and urging her to move away from Reiko. The physical compulsion to put a safe distance between them is accompanied by a bodily urge to throw up, that is, to refuse and expel an understanding she might have achieved in despite of herself. Her reactions can be read as the reactions of a cultural order expressing utter rejection of a woman who contravened social expectations of maternal propriety and who seems to have turned, at least momentarily, into a being devoid of humanity. In the end, *Watashi* leaves the house and it is only as she traverses a space that is at a safe distance from Reiko's presence that she is able to express what has so far only faintly surfaced at the threshold of verbal articulation:

> [...] my mind was pursuing restlessly what happened inside Reiko. I never thought that she had pushed the child off the cliff with her own hands. Yet, she might have been in a position from where she could have saved him. Maybe while the child was [still] clinging at the grass with his hands, she had [even] made to intervene, the sandy soil of the crumbled hillside hampering her movements, but then she had perhaps stood where she was. Only [his] face was still left above the cliff, strangely grotesque so flushed and congested. And maybe, for the several tens of seconds during which that face had gazed persistently at Reiko, she had too stared fixedly at it. Perhaps, while she was holding her breath, her body held stiff, she had watched as an accidental opportunity erased the child's existence. I wondered what the child might have seen. Maybe it was the rapt look, almost serious, of his mother who was just staring without even trying to reach out to him. I wondered if that was what the child had seen with his own eyes, his last sight of this world as he had fallen screaming through the blazing air made red by the setting sun.
>
> Maybe it had happened like that. Maybe not. Why, then, was I picturing it like that? And yet, if that was indeed what had happened, what would that mean? (103)

A forthright articulation of murderous desires at the very heart of the maternal experience becomes possible here only when the narrator is no longer dangerously close to the source of those dark impulses, and only after her resolution never again to return to Reiko's house. If Reiko's presence evokes the material possibility, the reality so to speak, of a maternal potential for violence, it is only when *Watashi* moves away from it that she becomes able to bring her own doubts unambiguously into discourse. Quite ironically, however, this retreat into a safe distance also signifies a withdrawal from the reality of maternal ambivalence into a realm of speculation. The narrator's monologue is interspersed with words that belong to the semantic field of conjecture: "my mind" (*watashi no atama*), "I never thought" (*kesshite…omowanai*), "might/perhaps" (*kamoshirenai*), "maybe/I wonder" (*darō ka*). Furthermore, her conclusions seem to deny the possibility of maternal ambivalence as they consider it: "Maybe it had happened like that. Maybe not." Even when such possibility is reinstated ("And yet…") the narrator still gropes for words to understand, and the question closing the passage can still be deemed complicit with an attempt to preserve the commonsensical and comforting notion of a maternal violent potential as defying meaning.

This episode, whose rhetorical implications and perspectival complexity I wanted to foreground, prepares the terrain for the narrator's long flashback which attempts to provide an answer to that final interrogative. *Watashi* recalls the time when they were both university students and Reiko and her fiancé Seishi were making plans for a future together. We come to know that during that summer the narrator had a secret affair with Seishi which resulted in his growing disinterest for Reiko and his decision to move to the United States, leaving her behind broken and still unaware of the reasons behind his change of heart. Reiko had eventually accepted an arranged marriage with another man. One year later she was pregnant with Akiyuki, but having discovered that she could not get over her lost love, she had ended up projecting her ambivalent feelings onto her child.

Reiko's ambivalence is here carefully explained and entirely resolved, as it were, as the product of a resentment pouring out of her broken feelings and broken trust. The story could have ended at this point with a plot astutely planned and carefully developed, but this is not the case. As we approach its real conclusion, two apparently inessential episodes seem to draw us back insistently to what we may describe as a "dark shadow" in the depths of the maternal experience. Towards the end of the flashback, *Watashi* recalls her earlier visit to Reiko when Akiyuki was born: on that occasion Reiko had told her about her conflicting feelings and her dislike of the baby. As the narrator was leaving, Reiko had followed her to the front door and hurriedly confessed: "I can't sleep. Every night the baby cries! I want to sleep. And yet, the baby cries. He cries every single night, as if my hatred were rubbing off on him" (120). This image of a worn-out

Reiko torn in two by her maternal ambivalence ends the narrator's stream of memories. We now find *Watashi* by the seaside reflecting on the recent events. She observes a woman with child walking on the beach:

> A woman of my age and a boy who was about three were standing on the seashore. The two, who could be mother and child, were directly facing the sea holding their hands. The song that the woman was singing to herself sounded like some foreign children's song. Her voice had a peaceful, relaxed and quiet tone. I was reminded of Reiko and her dead child. Watching these mother and child in front of me what I had imagined about the child's death seemed an absurd misunderstanding.
> As I passed them, the song continued behind me. [...] Singing it too in my head, I left the seaside and crossed the sandy beach. [...] In that moment, I felt a tightness in my chest. Perhaps it was because all of a sudden I couldn't hear the song or maybe the woman with child had reminded me of Reiko. My feet, sinking in the sand at every step, were heavy. That weight called forth the burden of my body and evoked the heaviness in my soul. (121)

The apparent serenity of this female figure stands in stark contrast with the memory of a tired and torn Reiko. Looking at such an image of maternal tenderness the narrator herself is inclined to dismiss her previous interpretation of Reiko's story as a gross misunderstanding and a logical impossibility. The appearance on the beach of the maternal couple (which seems to embody social expectations of maternal love) has the effect of silencing once again any intelligible articulation of a maternal potential for violence. If we remain faithful to our understanding of the narrator as a synecdoche of the social order, her prompt acceptance of that erasure may be emblematic of society's eager desire to deny that potential the remotest chance to enter the realm of cultural intelligibility. However, the song's abrupt interruption comes to haunt society's stubborn refusal. *Watashi* might well have reached a place where the woman's voice can no longer reach her, but the sudden silence (as opposed to a gradual fading away of the voice) combined with the heavy pressure in the narrator's chest and the lingering image of a distressed Reiko conjure up a dramatic possibility: has the woman walked into the sea with her child? We cannot escape being recalled here of Fumiko Kimura walking along the desert beach of Santa Monica with her two children just before she waded into the cold waters of the Pacific Ocean. Given the frequency of cases of *boshi shinjū* in postwar Japan we may ask ourselves whether the readers of "Summer Abyss" might have had this possibility in mind when confronted with the story's finale. Takahashi certainly does not attempt to resolve its ambiguity, and we are just left to speculate whether it might indeed be fear that holds *Watashi* from turning around in the direction of the maternal couple to assuage her (or our?) anxiety.

***

In a vein that resonates with my analysis in the previous pages, my reading of "Incarnation" ("Keshin") highlights the ways in which the text offers a fictional dramatization of the resistance encountered when a maternal potential for violence threatens to become visible. As we have seen in my cursory exploration of "Summer Abyss," this resistance is twofold: on the one hand, it pertains to the realm of discourse and poses limits to a direct verbalization and intelligible articulation of a mother's violent impulses. On the other hand, it pertains to the realm of the psyche and betrays the inner conflicts triggered by a woman's growing awareness of such violent potential. In what follows I further investigate the working and implications of this multilayered form of resistance for the regulation of the conditions of appearance of maternal violence in the realm of discourse. Like in "Summer Abyss," here too a long flashback sheds light upon the death of a child, and here too the stage is set for a mother's confession. What makes "Incarnation" stand apart from the other stories analysed in this chapter is the fact that the two main characters are both mothers who have lost their only child (a daughter in both cases). The narrative structure of "Incarnation" thus becomes a unique opportunity to open up a dialogic space where these two mothers can engage in a tentative articulation of their violent potential. Yet, although this is a space shielded from judgement and moral condemnation, their narratives appear, nonetheless, haunted by the spectre of a profound incommunicability: as they search for words to translate their affective landscapes, these mothers must confront the taboo that surrounds "the heart of maternal darkness" (Rich 1976). Motherhood's darker impulses thus surface as much from the words that are said as from what is left unsaid, emerging, as it were, from the interstices of language.

The story begins when the narrator (here too identified only as *Watashi* [I]) receives a demand for relief supplies for the RR region[23] whose crops have been irreparably damaged by cold weather and heavy snow. Having resolved to send some clothes, *Watashi* goes to the storeroom and opens a chest of drawers where she keeps old kimonos that she brought with her when she married into her husband's family. Her fingers suddenly stop above one of the folded garments with "an indescribable feeling" (*nanika iiyō no nai kanshoku*) that crawls up her arm, runs through her spine and finally rises "cold and bleak" inside the room (Takahashi 1972: 35). With trembling hands she unfolds a silk *haori*[24] decorated with a rich pattern of large, white and crimson camellia flowers. In the past that *haori* was so much to her liking that she used to wear it every day and the fabric is now consumed and slightly darkened:

> That faint darkness was probably caused by dust, dirt or mould, but it also resembled the tinge of some dark emotion. Peeking through it, one could catch a glimpse of what could be even described as the shadow of a grudge strangely old and torn, or of a timeworn sorrow. (36)

Watashi makes a little package of it and sends it away, but from that moment she begins to have occasional hallucinatory visions of the *haori* floating in the sky like a living thing, drifting far away towards the RR region:

> [...] despite the gay design there was also a melancholy and eerie desolation in the sight of the *haori* rising off [in the sky]. Oozing from the inside of the floating *haori* was the glow of some persistent darkness similar to the shade of a passion buried and left behind or the gloom of distant memories. (37)

The two passages quoted above alert the reader from the start to something ominous exuding from the *haori* as though painful experiences or violent emotions had left an indelible trace on it. However, *Watashi* is still unable to fathom the nature of these emotions which she variously

---

[23] The use of only initials in the original Japanese identifies a fictional topography.
[24] *Haori* are hip- or thigh-length garments which serve as light coats to be worn over a kimono.

describes as dark passion (*kurai jōnen*), grudge (*urami*), sorrow (*hiai*), melancholia (*urayamashii*) and eerie desolation (*zotto suru sekiryōkan*). These passions seem to have taken on a life of their own that is independent from the character's conscious mind, the vision of the *haori* floating in the sky constituting a symptomatic reminder of how the spectre of these affective traces haunts *Watashi*'s narrative from the outset.

The discovery of the *haori* provides the textual occasion to know more about the circumstances surrounding *Watashi*'s life: since the death of her husband and her mother-in-law she has been living alone in the big family mansion. There was also a daughter, we are told, but for a brief, intense moment the narrator seems unable to recall what happened to her:

> And my daughter, my daughter…What happened to my daughter? For a moment I felt pain somewhere inside my head, aware of a lump of memories I wouldn't possibly remember even if I tried to. As the pain expanded and filled my head, I remembered. That's right, my daughter died of suffocation when she'd just turned two. (35–6)

The first pages of "Incarnation" thus appear to implicitly associate the dark emotions imbibed in the fabric of the *haori* with pain for the loss of the child. The forgetfulness that momentarily makes excruciating memories inaccessible could be explained as a psychic reaction to trauma that only allows these affective residues to exist as traces at the very margins of the narrator's consciousness.

Time passes by and two years later, while on a train trip, *Watashi* runs into a younger woman wearing a *haori* identical to the one she gave away. Underneath the lively design of the *haori* the young woman wears dark mourning clothes and a Buddhist rosary. The narrator is overwhelmed by a sense of nostalgia and intimacy for this woman "as if deep from distant memories some vague image had emerged and perfectly overlapped over [the woman's] face" (38). This feeling grows in intensity to the point that, as *Watashi* becomes certain that the *haori* is indeed hers, she is also struck by the impression of facing her past self:

> I looked at that *haori* which had been unmistakeably mine as if I were sucked into it. […] An indescribable nostalgia started flowing like a subter-

ranean current from inside me towards it. Or perhaps, quite the contrary, a fragment of my soul contained inside the *haori* was trying to gush forth towards me, feeling an unspeakable longing for me, its original home. Its colours, its pattern, its stained conditions, the shape of its sleeves, its red strings, its lining: all that I knew perfectly well. In all that lingered so vividly my own reflection. That's why now, as I gazed at it, I felt almost the illusion that the one wearing the *haori* was not her but me. It was as if the person wearing that *haori* and sitting in front of me in the train were my past self[.] (40)

As the two characters engage in polite conversation, we learn that the young woman is from the RR region and that she suffered a recent loss in her family. It has been only one week and she is on her way back from visiting the tomb. "You've lost a child, haven't you?" the narrator asks knowingly, causing her interlocutor to momentarily fall into an astonished silence. But this is only the first of a series of rhetorical questions that *Watashi* will pose causing an ever greater surprise: "Was it your only child? [...] It was a girl, wasn't it? [...] Right at a time when she was two and adorable, and yet..." (42) The young woman is astounded by the precision of the narrator's considerations and confirms that her daughter died of suffocation when she had just turned two. One night the pillow had accidentally covered the child's mouth making it impossible for her to breathe, and the morning after, when she had found her, she was already cold under the futon. "At the expression she showed every now and then," the narrator tells us, "I couldn't help feeling that *I had seen it before*" (41, emphasis in the original).

Watashi's words "I had seen it before" constitute the only passage that is emphasized in the original Japanese text. Despite the shared loss of a child that bonds the two women in similar grief, and notwithstanding the presence of the *haori* which blurs the distinction between past and present and between self and other, those words betray the narrator's stubborn refusal of any form of conscious identification. They epitomize the resistance she has been encountering all along in becoming conscious of her past emotions and experiences and which had already surfaced at several textual junctures. We have seen, for example, how the impressions emanating from the *haori* are consistently described as "undefinable" or "unspeakable" (*iiyō no nai*), how the feeling of nostalgia the narrator experiences remains "mysterious" (*fushigi na*) and how the woman's expression is *not* recognized as her own. Her choice of words suggests a form of profound alienation, a gap between the narrator and her own past feelings which, even when recognized, are resolutely cast outside of her despite being wrapped up in a film of nostalgic familiarity.

Takahashi expressed a deep fascination with the idea of the double or alter-ego which she extensively explored in her essay "Thought on the Doppelgänger" ("Dopperugengeru-kō," 1975), and it would seem not so far off the mark to understand the woman on the train as *Watashi*'s own double. Taking this possibility as a starting point, I want to suggest that the encounter between these two women could also be read as staging a "demand for recognition." The force of this demand surfaces in the following passage:

> We entered a tunnel. The view [outside the window] was interrupted and the windowpane created a black mirror in front of us. Her figure was reflected in the mirror. Her face was leaning a bit forward, as if she were crouching over some dark emotion. The *haori* decorated with camellia flowers really suited her. It merged perfectly with her as if it had been hers from the beginning. The train made a stumbling sound. In that moment she raised her eyes and looked at me in the mirror. That face, a face gleaming with a dark emotion which illuminated it from within. I could no longer take my eyes away from her in the mirror. That was my past self. It strikingly resembled my very self of about twenty years before. (44)

The mirror becomes here a narrative strategy to redouble the theme of the alter-ego: the narrator is looking at herself in the mirror in the form of the young woman's reflection. As the eyes of this younger self stare back at her, a contact is forcefully made which seems to foreclose any possible escape: *Watashi* can no longer divert her eyes from that reflection or, put it differently, she cannot not look at the "dark emotion" that exudes from the figure in front of her. Or so we are led to believe, however briefly. But the passage ends abruptly (and with it the episode of the train): textually this translates into a sudden interruption, the subsequent paragraph staged days after that encounter. We are told that, in that fatidic moment of apparent recognition, *Watashi* felt the urge to rush off the train at the first available stop, running away from her own reflection and implicitly reinstating the obdurate refusal to confer intelligibility to the dark shadow that loomed large between (and within) the two women. In her haste *Watashi* left behind a book that carried between its pages her visiting card, a narrative strategy that creates the conditions of possibility for a second encounter between the two women a few days later.

The turning point in the story occurs when *Watashi* receives a letter from the young woman from the train. Matsubara Mine—such is her name—explains her motivation for writing to her:

> Even though I met you for the first time, I experienced an indescribable nostalgia and I felt that I wanted you to listen to my sorrow and that you could probably understand. What I will now say, I haven't told anyone yet. (45)

What the narrator holds in her hands is a written confession of the darkest side of maternal ambivalence and of the murderous consequences it may spawn. The resemblance of Matsubara's words with those used by Reiko to frame her "confession" in "Summer Abyss" is striking: "You are the only one who can understand. I want you to hear everything" (Takahashi 1973a: 99) and "I feel relieved now that you've listened. I wanted someone to listen [...] No one has ever heard this story" (102). Both characters thus embody a maternal position that feels the urge to speak the unspeakable. Not only do they want to bring their experience of motherhood's violent potential into the field of discourse, but they also harbour a desperate need to be heard and perhaps understood. For this to happen and for their articulation of a maternal potential for violence to become truly intelligible, they need to find an interlocutor that will not turn a deaf ear and will search for an easy escape in cultural idealization of maternal love and abnegation. Put differently, their voices need to be made *recognizable* by our very capacity to hear them, that is, our willingness *to stay with the thought of the violence they tentatively articulate*.

In the letter Matsubara explains how she experienced a period of extreme hardship as the RR region was stricken by a merciless winter and how poverty forced her to give her clothes away in exchange for food. It

5 Filicide and Maternal Animosity in Takahashi Takako's Early... 191

was at this time, she confesses, that a mysterious change occurred within her, albeit undetectable on the outside: her previous self was "receding like a shadow" and someone other than herself had started living inside her (Takahashi 1972: 46). She recounts several episodes that are symptomatic of this change and which testify to the mother's growing ambivalence towards her daughter:

> One day, both my husband and my parents-in-law were out in the fields. Since I hadn't fully recovered from a cold, I was shut up in the house sewing. With open arms and uncertain steps, my daughter (back then she was one year and nine months old) was coming up to me with loud, shrill crows. She was my first child and, of course, I loved her deeply: my daughter was my sole purpose in life.
>
> But somehow in that moment and with no reason, I felt hatred of my daughter whom I was supposed to love. She looked like a monstrous thing advancing toward me and producing strange, screeching sounds. The face swollen red, foam spurting abundant from her mouth, screaming words in the language of an unknown country, that monster clung to my shoulder […] When I came to myself, it looked like my hand had flung in the air and my daughter was lying down by my knees crying.
>
> After that, such things happened every so often. I had come to feel hatred towards my daughter, [a hatred] of which I could not fathom the reason myself. (46–7)

This first manifestation of the dark side of maternal ambivalence is accompanied by the naming of that feeling: hatred. The feeling of aversion that takes hold of Matsubara is experienced, however, as incompatible with the form maternal love is supposed to take, and this young mother feels compelled to repeatedly stress her love for her daughter, as if she were trying to make amends for her own negative emotions. There is also a subtle progression in the way she accounts for her loving feelings, which moves from a rather spontaneous affective reaction ("I loved her deeply") to a consideration of the social expectations vis-à-vis what a mother is supposed to feel ("I was supposed to love"). This rhetorical shift symbolizes the social pressure that is exerted upon mothers whenever they experience ambivalence towards their children, social pressure which becomes a major catalyst for maternal guilt.

In the passage above maternal ambivalence turns into an unexpected explosion of physical violence, but its manifestation undergoes a process of psychic and textual censorship: the moment in which the mother hits her daughter is hidden from consciousness and from textual representation by the mother's own blackout. Only the final result is there to be seen. Despite Matsubara's apparent capacity to acknowledge and name her negative emotions, the episode is traversed by a considerable resistance to an exhaustive verbalization of her maternal potential for violence. It seems to me that her act of naming should rather be understood as a narrative strategy necessary for her to act as *Watashi*'s alter-ego: to the extent that this young mother functions as the narrator's double, her power to bring to consciousness affects and experiences that *Watashi* has thus far repressed is directly proportional to her capacity to name, however fragmentarily, what we now understand to be their shared experience of motherhood's violent impulses. "Incarnation" revolves around this unresolved tension between the need to bring a maternal potential for violence into discourse and a fundamental hesitation to do so to the extent that the story can be said to stage a simultaneous doing and undoing of such an effort.

A second episode recounted in Matsubara's letter occurs when she receives a parcel from her younger brother which contains six tins of canned food. She is at home alone, and because for days they have been eating only potatoes and millet, she succumbs to a moment of weakness and hides the cans in the chest of drawers. That evening a meeting is organized at her house during which several members from the farmers' cooperative, her husband and her parents-in-law discuss possible measures to counter the conditions of extreme poverty and hunger they have been facing:

> Right when we were absorbed in discussion my daughter, who had been fast asleep on my lap, woke up suddenly. Then, without making a sound and with an expression somewhat discontented, she toddled toward the chest of drawers. What on earth was the matter with her? She reached out with both hands to the drawer where I had hidden the cans. Until now, she had never tried to open the drawers. I jumped. Since she had been taken to the fields inside a basket, she couldn't possibly know about the parcel.

She grabbed the handle of the drawer, looked back at me and released an eerie laugh. That was the impression I had. I hurried close to her and I made to hold her back. But she began to cry in a shrill voice "Wee! Wee!" Angry looks from the people in the room converged on us. Indeed her pants were already wet. "Come on! Change her quickly!" urged my mother-in-law from where the party was sitting. She looked as if she was going to get up any moment and do it herself. With my heart pounding I opened the drawer and took a pair of pants for my daughter. But what then?! In that moment my daughter's hand reached out all of a sudden. That hand looked like the hand of a terrifying giant no man had ever seen. In a flash she removed the [pair of] underwear that was covering the cans. As she discovered the tins with their colourful labels, she grabbed them crowing with delight.

There's no need to tell you in what kind of position I was put on that occasion. And yet, more than being ashamed at my pettiness for having concealed the cans, I somehow felt a chilling terror of my little daughter. (48–9)

In the mother's distorted perceptions her daughter assumes the features of a supernatural, malignant being who displays a mysterious knowledge of where the tins have been hidden, and who seems to express a malevolent desire to reveal the mother's shameful secret. On the other hand, to the eyes of family and guests the daughter is simply behaving as a normal child and it is, instead, the mother who bears the blame for not promptly performing her maternal duties. The scene portrays a neat contrast between the mother's anguished perceptions and the judgemental reactions of the other adults in the room. There is no openness to dialogue and this incommunicability conveys an impression of deep maternal isolation. It may also suggest that the very possibility of maternal ambivalence is hardly registered or even contemplated by the world of social and familial relations in which this young woman's existence is inscribed.

The two episodes considered here are similar in structure: they first provide a symptomatic depiction of the mother's ambivalent feelings (in the form of her altered perceptions of her daughter) and they end with the naming of those feelings (hatred and terror, respectively). As I have already suggested, however, it appears that what enables this mother to bring ambivalence into discourse is less the acquisition of adequate discursive tools and more the need of a narrative device by means of which *Watashi* is made to confront "the return of the repressed." This interpretation is confirmed by the following extract where, at the climax of her supposed crescendo of awareness, Matsubara remarkably fails to come to terms with that very ambivalence she seemed at first ready to acknowledge:

> I was probably mentally disturbed. I wonder if it was because of an illness that I have done what I am to tell you. This is so unacceptable that I cannot find another way to explain it. (50)

As this brief quote makes patently clear, madness and mental instability suddenly enter this young mother's narrative as powerful explanatory devices that, I contend, risk undermining the legitimacy of her affective experience. As she recounts the night when she smothered her child, she also seems to appropriate "commonsensical" views that consider maternal filicide so unacceptable that it ought to be attributed to insanity and nothing else. In so doing, the cultural intelligibility tentatively accorded to a maternal potential for violence is confined to a narrative of pathologization that reduces it to the unfathomable outburst of an (exceptionally) unstable mind.

> The night of my daughter's birthday, still wearing the *haori*, I lay down next to her with the intention to get up later to tidy up. I dozed off and as I woke up it was already late at night. My husband was sound asleep with his head buried under the futon and a loud snore was coming from the adjacent room where my parents-in-law slept. When that stopped, quiet expanded suddenly all around. A faint sound that I would even call the sound of silence was coming along from somewhere. —— —— Perhaps it was the sound of the falling snow slipping through the darkness.
>
> Under my chest, as if it were going to be crushed, was my daughter's face. In that moment I remembered that feeling somewhere between hatred and terror. Because of that my heart was [now] beating louder. The snow was making its silent sound. —— —— The night was so quiet that I could hear the drumming of my heart. I think I kept looking fixedly at my daughter's face for a long time. My chest got close as to cover her mouth.

5 Filicide and Maternal Animosity in Takahashi Takako's Early...

> I really don't remember much of what happened after. I dozed off again. What I wished for, what I wanted in that light indistinct sleep, I don't know. The next morning she was cold under my breast. (50–1)

Here the intensity of that maternal violent potential that seemed to be pushing its way from the edge of discourse is such that it defies words and can only be lived as an overflowing of sensorial perceptions. Symptomatic of a defence against its overwhelming magnitude is the fact that, just as the mother confesses her crime, she disappears from the scene as the agentic subject, receding into a psychically safe distance from where she observes the unfolding of events. She does not confess to having purposefully killed her daughter. Rather, her recollection makes a part of her body the subject of the action: "My chest got close as to cover her mouth." And as soon as this act is put into words a new blurring of consciousness occurs: she can't remember what happened afterwards. As she killed her child, she also drifted into a safe oblivion, unable to articulate her own desires. Her account seems to reveal the impossibility of gaining textual/discursive access to that experience. And while it may be argued that this is the nature of trauma, I am also inclined to read this episode as the culmination of the series of pauses, blackouts, interruptions and hesitations that constitute the distinguishing feature of both stories I have thus far analysed. In this respect, if we understand the process whereby a mother becomes aware of her ambivalence to depend on her capacity to articulate those feelings to herself, it seems legitimate to suspect that a failure to do so might be related to the lack of a discursive space where such articulation might be possible (and imaginable) in the first place.

After reading Matsubara's letter *Watashi* is plunged into a state of turmoil and confusion that lasts several days: "Time blurred and past and present overlapped. Then I remembered vividly the circumstances in which my daughter had died" (51). This is the closest she will ever get to admitting that she had too killed her own daughter, but she will never offer the reader a full-fledged confession. Instead, she will decide to pay a visit to Matsubara. Upon her arrival at the house, the narrator does not share with the young woman (who is still wearing the *haori*) her newly acquired awareness. She only admits that when she was younger and used to wear a similar *haori*, she lost her two-year-old daughter herself. However, when questioned about the cause of her death, she remains silent. "I didn't know how to answer," she admits to herself (54). Instead, she offers the woman a brand-new *haori* asking the old one in exchange so that she can burn it in front of her astounded interlocutor. To the alarmed Matsubara she explains: "Forgive such an action. And please, don't ask for an explanation. This is a ritual that by all means we had to perform. Please, wear this cotton *haori* and be happy" (ibid.). As the old *haori* turns to ashes, the narrator looks at Matsubara, but this time the empathy and intimacy that had once existed between the two of them has disappeared. Even the woman's expression, once so dear and familiar to the protagonist, has faded away: the person standing in front of her looks now like an ordinary wife from a farmer's house.[25]

As with "Summer Abyss," we cannot escape the ambiguity of the story's finale. Despite *Watashi*'s increased awareness, she seems unable to bring that awareness into discourse: even when confronted with Matsubara's unequivocal written confession, she cannot find words or answers. Their assumedly shared experience of a maternal potential for violence does not prompt the creation of bonds of female solidarity between the two characters. Surely enough, we may understand their private ritual as exorcizing the dark memories they share and take it as the confirmation of that silent forgiveness *Watashi* seems finally ready to offer her younger self. However, we cannot fail to acknowledge the loss of any chance of real communication, be it verbal or affective: any feeling of nostalgic intimacy is lost, and the narrator explicitly demands that the articulation of maternal ambivalence does not go any further. Although this final scene could perhaps be read as the coronation of a mother's journey towards awareness, it also seems to conjure up a rather bleak landscape, because the possibility of rendering a maternal potential for violence culturally intelligible is partially foreclosed by the characters' impossibility to elaborate further on the meaning of their experience.

---

[25] The plot of "Incarnation" and this last scene in particular buy into a cultural history of spirit possession in Japanese folklore of which Murasaki Shikibu's *Genji Monogatari* (eleventh century) offers the most well-known and discussed literary example. For a rich account of spirit possession in this classic of Heian literature, see D.G. Bargen, *A Woman's Weapon. Spirit Possession in* The Tale of Genji (1997). See also W. Pounds "Enchi Fumiko and the Hidden Energy of the Supernatural" (1990).

Both "Incarnation" and "Summer Abyss" portray an attempt to bring motherhood's violent potential into discourse while also foregrounding some of the resistances and defences which may hamper such an effort. Hegemonic discourse and cultural ideals of maternal love function here as a disabling obstacle to the very possibility that maternal ambivalence might be talked about and experienced differently. It is my contention that one of the things that make these stories so interesting is the implicit emphasis they place upon the absence or elusiveness of such positive discursive space, but also upon the struggle that such a discursive endeavour requires. On a more positive note, however, the existence of these stories as material objects that were (and are) circulated among a wider public can also be deemed symptomatic of that very struggle: they represent a vigorous intervention that aims at problematizing the politics of representation and opening the way to imagining otherwise.

Motherhood, Reproduction and Ambivalence in Takahashi's Early Fiction

"The freedom to give or not to give birth" (*umu umanu no jiyū*) is the title of a short essay Takahashi published in 1973 in the women's magazine *Fujin kōron* and reprinted in 1975 in the author's first essay collection *Soul Dogs* (*Tamashii no inu*). Although the text lacks any reference to *ribu*'s activism, its title and the date of its publication unmistakeably recall one of *ribu*'s most important battles: the fight to preserve women's access to abortion that exploded in reaction to the proposed amendments to the Eugenic Protection Law.[26] In this essay Takahashi explicitly disagrees with those changes in the law that would make it much more difficult for women to access abortion and argues that "[t]o be able to give birth or not to give birth according to one's own intentions is certainly desirable" (1975: 254). However, she also concedes that this freedom might also run the risk of encouraging women into careless sexual activity, knowing that they will be able to get rid of unwanted pregnancies. Takahashi also acknowledges some of the circumstances in which a woman might not

---

[26] See Chap. 3.

desire to have a child. She mentions the plight of unmarried mothers; she refers to the small number of children present-day families seem inclined to plan; she considers the possibility that women might simply not desire children (she places herself in this last category). Against the background of cultural ideals that identified womanhood with motherhood we can hardly overemphasize the revolutionary implications of these claims.

Takahashi also expressed aversion for representations of mother and child as a symbiotic totality which she believed denied woman full subjectivity. Her critical stance vis-à-vis cultural and linguistic conceptions of woman and child as an undifferentiated whole emerges in the opening passage of the essay "Woman-hating" ("Onna-girai," 1975), originally published in the pages of the *Mainichi shinbun* (one of Japan's major newspapers together with the Asahi and the Yomiuri):

> For a very long time the expression "*onna-kodomo*" [女子供, women-and-children] has appeared in the written language. Of course, those who write it are men. But when I was a child and I still didn't know that those who used such expression were men, every time I encountered the expression "women-and-children" I couldn't wrap my head around its meaning. Why were "*onna*" [woman] and "*kodomo*" [child] glued together? Being [still] unfamiliar with words, I even thought that a special noun "*onna-kodomo*" existed. Maybe it signified a female child. Or it could rather indicate a feminine child. That expression became such a concern that I ended up thinking such silly things. The reason was that, if human beings were distinguished into men, women and children, then the fact that only women and children were positioned differently seemed totally unreasonable. (1975: 229)

Here Takahashi is describing a linguistic specificity in the use of kanji (characters of Chinese origin) in written Japanese: the corresponding words in Japanese for "woman" and "child" are *onna* (女) and *kodomo* (子供). Expressions like "woman and child" or "women and children" would be rendered with the expression *onna to kodomo* (女と子供) where the two terms are joined by the particle "and" (to, と). However, by simply juxtaposing *onna* and *kodomo* without the mediation of any particle, we obtain a single new noun (*onna-kodomo*, 女子供) made up of more than one character (known in Japanese linguistics as *jukugo* or "multi-kanji compound word") whose "oneness" I have tried to emphasize in my translation using hyphens to unite its terms in an organic whole.

It seems to me that the passage above denounces the phallogocentrism of Japanese language, pointing to a masculine linguistic habit that "lumps together" woman and child. But Takahashi is also referring here to the process whereby a child is socialized into such a language, and she may be suggesting that the cultural expectation that woman and child be naturally bound together is produced and maintained via linguistic habits repeated through time. On the other hand, by remembering how her childhood self struggled to make sense of a seeming illogical linguistic rule while at the same time tentatively formulating fanciful alternatives to its "correct" meaning, the author is foregrounding both the violence of the process of acculturation and the possibility that linguistic repetitions might fail to bring about their intended outcomes.

A strong conviction about men's profound investment in images of mother-with-child is a distinctive feature of yet another essay whose title "Eve and Mary" ("Ibu to Maria," 1977b) is indicative of the author's growing interest in Christianity. After having travelled widely in Europe, Takahashi describes her amazement at the countless artistic representations of the Virgin Mary with baby Jesus, and she voices her suspicion that, far from being symptomatic of a religious devotion shared by men and women alike, these images might in fact be the expression of fantasies that are specifically male:

> Let's state in advance my conclusion. The Holy Mary is an illusion that men—who represent half of humanity—have continued to embrace for hundreds of years. It's nothing but a mere illusion that again and again the power of men's imagination has projected onto and expected from women. It seems to me that the paintings and sculptures of Mary holding baby Jesus in her arms that have remained in such copious amount in Europe show with how much persistence such male fantasy has been inherited unchanged across the centuries. And could it possibly be that, because the illusion envisioned by men found artistic expression in paintings and sculptures, women too have been confronted for centuries with that illusion as if it were their own? However, should we indeed think that

women—who constitute the other half of humanity—feel from the bottom of their heart that the Holy Mary deserves to be remembered, to be thought of and to be made the object of artistic representations time after time to such an extent? For me, at least, [the answer] is "no." (1977b: 110–11)

The points Takahashi raises in this passage echo those in "Woman-hating": a growing suspicion towards man-made notions of woman-and-child (here represented by the Virgin Mary and baby Jesus), a belief in their (re-)production and enforcement by means of their repetition through time in discourse—be it language or iconography—and the acknowledgement of the way in which women are made to internalize them. It is my contention that the recurrent problematization of the mother/child bond in Takahashi's early literature and her frequent depiction of women who explicitly despise motherhood and reproduction can be understood as the author's attempt to short-circuit these man-made illusions and to actively create the possibility for alternative forms of imagining to circulate in the public sphere. Many of her stories portray female characters who perpetrate acts of violence on small children, and it's not rare for such episodes of abuse to take the extreme form of child murder. Representative of such female animosity against children are stories such as "White Night" ("Byakuya," [1966] 1972) and "Eyes" ("Me," [1967] 1972) whose protagonists end up killing a child. Another example is Takahashi's award-winning novel *To the End of the Sky* (1973b) where the protagonist abandons her child in a burning house during an air raid and then sends her husband to the rescue, perfectly aware that he will not survive. This same character will later steal the newborn daughter of a woman she dislikes with the devious purpose of twisting her development and "warping her personality through cruel treatment" (Bullock 2010: 47). Similarly, the protagonist of the story "Lonely woman" ("Ronrii ūman," 1977c)[27] manifests a profound aversion for children to the point that, on occasion of a series of arsons in local elementary schools, she sadistically imagines "countless young children shrieking, roasting to a crisp in that

---

[27] The short story "Lonely Woman" originally appeared in 1974 on the pages of the literary magazine *Subaru*, but was republished in 1977 as part of the homonymous collection of interlocked stories.

inferno with no exit" (quoted in Mori 2004: xxxi). She will even come to fantasize that she is, indeed, the very criminal who caused the fires.

The story "Boundlessness" ("Byōbō," 1970) is exemplary of Takahashi's critical stance towards cultural idealizations of the mother/child relationship: its female protagonist is a woman who fails to develop a supposedly natural bond with the child she was once pregnant with.[28] The story also problematizes the bonds between family members: the boundlessness of the title is the vast expanse that the protagonist perceives as separating people and which represents the enormous distance she strives to overcome in her search for human connection. As the story begins, the main character Kiyoko is recovering from a recent miscarriage and dreaming of the foetus being carried away by the slow current of a river:

> The foetus floated slowly down a murky river. From time to time it raised its pale expressionless face, turned toward me and shook its head as if to say no. "You're a complete stranger to me!" it almost seemed to be saying, "We don't have the slightest connection!" The foetus was still merely a formless lump of flesh. Only the eyes were shaped in two deep creases. Those quietly half-open eyes seemed to speak that way. As the eyes closed, the foetus floated away, bobbing up and down. The water level was high and the water murky like after the rain, but the river moved along absolutely languid with no ripples or foam. A soft sunlight was shining out of nowhere and tinged the water of a dull, translucent colour. The foetus floated down the river and disappeared into a sky of the same tinge and which was one with the river. In the vast expanse of that smoky and misty-looking sky there was nothing. There was no one.
>
> Kiyoko stood up from sofa in the living-room.

---

[28] The unnamed protagonist of the story "Kodomosama" (literally Honorable Child, 1969) similarly struggles with increasing fears and ambivalence as she goes through the final stages of her second pregnancy. The opening of the story portrays the mother's perception of her own heavily pregnant body and conveys an image of pregnancy as threatening and parasitical:

> With her right hand she caressed her swollen belly from atop the dress made from Indian chintz. Through the thin material her skin felt a bit sweaty. Even the fabric was slightly warm and damp. Probably because of that, from within the dyed pattern of people, animals, birds and flowers, the vermillion of the flowers seemed to stand out vividly. The big petals of an obscene carnivorous plant blooming in a tropical forest appeared as if they had suddenly expanded on her belly. (Takahashi, 1969: 55)

> "It went away." She said in a small voice. Those were the words she softly whispered when she was alone. (Takahashi 1970: 134–5)

Kiyoko's feelings of separation and disconnection from the foetus stand in stark contrast to her husband's sadness at the loss of the baby or to her mother-in-law's insistence on the inexhaustible fertility of a woman's womb. The foetus' silent communication in Kiyoko's daydreaming seems also to question the idea of a supposedly natural mother–child bond. Although the dream could still be interpreted as the manifestation of feelings of inadequacy at her failure to become a mother, the words she whispers to herself do not convey an emotional struggle to overcome this perceived failure, but a sense of relief. In fact, as she reflects upon her husband's reaction to her miscarriage and upon her mother-in-law's insistence that "a woman's body is like Mother Earth" (135), Kiyoko repeats those words one more time, as if to taste their reassuring power and confirm her renewed sense of integrity.

Kiyoko also wonders whether she might have unconsciously caused the death of the foetus. Days after her return from the hospital she happens to see a schoolboy walking down the street and she follows him from a distance. She watches him as he sneaks into a farmyard and crushes a freshly laid egg under his sneakers: at this sight she is overwhelmed by confusion and by an incomprehensible fear of the boy. The hens' screams of alarm attract people to the windows of the farm and out in the garden, but the boy is now walking away innocently and she ends up being the one they scowl at. Suddenly, she feels as if she were the real culprit and breaks into a guilty escape. She now experiences a "mysterious intimacy" with the child and she is "struck by the sudden thought that without doubts she unconsciously killed the foetus" (137). The child can be read here as Kiyoko's double who acts out desires the full awareness of which remains fearful and threatening to the narrator. His actions allow Kiyoko to become conscious of her hostility towards motherhood and reproduction: she wanted to destroy the egg/foetus and the child simply translated into action a desire whose name she did not dare to speak, the angry looks of the people at the farm symbolizing society's harsh disapproval of her betrayal of her "female reproductive destiny."

The protagonist's rejection of women's traditional participation in extending the family system by means of their reproductive potential stands in marked contrast to a grotesque fantasy of reproduction that Kiyoko imagines at the heart of her mother-in-law's dreams. Here the mother-in-law is pictured giving birth to an endless chain of potatoes:

> Where the stem touched the ground, there were mother-in-law's genitals. She spread her thighs wide apart, giving birth to innumerable potatoes. They were all [...] strung out through the roots similar to capillary tubes. Maybe mother-in-law was now avidly dreaming such a dream of reproduction, with her belly laid down like a huge, obscene earth, pouring warm fluids on a swarm of potatoes buried in the ground. (139)

Living side by side with a woman who still exudes a sensual fertility despite her age and seven pregnancies, and whose relationship with Kiyoko's husband constitutes an ominous reminder of biological interconnectedness, the protagonist is painfully aware that she does not belong to this familial community. She is even proud of her body's refusal to become fertile again in the face of her mother-in-law's insistence that it is easier to get pregnant after a miscarriage.

Kiyoko's rebellion against her "biological destiny" brings about real or fantasized episodes of unrestrained violence against small children or pregnant women. These explosions of violence should be read side by side with the protagonist's spiteful rejection of those female characters whose normative femininity becomes complicit with the stifling working of society's gender organization. A first episode occurs when she is on a train and she is seized by the irresistible impulse to stab a baby's leg with her embroidery needle right before joining hastily the crowd who is getting off the car. Yet, as she stands still on the platform and looks back at the now empty rails, Kiyoko is left dumbfounded by her own actions: "Why, why, Kiyoko murmured to herself. Why did I do such a thing? But only the deed itself was certain" (tr. in Mori 1994: 35). The passionate insistence of her self-questioning accompanies the psychic difficulty of becoming aware of one's own violent inclinations that we have repeatedly encountered in previous stories.

Kiyoko also strikes up an acquaintance with an eccentric woman who speaks boldly of having had a mastectomy and whom the protagonist perceives as a possible twin soul, a person with whom she could communicate beyond the constraints imposed by prescriptions of feminine and maternal propriety. However, at the end of the story Kiyoko discovers that this woman is now happily pregnant, and that she and her husband-to-be have recently moved to her neighbourhood. She feels betrayed by the woman's joy in embracing the traditional feminine roles of wife and mother, and as the woman cheerfully converses with Kiyoko's husband and mother-in-law about her plan to have five children, Kiyoko's rage fuels a fantasy of assaulting her belly with a drill:

> Kiyoko stretched up her arm. She was trapped in the group's conversation, but her right arm reached across the five or six meters to the tool box. Softly it removed the drill. The woman's yellow sack dress hung before Kiyoko's eyes. Her lower abdomen rose in a gentle curve. Kiyoko placed the tip of the drill on the woman's abdomen. Supporting the tool with her left hand, she began turning the handle with her right. She ground vigorously. The spiral-shaped slender metal rod ripped through the woman's skin and bore into the uterus. This time I *do* have a reason, thought Kiyoko. Reproduction is destruction. She intensified her efforts. She drilled on. Her fingers ached. But she must keep on drilling. The woman's womb, and the fetus along with it, were gouged out by the screw-shaped tool. (translated in Mori 1994: 35)

This last hallucinatory scene marks the moment when the protagonist becomes finally aware of her negative emotions and her potential for violence. Those unfathomable violent outbursts that in the past left her lost and confused are now replaced by a form of consciously "justified" murderous aggression. This constitutes an undeniable powerful shift from the more discreet daydream that opened the story and which allowed Kiyoko only a cautious expression of relief, half-whispered in the afternoon solitude of an empty living room. The passage above also articulates a sort of programmatic declaration that seems to provide an explanation of the repugnance of and resistance to the maternal many of Takahashi's female protagonists share: the passage that Maryellen T. Mori translates as "reproduction is destruction" (*hanshoku wa sonzai no horobi na noda*) could be rendered more literally (but less beautifully) as "reproduction is the destruction of the existence." Mori's poetic translation effectively reproduces the oxymoronic association between "reproduction" and "destruction" that we find in the Japanese original. However, it seems to me also to suggest too simplistic an overlap between the destruction that reproduction is said to be and the destruction that is imaginarily performed by Kiyoko (to the extent that we could understand her words to mean "reproduction calls for its own destruction"). Whereas this interpretation may not be that much off the mark, I believe that the term left out in Mori's translation (*sonzai* = being, existence) is a fundamental element in the oxymoronic relation where the contrast is also intended to be between "reproduction" (i.e. the biological proliferation of life performed through woman's biological potential and upheld by society's gender norms) and "existence," that is, woman's very possibility to claim her being in excess of those very norms. This conflict between cultural idealizations of woman's reproductive potential and women's search for meaning/subjectivity will reappear in the last two stories analysed in this chapter.

The Demonic and the Maternal in Women

In her essay "Sexuality—The Demonic and the Maternal in Women" ("Sei—onna ni okeru mashō to bosei," 1977b), Takahashi associates what she calls the "demonic woman" with female awakening and places these ideas in stark opposition to motherhood. Against a notion of the maternal as selfless love and devotion, the author describes the "demonic woman" as a female subject who has awakened to her own self by virtue of antisocial behaviours and the violent breaking of society's laws and taboos:

> I have been made to realize that every time I write fiction, the female protagonists that emerge from me and make their appearance in [my] novels are all demonic women. [...] I began to suspect that whenever a woman really releases her [inner] self, the demonic manifests. It is generally thought

that women harbour the maternal, the polar opposite of the demonic. But no matter how many novels I write, the maternal never flows from me and into my work. The maternal upholds order, the demonic encourages upheaval. The maternal supports morality, the demonic incites immorality [*handōtoku*]. Something maternal makes women restrain themselves; it directs female energy toward the children produced by woman-as-mother; it makes women devote themselves to family harmony and their offspring's prosperity. In the sort of society in which people normally live, this is desirable and maybe even necessary. But if women have been drugged by the reassuring notion that they are essentially maternal beings, I wish to contend that there is more to woman than this. (Takahashi 1977b; quoted in Mori 1994: 32–33) (translation amended)

Despite Takahashi's conversion to Catholicism, her use of the term "demonic" ought not to be understood in religious terms and certainly not as suggesting a supposedly sinful female nature. Quite to the contrary, the "demonic" is used here as a positive term to signify a liberatory potential within woman which enables her to break free from stifling cultural understandings of womanhood and femininity. Takahashi's use of the word *handōtoku* (literally anti or against morality) instead of the more usual *fudōtoku* (literally immorality, non-morality) clearly suggests that the "demonic woman" embodies powerful counter-cultural impulses, while the association of the maternal with ideas of family harmony and offspring's prosperity points at the institution of the family as a pernicious site where stifling gender norms are reproduced and subtly enforced. The author also argues that

> [i]t is men those who classify women by distinguishing among them the two types of the diabolic and the maternal woman, the prostitute and the mother. But I can hardly think of them as two distinct types. The woman that [...] happens to awaken to her self is the diabolic woman. And I wonder whether the majority of those who are not awake are merely keeping that diabolic part buried alive. (Takahashi 1977b: 88)

Takahashi further explores this problematic dichotomy in the essay "Eve and Mary" (1977b) where she considers a fresco of the "Downfall of Adam and Eve" by Michelangelo that she happened to see in the Sistine Chapel in Rome (Italy). The painting portrays Adam and Eve in the Garden of

Eden and the tempting snake coiling around the forbidden tree with its upper body transfigured into that of a woman. Takahashi identifies two women in the fresco and confesses that it is the relationship between these two female figures that always constituted for her a source of curiosity and reflection. In the essay "Sexuality—The Demonic and the Maternal in Women," she further suggests that the snake might represent Eve's awakening to her own self (here specifically identified as Eve's awakening to sexuality), and she argues that the awakening to one's inner self "occurs in the form of the breaking of a taboo. Awakening goes against the moral [*handōtoku*]" (1977b: 98). Considered in this light, Eve is understood as a "real being" (*riaru na sonzai*) ("Ibu to Maria," 1977b: 112) as opposed to man-made representations of Mary-as-mother: "There's no Mary inside woman," Takahashi claims, "there's only Eve" (113):

> Mary stands as the symbol of the maternal in women, as the woman who has nothing but her motherhood. Mary is always contented and she's not unsettled like Eve (or women like Eve). Within the relationship with her own child she accepts reality and confirms the status quo. In the bond with her child she carries on a safe existence. (Sei—onna ni okeru mashō to bosei," 1977b: 98)

Whereas Takahashi seems to unambiguously identify the woman who is not awake with the maternal woman—thus suggesting that mothers may suffer from a form of false consciousness that buys into man-made myths of maternal love and abnegation—we may be left wondering what form the "demonic woman" might assume. One of the literary examples of "demonic woman" that the author provides is Thérèse Desqueyroux. The main character of François Mauriac's homonymous novel that Takahashi translated from French into Japanese in 1963, Thérèse is a young woman who endures the demands of motherhood and marriage and who embarks on a blind search for "something" that eventually leads her to unsuccessfully poison her husband. Takahashi describes Thérèse as a woman who is distinctly awakened albeit still unaware of what she really desires: her crime is not carefully planned but it stems instead from the depths of her unconscious. It is her unconscious that is suffocating and which resorts to murder in an attempt to escape from a life that resembles a prison. Takahashi recalls an exchange between Thérèse and her husband where he asks what she actually wanted when she tried to poison him:

> What I wanted? It would probably be easier to say what I didn't want. I didn't want to keep on playing a role, affecting [my] gesticulation, speaking only set formulas; in other words, live by constantly stifling to death another Thérèse. That's what I didn't want! (1977b: 91)

The reference to "another Thérèse" evokes a double structure or an internal split in Thérèse's subjectivity that reminds of Takahashi's reflections on Eve and the snake. There appear to be two women within Thérèse: one who conforms to society's conventions and norms of feminine propriety and "another woman" (*mō hitori no onna*) who exists in latent form inside her, and who is confronted with the choice of either dying away or struggling to live and be set free. But to awake also means for Thérèse that the "demonic woman" will venture onto a path that may turn harmful to both others and herself (her attempted murder bringing about the risk of imprisonment and social ostracism):

> In contrast to a secure self that is maintained on the outside, the content of that self that piles up on the inside is perceived as something terribly dangerous. It is an unconscious part of the personality that cannot be analysed at a conscious level and which, while existing inside, comes to act as if it were outside. And it always operates through the destruction of the status quo. (1977b: 98)[29]

I contend that the murderous mothers of Takahashi's fiction and those who are portrayed as harbouring filicidal fantasies are all manifestations of the "demonic woman." They are caught in this process of awakening, portrayed as they surprise their conscious selves with unpredictable outbursts of violence against social prescriptions of femininity and motherhood, while still lacking full awareness of what drives them into such antisocial behaviours. It is in light of these considerations that my partial

---

[29] While the parallel between Takahashi's wording and *ribu*'s rhetoric is way too obvious to be ignored, I don't want to overload an already lengthy chapter with such considerations. I will postpone my reflections about any overlap in terms of imagery and vocabulary to the Conclusions.

5 Filicide and Maternal Animosity in Takahashi Takako's Early... 209

readings of "Yonder Sound of Water" (1971a) and "Congruent Figures" ("Sōjikei," 1971b) will now be elaborated. These stories portray two more examples of women who are increasingly at odds with their roles as wives and mothers. Painfully alienated from other family members and from ideals of familial happiness, these women manifest their discomfort and internal conflicts in murderous fantasies where the victims are their own daughters. Yūko, the protagonist of "Yonder Sound of Water," lives with her inconclusive husband and her odd little daughter Mariko in a *danchi*-type apartment complex.[30] She describes the estate where her family lives as a small town made of concrete where all blocks look alike and are partitioned according to an alienating, identical pattern. In her eyes the housing complex looks like a factory that produces pregnant women: on each floor there is always an expectant mother and even when a woman fails to conceive, someone else does, so that there always seems to be a fixed number of pregnant women in the complex. The protagonist recalls her shame, when she was pregnant with Mariko, at being incorporated in such a mechanism.

Yūko also experiences a profound alienation from the familial intimacy that Mariko and her father share, and she longs for the lost vitality and individuality of her younger self. She thinks she can recognize such an independent self in an old photograph of herself when she was 14: "I want to look like that person," she thinks, "I wonder whether she still exists" (1971a: 68). She feels that the presence of her husband and daughter has cast a dark shadow that erased that younger self and made it impossible for Yūko to live a life as a full individual. "To live," she ponders, "is to be consumed by the shadows of others" (ibid.). A similar image can also be found in "Congruent Figures": one summer evening, the protagonist Akiko (who is both a wife and a mother) puts red lipstick on and contemplates her reflection in the mirror:

---

[30] The multiunit, urban housing estates known as *danchi* became the typical accommodation of post-World War II families. During the 1950s, 1960s and 1970s, the Japan Housing Corporation, founded in 1955, built many such low-rent apartment complexes in the outskirts of urban areas to confront the housing demands of the Japanese growing population. With the proliferation of consumer and electrical goods, the *danchi* became envisioned as the modern housing for the now expanding Japanese middle class. See Hoshino (1964), Waswo (2002) and Ronald (2007).

I saw the gay face of a woman in the mirror. It was another face buried under the dark layers and layers of life. I thought I could have lived with such a face. [...] But I did not do so. I never regretted it at all. Yet I did think about the gorgeous woman which had been crushed inside of me. If given a chance it could have bloomed into a large flower spreading its pink petals and wafting around a sweet fragrance. Such a flower which could not bloom existed inside of me. It existed inside of me without shrinking or withering, no, containing a still richer fragrance precisely because it could not bloom fully. (translation Mizuta Lippit 1991: 168)

Both mothers mourn the loss of a richer, younger self which is thought to harbour either the potential of individual plenitude or the energy of a fully bloomed sexual vitality. Meditations about an existence that has not been allowed to thrive are accompanied by a growing sense of alienation towards these mother's children. Like many of Takahashi's characters, the protagonist in "Yonder Sound of Water" has a hard time understanding her daughter and increasingly perceives her as an utterly foreign, inscrutable being:

A child that was supposed to have come from inside her was [now] growing into a mysterious other. Had she been a stranger from the start, it probably wouldn't have felt so weird. When [such] a human being, emerged as a part of Yūko's body which had then acquired separate existence, moved around out of the reach of Yūko's hands, she found herself stirred by a feeling of restlessness as if her own living flesh wandered about toward a space that was inaccessible to her will. (1971a: 71)

As these feeling of alienation and incommunicability multiply, Yūko discovers to her own surprise that she is capable of harbouring murderous desires towards her own daughter. The following scene reveals to her the violent impulses lurking in the shadows of her maternal ambivalence:

The shrill voices of children rose up from the courtyard. Yūko opened the door and stepped out in the long corridor. She recognized Mariko's figure. But it wasn't the usual view. She was walking on the concrete balustrade of that same corridor on the third floor, with hands spread out horizontally to keep the balance. The shouts of children who seemed to be looking up at

5 Filicide and Maternal Animosity in Takahashi Takako's Early... 211

her were rising up from the courtyard with an air of irritation and enjoyment.
    She was about to shout: "Mariko, what are you doing?," but she refrained herself. Startled by the sound of her voice Mariko could even fall. That being which was made of Yūko's own living flesh seemed suddenly to stiffen on the balustrade and, for an instant, twitched her body, unsteady. Immediately she leaned on one side and fell gently, drawing a parabola against the background of the clouded sky. Midway the head turned upside down under its weight and she acquired speed. Reaching the ground in a straight line, upside down like that, the head would perhaps split in half like a watermelon. At that idea she froze, as she had realized she was at the same time wishing that to happen. Had that happened, her living flesh would have stopped wandering around in unknown places. Mariko jumped down from the balustrade [back] in the corridor. (72)

Yūko's maternal potential for violence manifests here in an unexpected intermingling of reality and imagination: the description of Mariko walking dangerously on the balustrade merges with what we only later discover to be Yūko's own hallucinatory state of mind. Yūko herself becomes aware of it only after having unconsciously indulged in her murderous fantasy. Her reactions are particularly significant because, even though she "freezes" at the awareness that for a brief, intense moment she wished her daughter's death, she does not seem at all horrified or ashamed by her "deviant proclivities," and she does not vent negative judgements against herself as an unnatural or immoral mother. Instead, her reflections take the shape of a final reclamation of her independent subjectivity: had Mariko fallen for real, Yūko speculates, she would have finally been able to reappropriate the individuality that her daughter's existence and the humdrum of family life had irreparably undermined.

A similar fantasy also appears in "Congruent Figures" which arguably offers the most explicit problematization of motherhood among the stories I have considered in this chapter. The story opens with the main character Akiko who receives a letter from her daughter Hatsuko with whom she hasn't been in touch for years. Hatsuko informs her that she now has a child and that she is planning to pay her a visit soon. In the letter she confesses that from a young age she had felt disliked by her own mother and she compares Akiko's face to a Noh mask, where glimpses of sudden emotions emerge only to quickly disappear in its seemingly expressionless surface. The day when Hatsuko had become aware of this particular feature of her mother's face was during a summer vacation: while the family was on a boat trip, Hatsuko had noticed that her mother was staring oddly at her. Extremely uncomfortable because of the intensity of her gaze, she had stood up abruptly and she had fallen from the boat:

> I came to realize that your large eyes were fixed on me across father's shoulders. I wondered why you gazed at me in such a way. Your face was like that of a Noh mask. As the boat swayed, your face titled slightly and a certain vivid emotion seemed to appear on it, but your face kept its overall expressionless. I could not stand such a gaze and stood up suddenly. Because of it, the boat almost turned over and I fell into the ocean. Do you remember? I sat down again in the back of the boat after father and brother helped me back in. My eyes hurt because the sea water got into them, and the tears continued to flow. This time I looked at my mother through a veil of tears. Then you quietly looked aside, showing your pale profile, and from that time you continued to gaze vacantly far away, looking into the open air.
>
> From around that time you did not talk to me frequently. What were you angry with me about? [...] Sometimes you looked at me with a hard face devoid of emotion, and after that you always looked aside coldly. (translation Mizuta Lippit 1991: 169–70)

Most of the narrative of "Congruent Figures" consists of Akiko's memories as she recalls her growing feelings of hostility towards Hatsuko. The story is a classic fable of mother–daughter rivalry which recounts a mother's ambivalence towards a daughter perceived as a vampire-like, persecutory double. Akiko recounts of the growing, disconcerting similarities between the two of them: "I felt as if there was a miniature me beside me" (173) and "Her appearance resembled mine, her habits resembled mine, her feelings resembled mine" (179).[31]

In due time the narrative provides us with Akiko's own perspective on the boat accident: on that trip, the mother realized how an episode at school that had once revealed some of Hatsuko's dark, antisocial behav-

---

[31] It remains beyond the scope of this chapter to investigate the mother–daughter theme in Takahashi's fiction. For a detailed consideration of this theme in relation to "Congruent Figure," see Sakane (1998) and Alvis (2000).

iours perfectly overlapped with Akiko's memories of her own childhood. The feeling of being robbed of her individuality had been too much to bear and the eerie expression Hatsuko had seen on her mother's face was the result of the surfacing of this violent frustration. It is on this occasion that, while Hatsuko is being pulled up from the water and back into the boat, her mother has a first murderous fantasy about her:

> I looked far away, taking my eyes off Hatsuko. Stretched waves marked the few stripes on the surface of the sea. They were constantly moving, but as a whole the same striped shapes remained all the time. As I looked at it vacantly, the sea appeared immobile, as if it were a shining steel sheet. The vision of a shark springing up to break that surface crossed my sight bewitchingly. I could see before my eyes a vision of Hatsuko's body, swallowed by its sharp, wide-opened mouth, shining more vividly red than in reality. (180)

It is here that Akiko first becomes aware of the hostility she harbours towards her daughter. According to Hatsuko this is also the moment when her mother almost stopped talking to her. In line with my argument throughout this chapter, I suggest that one read this growing incommunicability as a reaction formation to the surfacing of a maternal violent potential to consciousness: social expectations of maternal propriety and the mother's own resistance to acknowledging her conflicting emotions inhibit access to linguistic articulation. Those same expectations and internalized norms force her to seal "deviant" emotions behind an expressionless mask: "She could not know the reason, for I made it my task to hide it from her" (ibid.).

A second murderous fantasy occurs on a day when Hatsuko is outside on the slope that climbs up to the woods and an indisposed Akiko is in bed resting and looking at her daughter through the window:

> Hatsuko's figure was striking and vigorous. [...] [I]t seemed as if the colors of her clothes were brought out not by the setting sun but by the life inside her. The book of home economy into which I was entering the household expenses was lying next to the pillow; I stretched my hand to it and picked up the pencil. I raised the upper half of my body from the mattress. The pencil was cut so as to show the long wooden surface and the lead was thin

and sharply pointed. Holding the middle part between my thumb and middle index finger, I placed the end of the pencil before my right eye. Closing my left eye, I aimed so that the tip of the pencil was pointed toward Hatsuko. I aimed the gun, so to speak. Hatsuko was still standing in the brightness of the setting sun, looking in the air somewhere far away, showing her profile to me. Hatsuko, move away quickly. If you don't, mother will shoot you. Hatsuko did not move. I held the pencil still. Quickly retreat to some place where mother cannot see you. The pencil in my hand felt heavy and hateful. When Hatsuko's figure moved slowly from my sight and disappeared, I felt relieved and at the same time tired. (184)

Of all the images I have analysed thus far, this is perhaps the most explicit. A mother is here consciously fantasizing of aiming a gun at her daughter and openly declares her intentions: mother will shoot you. As we have learned to expect from Takahashi's stories of maternal animosity, there is, emerging from this passage, a profound sense of inner conflict: a sense of restlessness accompanies Akiko's manifestation of hostility and the pencil becomes heavy and "hateful." In the solitude of the empty room, the protagonist's maternal potential for violence finds partial articulation. Yet, instead of confronting her own emotions, Akiko focuses more on her daughter, projecting onto her, so to speak, the mysterious power that is "making her" hold the pencil/gun. Akiko's words seem to imply that, if her daughter disappeared from view, she wouldn't feel compelled to make her the target of such dark fantasies. However, we may also notice that, like Yūko in "Yonder Sound of Water," she does not experience her emotions as deviant or exceptional. Rather, she recognizes them as feelings that find their way, sooner or later, in every mother's heart: "Was it something special that I felt about Hatsuko? Was my feeling about her abnormal? No, I don't think so. *It was an emotion that all the mothers of this world must have felt about their daughters*" (170, emphasis added).

In Akiko's neighbourhood used to live an old, crazy woman whom Akiko believed owned the mysterious power to see through the mind of others. Always concerned that her emotions remained concealed behind a façade of maternal propriety, Akiko had tried to avoid her on the street, as if she were scared that the woman's alleged powers could expose her innermost secrets. One night, during the time when her daughter was

5 Filicide and Maternal Animosity in Takahashi Takako's Early...

still living with her, Akiko has a dream where she chases after the old woman up to her dilapidated house at the foot of the mountain. There the woman gives her an old copper mirror and asks her to look at her own reflection:

> "It's my eyes. Reflect your face into my eyes." Hesitating, I looked at the old woman. Her gray hair hung down, dry like straw. Retaining no moisture, her skin was like leather.
> "You don't know. Look into this mirror," the old woman insisted stickily.
> I looked into the mirror. My face was reflected in vague outline on the dull surface. While I stared at it the face began gradually to change. Or I should say that from behind the blue brown surface of the mirror a strange, unfamiliar face emerged vaguely, and it overlapped my face. The face which revealed itself contained anger.
> "It is the face of mother." At these words of the old woman, the image on the mirror's surface disappeared.
> "It was not my mother's," I said. Then the coppered mirror in my hand disappeared too, and looking up I saw the old woman's eyes were gazing at me with the same color as the mirror's surface.
> "It is the face of mother itself in general." The old woman laughed with a husky voice. (190–1)

Reading the passage above, we have the impression that the whole episode unfolds in a realm of shared female knowledge and that the old crone is voicing a timeless, secret wisdom, laying bare an obscure truth about the dark potential at the heart of the maternal experience.[32] Far from being the image of eternal and self-sacrificial love, the reflection of Akiko-as-mother is transfigured by violent emotions. Akiko does not recognize her reflection, though: the face she sees is unfamiliar and this suggests her inability to face both her maternal ambivalence and that "other self" that remains buried and concealed inside her (the "demonic

---

[32] The old woman in Takahashi's story may remind a reader well-versed in Japanese literature of the *yamamba* (or *yamauba*), a well-known figure of Japanese folklore who appears in the literary tradition sometimes as an old woman who lives alone in the mountains, sometimes as a man-eater female demon or even a cannibal mother figure, just to name a few of her most striking manifestations (Viswanathan, 1996; Yamaori, 1997; Fisher, 1997; Hulvey, 1999; Reider, 2005).

woman" within Akiko?). The comments of the old woman further suggest that what we see in the mirror should not be limited to the idiosyncratic experience of a single woman: the face of anger and fury that the mirror sends back to us is the face of all mothers which remains hidden under the controlled expressionless of the mask of maternal propriety. Among the many manifestations of a mother's aggressive impulses and murderous potential that have punctuated this final chapter, this last passage holds an almost unique rhetorical charge because it portrays such violent potential as a natural facet of the maternal experience. This "heart of maternal darkness" flows often unnoticed under the deceptive myth of maternal boundless devotion, and threatens to break through it, erupting (in fantasy or reality) with unsettling and sometimes tragic consequences.

There is a second climactic moment in Akiko's visions with which I would like to bring my argument to a close, and that is when her dream turns into a nightmare: with her bare hands the old woman cuts her own wrists and disappears. Only her dry laughter still lingers in the air as her blood displaces the darkness:

> [...] and the voice of the old woman could be heard from far away saying it was the blood of women, and the sky was filled with a red-black sticky secretion, and the old woman stretched out her hands and scooped it up saying that it was the blood of women, look there is a limitless amount, scooped and scooped and it was still there; it is transmitted to the woman who comes out of your stomach, then to another woman who comes out of that woman, and what is transmitted is woman's karma, here try to scoop it, where can you find maternal love? It is nothing but an illusion manufactured by men. Look, look, there, there is only blood, why is there such a thing? (191)

Against the background of a gruesome oneiric landscape flooded with blood, Takahashi's story strikes a profound and unrestrained blow to cultural idealizations of the maternal. Reproduction becomes a tragedy and a curse: in all the stories I have explored Takahashi seems relentlessly to argue that, in a society that recognizes women only in their roles as wives and mothers, becoming a mother is inevitably associated with the endless and meaningless repetition of stifling gender norms which hamper the development of woman's autonomous subjectivity. Against this background, maternal violence may be read as the symptomatic manifestation of the "demonic woman" within Takahashi's female characters. And whereas these women utter with only great difficulty their unnameable desires, their actions have the effect to leave the reader mesmerized and disoriented vis-à-vis the realization that the myth of maternal love has been shattered in thousand fragments.

6

Conclusions

In her introduction to the volume *Nations, Language, and the Ethics of Translation*, Sandra Bermann (2005: 2) describes language as "a site of power, a means of active communication, and a scene of epistemological reflection." As a multiperspectival appreciation of the complexity of the linguistic dimension, her definition is well suited to foreground some of the key preoccupations that motivated the writing of this book. To investigate the discursive articulation of a maternal potential for violence meant not only to identify what was said about mothers who killed their children, but also to account for how it contributed to the production, circulation and resilience of specific ways of understanding motherhood's violent potential. It also meant to foreground the emergence of different discourses that provided alternative schemes of conceptualization for understanding cultural articulations of the "dark side" of the maternal.

Translating Maternal Violence recognized the extent to which media coverage of maternal filicide, *ribu*'s interventions in solidarity with mothers who killed their children and Takahashi's literary depictions of maternal animosity did not constitute isolated instances of an unprecedented preoccupation with maternal violence. Instead, they represented a historically and culturally specific tactical configuration of discourses that engaged in a passionate struggle over the meaning of womanhood, femininity and motherhood. *Ribu*'s political appropriation of a maternal potential for violence in the figure of the child-killing *onna*, its efforts to establish new forms of relationality with mothers who killed their children and Takahashi's portrayal of murderous mothers' psychic landscapes operated as powerful counter-discourses that challenged hegemonic understanding of maternal violence as a pathological or diabolic aberration. In this respect, both the *kogoroshi no onna* and Takahashi's "demonic woman" functioned as figures of resistance and were instrumental in what seemed to be a collective attempt to dismantle the myth of maternal love. In these concluding remarks, I want to draw attention to some of these connections between my archives that the reader certainly did not fail to recognize, but which could only be hinted at due to constraints of space, structure and flow. I will also take this opportunity to reposition my analysis in the context of the broader discussion about the ethics and politics of translation with which this book began.

Translating Maternal Violence maps the emergence in late postwar Japan of a distinctive constellation of discourses whereby multiple portrayals of maternal filicide and a maternal potential for violence were produced and circulated. The project was partially born out of a desire to know what had been said about mothers who kill their children at a time when the birth of a women's liberation movement announced women's growing dissatisfaction with cultural assumptions of womanhood and femininity. A founding suspicion remained, however, as to the effects of these discursive constructions of murderous motherhood, because the frequency with which representations of filicidal mothers appeared in the discursive arena did not by necessity indicate that maternal violence had finally stopped being the object of a deep-seated cultural taboo. Silences, erasures and omissions became then as important as the things said, suggesting that, at the very moment when a maternal potential for violence seemed to make its way into the realm of cultural intelligibility, forms of conscious and unconscious resistance limited the extent to which a renegotiation of the meaning of the maternal was allowed to take place.

The analysis of Japanese newspapers in Chap. 2 shed light upon the effort of news media to make sense of the frequency with which mothers seemed to harm their children. Although it would be naïve to conceive of media coverage as internally homogeneous, it was possible to identify a set of rhetorical and editorial strategies whereby filicide came to be portrayed as a phenomenon of alarming proportion, while mothers were simultaneously made into the main target of social criticism and public condemnation. A close reading of newspaper articles exposed the ways in which Japanese news media sought to contain the threat to the social fabric and its gender order that filicidal mothers represented. Stock stories of the "bad" and the "mad" mother so familiar to a Western audience combined with a widespread lamentation for an era marked by "the loss of motherhood" and "the suffering of children." Although somewhat at odds with it, recurrent portrayals of murderous mothers as cruel monsters, demonic creatures or unfortunate victims of mental illness combined with a narrative of filicide as a social phenomenon (i.e. as a common albeit tragic occurrence) and operated as a safety valve: by implicitly suggesting the exceptionality of the accidents, those narratives were meant to relieve the excessive pressure that such manifestations of violence exerted upon society's idealization of motherhood. We could arguably conclude that despite the growing visibility of episodes of maternal filicide, the violence perpetrated by these mothers was tamed: its threat was exorcized and made socially "digestible," while its implicit call for a re-examination of the myth of maternal love was successfully sidestepped.

As we have seen, one of the most striking features of Japanese media coverage on maternal filicide was the employment of the categories of *boshi shinjū* and *kogoroshi* which allowed a systematic and differential treatment of maternal violence. The notion of *kogoroshi* carried in itself the semantic traces of an unambiguous violence in the nominalization of the verb *korosu* (to kill). Those mothers who committed *kogoroshi* came to be portrayed as the most dangerous transgressors of cultural norms of motherhood and femininity, and their violence perceived accordingly as a monstrous aberration. Filicidal mothers (*kogoroshi no haha*) were stripped of their maternal identities and plunged into a realm of social abjection, while the maternal potential for violence they embodied was made into the very limit against which norms of appropriate maternal behaviour were continually re-established.

On the other hand, when the killing of a child by a mother was reported under the category of *boshi shinjū* it was arguably met with greater social acceptability and understanding. The use of this category made it possible to subsume a mother's killing of her child and her own suicide under the romanticized notion of a double-suicide committed out of love. At the same time, this rhetorical move collapsed the identity of the child with that of the mother and erased the child's status as a victim in its own right. By foregrounding the emotional bond between mother and child and sidestepping any overt reference to the violence perpetrated by the mother, the category of *boshi shinjū* actively hindered the intelligible articulation of a maternal potential for violence. Arguably, it was *because* subjected to these conditions of erasure that maternal filicide in the form of *boshi shinjū* could acquire a considerable degree of social acceptance.

However, can *boshi shinjū* be read otherwise? I have written extensively on how this category draws on the image of the double-suicidal pact between lovers (*shinjū*) and how *shinjū* was traditionally understood as the dramatic expression of an unresolvable tension between social obligations (*giri*) and emotions (*ninjō*). If the conflict between *giri* and *ninjō* often found resolution in dramatic forms of double-suicide, would it be that far off the mark to argue that in these instances *shinjū* becomes tinged with the colours of a *transgression* against those social norms that asserted external social obligations over the emotions of the individual? Also, if we consider that *giri* prioritizes the individual's belonging to the group—whose values are understood to eclipse individual subjectivity—we could also read the double-suicidal pact between two lovers as the affirmation of the individual *against* the group. Can this interpretation of *shinjū* pave the way to a more subversive understanding of *boshi shinjū*? To what extent does the *shinjū* in *boshi shinjū* open up the possibility of recognizing a culturally sanctioned form of social protest in this distinctive configuration of maternal child-killing? Can this interpretation confer to the mother who kills her child and then kills herself an agentic consciousness that rebels against the status quo of Japanese society and its expectation of maternal propriety? The erasure of the child in *boshi shinjū* reproduces cultural assumptions about the child being a non-person and as being part of the mother's own self. In so doing, it points at specific features of *boshi shinjū* that clearly distinguish it from the traditional understanding of *shinjū*. However, the fact that such subversive potential of *boshi shinjū* —however partial and certainly speculative—never emerged in media coverage of maternal filicide (where the romanticized and literary dimensions of *shinjū* remained prevalent) is indicative of the effacement that the idea of a maternal potential for violence suffered at the very site where its frequent appearance in public discourse should have made it all the more visible.

Media representations of maternal filicide constituted the background against which *ribu*'s manifestations of solidarity with mothers who killed their children acquired the clear status of counter-hegemonic acts of dissent (Tyler 2013). In the context of a broader critique of the gender organization of modern society and their attempts to establish the conditions of possibility for new forms of relationality, *ribu* activists opposed the media's biased portrayals of filicidal mothers. They denounced the criminalization, stigmatization and pathologization of these women and the process whereby the individual mother was singled out and declared the exception to a norm that remained unquestioned. The unfair treatment meted out to these mothers was understood to deny them the status of agentic subject and rational human being, and to create a separation between their experience and the average woman. In order to counter such widespread and "commonsensical" understandings of maternal filicide, *ribu* aimed at creating an alternative discursive space where a mother's potential for violence could be conceived in more human and sympathetic terms. Shigematsu (2012) called this approach a "feminist praxis of critical solidarity and radical inclusivity": a modality of political contestation that relied on the programmatic expression of solidarity with socially abjected or criminalized individuals, and which aimed to raise awareness of one's own complicity with the system of discrimination and social injustice that was understood to spur those criminal behaviours.

Yet, we have also recognized a degree of ambivalence and ambiguity in the way murderous mothers came to be represented in *ribu*'s rhetoric. One of the reasons was certainly *ribu*'s heterogeneous composition and the relative independence of the various groups that constituted its choral voice. On the other hand, I also pointed out that the possible contradictions or inconsistencies in the movement's multiple portrayals of mothers who kill may well have stemmed from the mutual interference of two potentially irreconcilable desires. First, the movement's emphasis on relationality urged *ribu* activists to strive to establish an encounter with filicidal mothers and provide a discursive space where their voice could be heard. In this respect, even though the voices of these mothers do not seem to have left material traces in the archival material this book draws upon, their presence can be somehow perceived, at times, as the ghostly addressee of some of *ribu*'s rhetorical interventions.

The second motivation that fuelled *ribu*'s discursive engagement with maternal filicide was its desire to articulate an alternative understanding of the phenomenon that was in line with the movement's political agenda. Arguably, the production and circulation of images of murderous mothers that certainly constituted an important discursive intervention in the context of *ribu*'s multiple struggles for social transformation might also have exposed the tragic experiences of these mothers to the danger of co-optation. In other words, *ribu* may have sometimes slipped into an appropriation of the notion of maternal filicide for political purposes which might have inadvertently relegated the *actual* experience of mothers who killed their children to the fringes of discourse. This could explain why these mothers cannot be identified as a consistent and material presence in the language of *ribu*. Whether or not the voicelessness of these mothers was sometimes exacerbated by *ribu*'s rhetorical engagement with the notion of maternal filicide remains an open question. Yet there is enough evidence to suggest that, while the two driving forces behind such engagement were not necessarily mutually exclusive, they may have at times shaped *ribu*'s discourse on maternal violence in unpredictable directions.

Ribu's discourse(s) on maternal filicide were born out of the movement's urgent desire to challenge the biased portrayals of mothers who killed that appeared with alarming frequency in the media coverage of the time. It is therefore striking that the silences that traverse *ribu*'s archival material betray what appears to be a failure to engage (or, possibly, a purposeful choice not to engage) with instances of maternal violence in the form of *boshi shinjū*. In fact, it was *kogoroshi* and not *boshi shinjū* that became a buzz-word in the context of *ribu*'s numerous interventions to reclaim a maternal or, rather, female potential for violence. *Ribu*'s

6 Conclusions

emphasis on *kogoroshi* could be understood in light of the movement's politicization of women's relationship with violence (Shigematsu 2012). By embracing *kogoroshi*, women activists were also purposefully embracing the unambiguous violence that distinguished it vis-à-vis the romanticized (and tamed) image of *boshi shinjū*. In this respect, it could be argued that it was because news media denounced the violent nature of *kogoroshi* as aberration that *ribu* reclaimed the term and its violence, associating it to the notion of *onna* as a new political subject. Therefore, this may well have constituted a conscious strategy to counter those representations of murderous mothers that were most damaging to women's efforts to articulate a female identity freed from the shackles of cultural prescriptions of femininity and womanhood. On the other hand, *ribu*'s lack of engagement with a common understanding of *boshi shinjū* and its use by the media to portray more "acceptable" forms of maternal filicide may also identify a lacuna in the movement's intervention on maternal violence. A selective focus on *kogoroshi* to the detriment of *boshi shinjū* may even nourish the suspicion that many *ribu* activists did indeed buy into the romanticized image of *shinjū*. In doing so they might have become inadvertent accomplices in specific forms of erasure of motherhood's violent potential.

In Chap. 5 the analysis of early works of fiction by Japanese writer Takahashi Takako offered the chance to consider the extent to which women's literature might have participated in the redefinition of female identity in late postwar Japan. Investigating the multiple configurations of maternal violence that surface in Takahashi's literature led us to the recognition of just how deeply her literary representations of maternal animosity resonate with *ribu*'s commitment to social change. Her works lend themselves to being read as the manifestation in literary form of a programmatic effort to challenge cultural prescriptions of femininity and norms of appropriate maternal behaviour. And although Takahashi never referred to *ribu* in explicit terms nor ever expressed support for its struggle, it is my contention that a careful analysis of her writings places her in a legible relation to the women's movement. Her preoccupation with the proposed changes to the law that regulated women's access to abortion, her support for women's freedom to decide not to give birth, her acknowledgement (however cursory) of the plight of unmarried mothers and her fierce critique of the institution of the family reveal Takahashi as an acute and engaged social commentator, despite her claims to the contrary.[1]

Furthermore, the specific vocabulary and imagery she employs in many of her non-fictional writings show such striking similarities with the rhetoric and language of *ribu* that one may well be tempted to read them both as refracted manifestations of a single revolutionary consciousness. Those instances in which Takahashi indicates woman's awakening to sexuality as a preferential route towards a liberated self find a suggestive correspondence in *ribu*'s emphasis on the promotion of woman's knowledge of her body as key to the articulation of a new female subjectivity. Even more reminiscent of *ribu*'s rhetoric is Takahashi's claim that, just like the "mother" and the "prostitute" had once been exposed as two sides of the same coin (perceived as opposites only within man's split consciousness), the categorical distinction between the "diabolic" and the "maternal" woman was also understood as the inaccurate (and damaging) result of man's classificatory system.

The disturbing fascination that Takahashi's depictions of maternal animosity exerted (and still do) upon her readers is indicative of the potential of literature to constitute a counter-discourse that may interfere with hegemonic understandings of maternal violence. The insistency with which mothers who kill appeared in her early writings constituted an affront to cultural idealizations of maternal love and selfless devotion. These repeated provocations may have performed an intervention into the Symbolic, expanding the conditions of appearance of a maternal potential for violence in public discourse. The cultural and representational challenge that traversed Takahashi's literature was further amplified by the emergence, at that time, of a new generation of women writers whose disturbing fantasies of female transgression produced an effect of kaleidoscopic reflections and reciprocal amplifications.

Literary representations of "aberrant" motherhood certainly contributed to the dismantling of the myth of maternal love. However, it is the disconcerting similarity between Takahashi's "demonic woman" and

---

[1] In "My Obtuseness" (*Watashi no donkansa*, 1977b), for example, Takahashi confesses her lack of political and historical consciousness at the time she was attending university.

the "child-killing *onna*" of *ribu*'s rhetoric that is most suggestive of the ways in which these two discourses might have jointly participated in the reclaiming of a female potential for violence. Takahashi theorized the demonic woman as the embodiment of a female awakening to a new self. Positioned in stark opposition to the maternal—which, in turn, was conceived unequivocally as a condition of lethargy and sleep-walking— the "demonic woman" was described as caught in a struggle for survival underneath the mask of feminine propriety. Thérèse Desqueyroux's split subjectivity was taken by Takahashi to exemplify this existential conflict, and "the other woman" within Thérèse to be the true origin of Thérèse's murderous desires. The real culprit, so to speak, was not Thérèse-the-wife or Thérèse-the-mother (i.e. the Thérèse whose identity society recognized), but the image darkly forming of this "other woman" within Thérèse.

When we read Takahashi's fictional portrayals of mothers who kill in light of the figure of the "demonic woman," we come to understand that one who perpetrates the violence is not the mother, but the demonic woman within/underneath (the mask of) the mother. In similar fashion, *ribu* claimed that that who laid her hands on the child was not the woman-as-mother but the *onna*-within-the-mother. These considerations make it extremely tempting to read the "demonic woman" and *onna* as twin figures that remind us of the reciprocal permeability of the two counter-discourses from which they emerged. In similar ways in which *onna* was understood to harm the child (and eventually herself) in a desperate, blind attempt to break free from the prison of an inauthentic self (that self-that-was-not-a-self), a woman's awakening to her "demonic" self (her "real" self) often brought about the breaking of the taboo of a female/maternal potential for violence.

Takahashi's depictions of mothers who kill their children also made it possible to explore in fictional form the psychic dimension of maternal violence. Literary portrayals (re-)produced mothers' intimate experience of their murderous desires, and imagined the fractures these could generate in women's identities as mothers and wives. Essay titles such as "Moving backward toward the world of the unconscious" ("Senzai sekai e no gyakkō," 1977b), "To dig into the unconscious" ("Muishiki wo horu," 1980) and "Subconscious landscapes" ("Senzai ishiki no kōkei," 1977b) testify to the importance Takahashi attributed to the subconscious and the inner workings of the psyche. "The act of writing fiction," she once claimed, "is the act of digging into the unconscious" ("Muishiki wo horu," 1980: 96). Accordingly, literature became for Takahashi a realm where she could unearth desires, passions and dark emotions that social mores made barely acceptable, when they did not simply repress and expunge them from the realm of cultural intelligibility.

Commenting on literature's transformative potential, Takahashi also argued that, by means of writing about a character's dark impulses and criminal deeds, the author could undergo those same experiences and be transformed by them ("Shōsetsu wo kaku kekka" [Writing a novel], 1980). In the essay "A literature of crime" ("Satsui no bungaku," 1975) she further elaborated on this aspect and considered that writing about individuals who committed crimes in solitude had become for her a way to experience an otherwise inaccessible existential journey during which she could share the deep incommunicability that separated the person who had committed the crime from those who had not committed it. We would have expected that, as a result of such an approach to writing fiction, Takahashi's portrayals of mothers who kill would have succeeded in retrieving a maternal potential of violence from the realm of psychic repression and in conferring to it a fully intelligible formulation. However, what we encounter in her stories is a tenacious resistance to discursive articulation, resistance that takes the form of multiple interruptions, hesitations, pauses and silences. It could be argued, therefore, that Takahashi's portrayals of murderous mothers fall short of their promises (i.e. a complete salvaging of a maternal potential for violence from the repressions performed by cultural taboos and linguistic prohibition). On the other hand, they could also be understood as forms of implicit denunciation of the most dramatic form of erasure, where verbal articulation is not simply prohibited from without but from within, and collapsed into the physicality of symptoms.

From these considerations two things become clear: first, that "language can never be viewed as a simple mental tool, or a transparent medium of representation"; second, that cultural practices and texts "produce and sustain—and are in turn sustained by—the lexicon and syntax of a given language" (Bermann 2005: 4). This takes me back once again to the translational framework that from the outset intersected this investigation on multiple levels and which was the expression of a sense of urgency for a critical transnational feminist inquiry on maternal violence. In many respects, the kind of work that I undertook in writing *Translating Maternal Violence* was conceived as a way to respond to Lila Abu-Lughod's (2010: 220) rather bleak pronouncement that "[a]s long as we are writing for the West about 'the other,' we are implicated in projects that establish Western authority and cultural difference." In embracing an ethics of translation as a theoretical and methodological strategy to open up the space for a dialogic encounter between Western readership and non-Western conceptualizations of a maternal potential for violence, I attempted to problematize what it means writing "for the West."

I also tried, more or less explicitly, to dislodge the assumed universality of Anglo-American or, alternatively, Eurocentric (feminist) categories used to conceptualize a maternal potential for violence. *Translating Maternal Violence* argues for and performatively undertakes a dislocation and dispersal of the West (Sakai 2005), while also attempting to think theoretically about "the East." According to Margaret Hillenbrand (2010: 317) to do so requires "writing about the region in ways that [...] challenge the very cartography of global knowledge." It means "to theoretically dislocate the sign [...] from the West toward new decolonial geographies and languages" (de Lima Costa and Alvarez 2014: 561–2). In this respect, translation is always already political, and the study and practicum of translation become strategies to expose, explore and intervene in existing power relations.

It may be productive at this point to juxtapose these ideas of decentring, dislocation and dispersal with the concept of *defamiliarization*, which often also carries with it a sense of *disorientation*. Sara Ahmed's theoretical engagement with questions of orientation and failed orientation becomes useful here. As I began to explore my archives I made a deliberate effort not to superimpose on them categories stemming from Western feminist investigations of motherhood and maternal ambivalence in order to avoid the inadvertent erasure of the particularities of the Japanese experience. Certainly, such superimposition would have made the Japanese case study familiar to a Western reader (bringing the foreign author to the reader, as it were), but as Ahmed aptly put it, "in a familiar room we have already extended ourselves" (2006: 7). This, in turn, hinders a desire to prioritize the unknown over the known (Hemmings 2011). As we extend ourselves in search of the familiar or, rather, creating the familiar, we also determine in advance what will come into view and what will take its place in the line of our horizon: "The starting point for orientation," Ahmed rightly argues, "is the point from which the world unfolds" (2006: 8). And if an object takes the shape that it does as a result of our specific orientation towards it, of the position we occupy when we attend to it, then to set out to investigate Japanese archival material with the employment of analytical categories formulated in the context of Western feminist theorizations of the maternal would have set in advance the terms in which we might have apprehended our object, constituting in ultimate analysis an instance of Western narcissism.

Yet, a reflection about the concept of orientation requires that we also attend to what it means to experience moments of *dis*orientation, those instances when the world that we inhabit loses its familiarity. At this regard, Ahmed observes that "getting lost" still takes us somewhere (7), and she encourages us to imagine how an object might appear when it is no longer familiar (35). As she foregrounds the epistemological value of these moments of failed orientation, she also points at the potential for a collective repetition of such moments of *de*familiarization to *create a new orientation* (61). "Becoming reorientated," she reminds us, "involves the disorientation of encountering the world differently" (20). An engagement with translation thus provides a fresh perspective on how we might engage with and experience these moments of disorientation and sheds light upon some of the lessons we may learn from them. Considered in this light translation offers itself as a category of action (Bachmann-Medick 2009: 3), and untranslatability, far from simplistically representing a failure in communication, can carry with it the potential for unforeseen moments of disorientation and reorientation. Apter (2008: 587) describes this as the "effect of the noncarryover that carries over nonetheless" because it causes in the reader a moment of estrangement in a foreign tongue and prompts her "to reverse the order of comparison" (590). As we face the "untranslatable" or others forms of translational troubles we are confronted with the fact that "translation failure demarcates intersubjective limits," but also with the transformative awareness that translation can be "a significant medium of subject formation and political change" (Apter 2006: 6) which relentlessly urges us to become polyglots.[2]

---

[2] For a theoretical elaboration of the polyglot, see Rosi Braidotti's *Nomadic Subjects* (2011) and Sandra Ponzanesi's "Translating Selves: On Polyglot Cosmopolitanism" (2015).

Bibliography

Abu-Lughod, L. (2010) "Orientalism and Middle Eastern Feminist Studies." In *Feminist Theory Reader: Global and Local Perspectives*, eds. C. Mccann and S. Kim, 218–27. New York: Routledge.
Ahmed, S. (2006) *Queer Phenomenology: Orientations, Objects, Others*. Durham and London: Duke University Press.
Aki Shobō, ed. (1971) *Seisabetsu e no kokuhatsu—ūman ribu wa shuchō suru*. Tokyo: Aki Shobō.
Akiyama, Y. (1993) *Ribu shishi nōto. Onna-tachi no jidai kara*. Tokyo: Inpakuto Shuppankai.
Akiyama, Y., S. Ikeda, and T. Inoue (1996) "Zadankai: tōdai tōsō kara ribu, soshite joseigaku, feminizumu." In *Zenkyōtō kara ribu e*, ed. Onnatachi no ima wo tou kai, 38–70. Tokyo: Inpakuto Shuppankai.
Alcoff, L.M. (1995) "The Problem of Speaking for Others." In *Who Can Speak? Authority and Critical Identity*, eds. J. Roof and R. Wiegman, 97–119. Urbana: University of Illinois Press.
Allinson, G.D. (1997) *Japan's Postwar History*. Ithaca, NY: Cornell University Press.
Almond, B. (2010) *The Monster Within: The Hidden Side of Motherhood*. Berkeley, CA: University of California Press.

Alvis, A. (2000) "Fantasies of Maternal Ambivalence in Takahashi Takako's 'Congruent Figures'." *U.S.-Japan Women's Journal* 18, 58–83.
Anzaldúa, G. ([1987] 1999) *Borderlands/La Frontera: The New Mestiza*. San Francisco, CA: Aunt Lute Books.
Apter, E. (2006) *The Translation Zone: A New Comparative Literature*. Princeton, NJ: Princeton University Press.
Apter, E. (2008) "Untranslatables: A World System." *New Literary History* 39(3), 581–98.
"Asu wa wagami! 'Kogoroshi onna wa seishin shōgaisha' naru asahi shinbun no hōdō ni kōgi suru!" (1974). In Mizoguchi A., Saeki Y., and Miki S., eds. (1994), 379.
Avenell, S.A. (2010) *Making Japanese Citizens. Civil Society and the Mythology of the* Shimin *in Postwar Japan*. Berkeley: University of California Press.
Ayres, S. (2004) "'[N]ot a Story to Pass On': Constructing Mothers Who Kill." *Hastings Women's Law Journal* 15(1), 39–110.
Bachmann-Medick, D. (2009) "Introduction: The Translational Turn." *Translation Studies* 2(1), 2–16.
Bachmann-Medick, D., ed. (2014) *The Trans/National Study of Culture: A Translational Perspective*. Berlin and Boston: De Gruyter.
Baraitser, L., and I. Tyler (2010) "Talking of Mothers." *Soundings* 44, 117–27.
Bargen, D.G. (1997) *A Woman's Weapon. Spirit Possession in the Tale of Genji*. Honolulu: University of Hawai'i Press.
Barnett, B. (2005) "Perfect Mother or Artist of Obscenity? Narrative and Myth in a Qualitative Analysis of Press Coverage of the Andrea Yates Murders." *Journal of Communication Inquiry* 29, 9–29.
Barnett, B. (2006) "*Medea* in the Media: Narrative and Myth in Newspaper Coverage of Women Who Kill Their Children." *Journalism* 7, 411–32.
Barnett, B. (2007) "The Wounded Community: Myth and Narrative in Print News Articles about Women Who Kill Their Children." *Media Report to Women* 35(1), 13–21.
Barnett, B. (2013) "Toward Authenticity. Using Feminist Theory to Construct Journalistic Narratives of Maternal Violence." *Feminist Media Studies* 13(3), 505–24.
Bassnett, S. (1998) "The Translation Turn in Cultural Studies." In *Constructing Cultures: Essays on Literary Translation*, eds. S. Bassnett and A. Lefevere, 123–40.
Beaudry, M.C., Cook, L.J., and Mrozowski, S.A. (1996) "Artifacts and Active Voices: Material Culture as Social Discourse." In *Images of the Recent Past: Readings in Historical Archaeology*, ed. C.E. Jr. Orser, 272–310. Oxford: AltaMira Press.

Bellos, D. (2012) *Is That a Fish in Your Ear? The Amazing Adventure of Translation*. London: Penguin.
Benjamin, W. ([1955] 2007) "The Task of the Translator." In *Illuminations*, W. Benjamin, ed. H. Arendt, 69–82. New York: Schocken Books.
Berman, A. ([1984] 1992) *The Experience of the Foreign: Culture and Translation in Romantic Germany*. Albany: State University of New York Press.
Bermann, S. (2005) "Introduction." In *Nation, Language, and the Language of Translation*, eds. S. Bermann and M. Wood, 1–10. Princeton and Oxford: Princeton University Press.
Bhabha, H. (1994) *The Location of Culture*. London and New York: Routledge.
Borovoy, A.B. (2005) *The Too-Good Wife: Alcohol, Codependency, and the Politics of Nurturance in Postwar Japan*. Berkeley: University of California Press.
Boston Women's Health Book Collective, ed. (1973) *Our Bodies, Ourselves: A Book by and for Women*. New York: Simon and Schuster.
Boyer, E.J. (1985) "Mother Ordered to Trial in Two Child Drownings." *Los Angeles Times*. Retrieved from http://articles.latimes.com/1985-04-19/local/me-14958_1_child-drownings
Braidotti, R. (1997) "Mothers, Monsters, and Machines." In *Writing on the Body: Female Embodiment and Feminist Theory*, eds. K. Conboy, N. Medina, and S. Stanbury, 59–79. New York: Columbia University Press.
Braidotti, R. (2011) *Nomadic Subjects: Embodiment and Sexual Difference in Contemporary Feminist Theory*. New York: Columbia University Press.
Brookman, F., and J. Nolan (2006) "The Dark Figure of Infanticide in England and Wales: Complexities of Diagnoses." *Journal of Interpersonal Violence* 21(7), 869–89.
Bryant, T.L. (1990) "*Oya-ko shinju*: Death at the Center of the Heart." *UCLA Pacific Basin Law Journal* 8, 1–31.
Bryant, T.L. (1991) "For the Sake of the Country, for the Sake of the Family: The Oppressive Impact of Family Registration on Women and Minorities in Japan." *UCLA Law Review* 39(1), 109–68.
Buckley, S., and V. Mackie (1986) "Women in the New Japanese State." In *Democracy in Contemporary Japan*, eds. G. McCormack and Y. Sugimoto, 173–85. Armonk, NY: M.E.Sharpe.
Buckley, S. (1993) "Altered States: The Body Politics of 'Being-Woman'." In *Postwar Japan as History*, ed. A. Gordon, 347–372. Berkeley: University of California Press.
Buckley, S. (1994) "A Short History of the Feminist Movement in Japan." In *Women of Japan and Korea: Continuity and Change*, eds. J. Gelb and M. Lief Palley, 150–86. Philadelphia: Temple University Press.

Buckley, S., ed. (1997) *Broken Silence: Voices of Japanese Feminism*. Berkeley: University of California Press.
Bullock, J.C. (2006) "Fantasizing What Happens When the Goods Get Together: Female Homoeroticism as Literary Trope." *Positions* 14(3), 663–85.
Bullock, J.C. (2009) "Fantasy as Methodology: Simone de Beauvoir and Postwar Japanese Feminism." *U.S.-Japan Women's Journal* 36, 73–91.
Bullock, J.C. (2010) *The Other Women's Lib: Gender and Body in Japanese Women's Fiction*. Honolulu: University of Hawai'i Press.
Butler, J. (1990) *Gender Troubles: Feminism and the Subversion of Identity*. New York: Routledge.
Butler, J. (1992) "Contingent Foundations: Feminism and the Question of 'Postmodernism'." In *Feminists Theorize the Political*, eds. J. Butler and J.W. Scott, 3–21. New York: Routledge.
Butler, J. (2000) *Antigone's Claim: Kinship between Life and Death*. New York: Columbia Unversity Press.
Butler, J. (2004) "Betrayal's Felicity." *Diacritics* 34(1), 82–7.
Butler, J. (2008) "Sexual Politics, Torture, and Secular Time." *The British Journal of Sociology* 59(1), 1–23.
Butler, J. (2010) *Frames of War: When Is Life Grievable?* London and New York: Verso.
Butler, J. (2014) *Parting Ways. Jewishness and the Critique of Zionism*. New York: Columbia University Press.
Butler, J., and G.C. Spivak (2007) *Who Sings the Nation State?: Language, Politics, Belonging*. London, New York and Calcutta: Seagulls.
Carpenter, J.W. (1990) "Enchi Fumiko: 'A Writer of Tales'." *Japan Quarterly* 37(3), 343–55.
Castellini, A. (2014) "Silent Voices: Mothers Who Kill Their Children and the Women's Liberation Movement in 1970s Japan." *Feminist Review* 106, 9–26.
Cavaglion, G. (2008) "Bad, Mad or Sad? Mothers Who Kill and Press Coverage in Israel." *Crime, Media and Culture* 4(2), 271–8.
Cavanagh, K., R.E. Dobash, R.P. Dobash, and R. Lewis (2001) "'Remedial Work': Men's Strategic Responses to Their Violence against Intimate Female Partners." *Sociology* 35(3), 695–714.
Cerwonka, A. (2008) "Traveling Feminist Thought: Difference and Transculturation in Central and Eastern European Feminism." *Signs* 33(4), 809–32.
Chakrabarty, D. (2000) *Provincializing Europe: Postcolonial Thought and Historical Difference*. Princeton and Oxford: Princeton University Press.

Cheever, S. (2001) *As Good as I Could Be: A Memoir of Raising Wonderful Children in Difficult Times*. New York and London: Washington Square Press.

Cheung, M. (2005) "'To Translate' Means 'To Exchange'?: A New Interpretation of the Earliest Chinese Attempts to Define Translation (*fanyi*)." *Target* 17(1), 27–48.

Chow, R. (1993) *Writing Diaspora: Tactics of Intervention in Contemporary Cultural Studies*. Bloomington: Indiana University Press.

Chow, R. (2006) *The Age of the World Target: Self-Referentiality in War, Theory, and Comparative Work*. Durham and London: Duke University Press.

Chow, R. (2007) "Translator, Traitor; Translator, Mourner (or, Dreaming of Intercultural Equivalence)." *New Literary History* 37, 565–80.

Chow, R. (2014a) *Not Like a Native Speaker: On Languaging as a Postcolonial Experience*. New York: Columbia University Press.

Chow, R. (2014b) "Interview with Rey Chow, Author of 'Not Like a Native Speaker'." [online] Available at: http://www.cupblog.org/?p=14707 (accessed 27 October 2015).

Chūpiren (1972) "'Kogoroshi' ni tsuite." In Mizoguchi A., Saeki Y., and Miki S., eds. (1994), 246–7.

Cohen, S. ([1972] 2002) *Folk Devils and Moral Panics*. Third ed. London and New York: Routledge.

Connell, R. (2014) "Rethinking Gender from the South." *Feminist Studies* 40(3), 518–39.

Connell, R. (2015) "Meeting at the Edge of Fear: Theory on a World Scale." *Feminist Theory* 16(1), 49–66.

Copeland, R.L. (1992) "Motherhood as Institution." *Japan Quarterly* 39(1), 101–10.

Copeland, R.L., ed. (2006) *Woman Critiqued: Translated Essays on Japanese Women's Writing*. Honolulu: University of Hawai'i Press.

Covino, D.C. (2004) *Amending the Abject Body: Aesthetic Makeovers in Medicine and Culture*. New York: The State University of New York Press.

Coward, R. (1997) "The Heaven and Hell of Mothering: Mothering and Ambivalence in the Mass Media." In Hollway and Featherstone, eds. (1997), 111–18.

Davis, K. (2007) *The Making of Our Bodies, Ourselves: How Feminism Travels across Borders*. Durham and London: Duke University Press.

De Lange, W. (1998) *A History of Japanese Journalism: Japan's Press Club as the Last Obstacle to a Mature Press*. Surrey: Japan Library.

de Lima Costa, C., and S.E. Alvarez (2014) "Dislocating the Sign: Toward a Translocal Feminist Politics of Translation." *Signs* 39(3), 557–63.

de Man, P. (1985) "Walter Benjamin's 'The Task of the Translator'." *Yale French Studies* 69, 25–46.

Derrida, J. (1985) "Des Tours de Babel." In *Difference in Translation*, ed. J.F. Graham, 165–207. Ithaca and London: Cornell University Press.

Derrida, J. (2001) "What Is a 'Relevant' Translation?" *Critical Inquiry* 27(2), 174–200.

Di Marco, F. (2013) "Act or Disease?: The Making of Modern Suicide in Early Twentieth-Century Japan." *The Journal of Japanese Studies* 39(2), 325–58.

Di Marco, F. (2016) *Suicide in Twentieth-Century Japan*. London and New York: Routledge.

Dizdar, D. (2009) "Translational Transitions: 'Translation Proper' and Translation Studies in the Humanities." *Translation Studies* 2(1), 89–102.

Dodane, C. (2006) "Femmes et Littérature au Japon." *Cahiers du Genre* 3, HS, nr. 1, 197–218.

Doi, T. ([1973] 1981) *The Anatomy of Dependence*. Tokyo and New York: Kodansha International.

Dolan, M. (1985) "Two Cultures Collide over Act of Despair: Mother Facing Charges in Ceremonial Drowning." *Los Angeles Times*. Retrieved from http://articles.latimes.com/1985-02-24/news/mn-24484_1_criminal-charges

Dongchao, M. (2005) "Awakening Again: Travelling Feminism in China in the 1980s." *Women's Studies International Forum* 28(4), 274–88.

Dongchao, M. (2007a) "*Duihua* (Dialogue) In-between. A Process of Translating the Term 'Feminism' in China." *Interventions: International Journal of Postcolonial Studies* 9(2), 174–93.

Dongchao, M. (2007b) "Translation as Crossing Borders: A Case Study of the Translations of the Word 'Feminism' into Chinese by the CSWS." *Transversal* (4). Retrieved from http://eipcp.net/transversal/1107/min/en

Douglas, S.J., and M.W. Michaels (2004) *The Mommy Myth: The Idealization of Motherhood and How It Has Undermined All Women*. New York, NY: Free Press.

Ehara, Y. ([1985] 2012) *Josei kaihō to iu shisō*. Tokyo: Keisō Shobō.

Ehara, Y. (2005) "The Politics of Teasing" translated by Ayako Kano. In *Contemporary Japanese Thought*, ed. R. Calichman, 45–55. New York: Columbia University Press.

Enchi, F. ([1958] 1983) *Masks*. Translated by Juliet Winters Carpenter. New York: Aventura.

Endo, O. (1995) "Aspects of Sexism in Language." In Fujimura-Fanselow and Kameda, eds. (1995), 29–42.

Endō, M. et al. (1996) "Zadankai: ribu sen wo taguri yosete miru." In *Zenkyōtō kara ribu e*, ed. Onnatachi no ima wo tou kai, 204–51. Tokyo: Inpakuto Shuppankai.

Entman, R.M. (1993) "Framing: Towards Clarification of a Fractured Paradigm." *Journal of Communication* 43(4), 51–8.

Ericson, J.E. (1996) "The Origins of the Concept 'Women's Literature'." In P.G. Schalow and J.A. Walker, eds. (1996), 74–115.

Ericson, J.E. (2006) "The Resisting Woman Writer." In *Woman Critiqued*, ed. R. Copeland, 114–18. Honolulu: University of Hawai'i Press.

Fahmy, S., and T.J. Johnson (2007) "Embedded Versus Unilateral Perspectives on Iraq War." *Newspaper Research Journal* 28(3), 98–114.

Feldman, O. (1993) *Politics and the News Media in Japan*. Ann Arbor: The University of Michigan Press.

Feldman, P. (1985) "Mother Pleads No Contest in Drowning of 2 Children." *Los Angeles Times*. Retrieved from http://articles.latimes.com/1985-10-19/local/me-15043_1_murder-case

Firestone, S. ([1970] 1971) *The Dialectic of Sex: The Case for Feminist Revolution*. London: Paladin.

Firestone S., and A. Koedt, eds. (1971) *Notes from the Second Year: Women's Liberation: Major Writings of the Radical Feminists* (New York: Radical Feminism). Translated as *Onna kara onnatachi e: Amerika josei kaihō undo repōto* (1971), trans. and commentary Urufu no kai (Tokyo: Gōdō Shuppan).

Fisher, S. (1997) "The Devouring Mother: The *Yamamba* Archetype in Ōba Minako's '*Yamauba no bishō*'." In *Mothers in Japanese Literature*, ed. K. Tsuruta, 447–64. Conference Proceedings. Vancouver, BC: University of British Columbia.

Foucault, M. ([1972] 1992) *The Archaeology of Knowledge*. London: Routledge.

Foucault, M. ([1978] 1998) *The History of Sexuality 1: The Will to Knowledge*. London: Penguin.

Friedan, B. ([1963] 1965) *The Feminine Mystique*. Harmondsworth, England: Penguin Books.

Friedman, S.S. (1998) *Mappings. Feminism and the Cultural Geographies of Encounter*. Princeton, NJ: Princeton University Press.

Fujieda, M., and K. Fujimura-Fanselow (1995) "Women's Studies: An Overview." In Fujimura-Fanselow and Kameda, eds. (1995), 155–80.

Fujimura-Fanselow, K., and A. Kameda, eds. (1995) *Japanese Women: New Feminist Perspectives on the Past, Present, and Future*. New York: Feminist Press.

Bibliography

Gamson, W.A., and A. Modigliani (1989) "Media Discourse and Public Opinion on Nuclear Power: A Constructionist Approach." *American Journal of Sociology* 95(1), 1–37.

Gao, B. (2007) "The Postwar Japanese Economy." In *A Companion to Japanese History*, ed. W.M. Tsutsui, 299–314. Malden, MA: Blackwell.

Goc, N. (2003) "Mothers and Madness: The Media Representation of Postpartum Psychosis." In *Interdisciplinary Perspectives of Health, Illness and Disease*, eds. P.L. Twohig and V. Kalitzkus, 53–65. Amsterdam and New York, NY: Rodopi.

Goc, N. (2007) "Monstrous Mothers and the Media." In *Monsters and the Monstrous: Myths and Metaphors of Enduring Evil*, ed. N. Scott, 149–66. New York: Rodopi.

Goc, N. (2008) "Case Study 3: Media Narratives: The 'Murdering Mother'." In *Media and Journalism: New Approaches to Theory and Practice*, eds. J. Bainbridge, N. Goc, and E. Tynan, 213–23. South Melbourn, Vic. and Oxford: Oxford University Press.

Goc, N. (2009) "Framing the News: 'Bad' Mothers and the 'Medea' News Frame." *Australian Journalism Review* 31(1), 33–47.

Goc, N. (2013) *Women, Infanticide and the Press*. Farnham, Surrey: Ashgate.

Goel, R. (2004) "Can I Call Kimura Crazy? Ethical Tensions in Cultural Defense." *Seattle Journal for Social Justice* 3(1), 443–64.

Goodman, R. (2002) "Child Abuse in Japan: 'Discovery' and the Development of Policy." In *Family and Social Policy in Japan: Anthropological Approaches*, ed. R. Goodman, 131–55. Cambridge: Cambridge University Press.

Goodman, R., Y. Imoto, and T. Toivonen (2012) *From Returnees to NEETs*. New York: Routledge.

Grewal, I., and C. Kaplan, eds. (1994) *Scattered Hegemonies: Postmodernity and Transnational Feminist Practices*. Minneapolis: University of Minnesota Press.

Gurūpu Tatakau Onna (1970) "Naze 'sei no kaihō' ka." In Mizoguchi A., Saeki Y. and Miki S., eds. (1992), 210–12.

Gurūpu Tatakau Onna (1971a) "Haha e no rabu retā." In Mizoguchi A., Saeki Y. and Miki S., eds. (1992), 240–46.

Gurūpu Tatakau Onna (1971b) "Ondoro ondoro onna ga kodomo wo koroshiteku ondoro ondoro onna ga kodomo wo koroshiteku." In Ribu Shinjuku Sentā Shiryō Hozon Kai, ed. (2008a), 186–7. Also in Tanaka, M. (2010), 314–19.

Gurūpu Tatakau Onna (1971c) "Shiryō: onna no kogoroshi wo kangaeru kai" In Ribu Shinjuku Sentā Shiryō Hozon Kai, ed. (2008a), 188–95.

Gurūpu Tatakau Onna (1971d) "10-21 onna no shūkai" In Mizoguchi A., Saeki Y. and Miki S., eds. (1992), 250–1.

Hara, K. (1995) "Challenges to Education for Girls and Women in Modern Japan: Past and Present." In Fujimura-Fanselow and Kameda, eds. (1995), 93–106.

Hara, Y. (1987) "The Significance of the U.S.-Japan Security System to Japan: The Historical Background." *Peace & Change* 12(3–4), 29–38.

Hartley, B. (1999) "The Mother, The Daughter, and the Sexed Body in Enchi Fumiko's 'Fuyu momiji'." *PMAJLS* 5, 250–62.

Hayashi, K.K. (1985a) "An Act of Despair or Violence?" *The Corsair* 55(24), 2. Retrieved from http://cdnc.ucr.edu/cgi-bin/cdnc?a=d&d=CRS19850313.2.8.4

Hayashi, K.K. (1985b) "Understanding *Shinju* and the-Tragedy of Fumiko Kimura." *Los Angeles Times*, 1985 April 10, p5.

Hayashi, K. (2000) "The 'Home and Family' Section in the Japanese Newspaper." In *Tabloid Tales: Global Debates over Media Standards*, eds. C. Sparks and J. Tulloch, 147–62. Oxford: Rowman & Littlefield Publishers.

Heine, S. (1994) "Tragedy and Salvation in the Floating World: Chikamatsu's Double Suicide Drama as Millenarian Discourse." *The Journal of Asian Studies* 53(2), 367–93.

Hemmings, C. (2011) *Why Stories Matter: The Political Grammar of Feminist Theory*. Durham and London: Duke University Press.

Hillenbrand, M. (2010) "Editorial: Communitarianism, or, How to Build East Asian Theory." *Postcolonial Studies* 13(4), 317–34.

Hollway, W., and B. Featherstone, eds. (1997) *Mothering and Ambivalence*. London: Routledge.

Hook, D. (2001) "Discourse, Knowledge, Materiality, History: Foucault and Discourse Analysis." *Theory and Psychology* 11(4), 521–47.

Hoshino, I. (1964) "Apartment Life in Japan." *Journal of Marriage and Family* 26(3), 312–17.

Huckerby, J. (2003) "Women Who Kill Their Children: Case Studies and Conclusions Concerning the Differences in the Fall from Maternal Grace by Khoua Her and Andrea Yates." *Duke Journal of Gender Law and Policy* 10, 149–72.

Hulvey, S.Y. (1999) "Man-Eaters: Women Writers and the Appropriation of the *Yamauba* Motif." *PMAJLS* 5, 240–49.

Inoue, T. (1980) *Joseigaku to sono shūhen*. Tokyo: Keisō Shobō.

Jakobson, R. ([1959] 2000) "On Linguistic Aspects of Translation." In *The Translation Studies Reader*, ed. L. Venuti, 113–18. London and New York: Routledge.

Jackson, P.A. (2003) "Space, Theory, and Hegemony: The Dual Crisis of Asian Area Studies and Cultural Studies." *Sojourn: Journal of Social Issues in Southeast Asia* 18(1), 1–41.

Johnson, B. (1985) "Taking Fidelity Philosophically." In *Difference in Translation*, ed. J.E. Graham, 142–48. Ithaca and London: Cornell University Press.

Johnson-Cartee, K.S. (2005) *News Narratives and News Framing: Constructing Political Reality*. Lanham : Rowman & Littlefield Publishers.

Jones, A. ([1980] 2009) *Women Who Kill*. New York: The Feminist Press.

Jones, G. (2003) "The 1960s and 1970s Boom in Women's Writing." In *The Columbia Companion to Modern East Asian Literature*, ed. J. Mostow, 221–9. New York: Columbia University Press.

Jones, T. (1985) "Mother Who Killed Children Trapped in Culture Conflict." *The Evening News* 1985, Oct 21, p. 8C. Retrieved from https://news.google.com/newspapers?nid=1982&dat=19851021&id=eZJGAAAAIBAJ&sjid=nzMNAAAAIBAJ&pg=1432,1981325&hl=en

K., K. (1973) "Kogoroshi no oya to shōgaisha to no deai." In Mizoguchi A., Saeki Y. and Miki S., eds. (1994), 363–4.

Kan, H. (1987) "The Significance of the U.S.-Japan Security System to the United States: A Japanese Perspective." *Peace & Change* 12(3–4), 11–28.

Kanō, M., ed. (2003) *Ribu to iu "kakumei": gendai no yami wo hiraku*. Tokyo: Inpakuto Shuppankai

Kato, M. (2009) *Women's Rights? The Politics of Eugenic Abortion in Modern Japan*. Amsterdam: Amsterdam University Press.

Kato, S. (1983) *The History of Japanese Literature*, Vol. 2. London: Macmillan.

Kawanishi, Y. (1990) "Japanese Mother-Child Suicide: The Psychological and Sociological Implications of the *Kimura* Case." *UCLA Pacific Basin Law Journal* 8, 32–46.

Kearney, R. (2006) "Introduction: Ricoeur's Philosophy of Translation." In P. Ricoeur ([2006] 2008), vii–xx.

Kersten, R. (1996) *Democracy in Postwar Japan: Maruyama Masao and the Search for Autonomy*. London and New York: Routledge.

Kersten, R. (2009) "The Intellectual Culture of Postwar Japan and the 1968–1969 University of Tokyo Struggles: Repositioning the Self in Postwar Thought." *Social Science Japan Journal* 12(2), 227–45.

Kim, N.S. (1997) "The Cultural Defence and the Problem of Cultural Preemption: A Framework for Analysis." *New Mexico Law Review* 27(1), 101–39.

Kobayashi, F. (1999) "Killing Motherhood as Institution and Reclaiming Motherhood as Experience: Japanese Women Writers, 1970s–90s." In *Transnational Asia Pacific. Gender, Culture, and the Public Sphere*, eds. S.G. Lim, L.E. Smith, and W. Dissanayake, 134–44. Urbana: University of Illinois Press.

"Kogoroshi: Shiryō. ...san e tayori shita watashi kara." (1971). In Ribu Shinjuku Sentā Shiryō Hozon Kai, ed. (2008a), 310.

Kōno, T. ([1961] 1996) "Toddler-Hunting." Translated by Lucy North in Kōno Taeko (1996), *Toddler-Hunting & Other Stories*, 45–68. New York: New Directions.

Kōno, T. ([1964] 1996) "Ants Swarm." Translated by Lucy North in Kōno Taeko (1996), *Toddler-Hunting & Other Stories*, 166–84. New York: New Directions.

Kouno, A. (1995) "Child Abuse and Neglect in Japan: Coin-Operated-Locker Babies." *Child Abuse & Neglect* 19(1), 25–31.

Kristeva, J. (1982) *Powers of Horror: An Essay on Abjection*. New York: Columbia University Press.

Kurisu, E. (1974) "Kodomo no yōiku ni kan suru shakai byōriteki kōsatsu." *Jurisuto* 577.

Lai, M.Y. (2008) *Nativism and Modernity: Cultural Contestations in China and Taiwan under Global Capitalism*. Albany, NY: State University of New York Press.

Lang, L.J. (2005) "To Love the Babe That Milks Me: Infanticide and Reconceiving the Mother."*Columbia Journal of Gender and Law* 14(2), 114–41.

Lazarre, J. ([1976] 1997) *The Mother Knot*. Durham and London: Duke University Press.

Lebra, T.S. (1976) *Japanese Patterns of Behavior*. Honolulu: University of Hawai'i Press.

Lee, J.B. (1985) *The Political Character of the Japanese Press*. Seoul: Seoul National University Press.

Lin, C. (1997) "Finding a Language: Feminism and Women's Movements in Contemporary China." In *Transitions, Environments, Translations: Feminisms in International Politics*, eds. J.W. Scott, C. Kaplan, and D. Keates, 11–20. New York: Routledge.

Liu, L.H. (1999) "The Question of Meaning-Value in the Political Economy of the Sign." In *Tokens of Exchange: The Problem of Translation in Global Circulations*, ed. L.H. Liu, 13–41. Durham, NC: Duke University Press.

Loftus, R.P. (2013) *Changing Lives: The "Postwar" in Japanese Women's Autobiographies and Memoirs*. Ann Arbor, MI: Association for Asian Studies, Inc.

Lowy, D. (2004) "Love and Marriage: Ellen Key and Hiratsuka Raichō Explore Alternatives." *Women's Studies* 33(4), 361–80.

Lowy, D. (2007) *The Japanese "New Woman": Images of Gender and Modernity*. New Brunswick, NJ: Rutgers University Press.

Lule, J. (2001) *Daily News, Eternal Stories: The Mythological Role of Journalism*. New York and London: Guilford.

Mackie, V. (1992) "Feminism and the Media in Japan." *Japanese Studies* 12(2), 23–31.

Mackie, V. (2003) *Feminism in Modern Japan. Citizenship, Embodiment and Sexuality*. Cambridge: Cambridge University Press.

Mackie, V. (2016) "From Hiroshima to Lausanne: The World Congress of Mothers and the Hahaoya Taikai in the 1950s." *Women's History Review*. Available online at: http://www.tandfonline.com/doi/pdf/10.1080/0961202 5.2015.1114317. Last accessed 21 May 2016.

Marotti, W. (2009) "Japan 1968: The Performance of Violence and the Theatre of Protest." *The American Historical Review* 114(1), 97–135.

Marvin, S.E. (2010) *Heaven Has a Face, So Does Hell: The Art of the Noh Mask*, 2 Vol. Warren, CT: Floating World Editions.

Matsui, M. (1990) "Evolution of the Feminist Movement in Japan." *NWSA Journal* 2(3), 435–49.

Matsumoto, A. (1995) "A Place for Consideration of Culture in the American Criminal Justice System: Japanese Law and the Kimura Case." *Journal of International Law and Practice* 4, 507–38.

Mauriac, F. ([1927] 2012) *Thérèse Desqueyroux*. Paris: Librairie Générale Française.

McCombs, M. (2005) "A Look at Agenda-Setting: Past, Present and Future." *Journalism Studies* 6(4), 543–57.

Metropolitan (1971) "8-1 wansaka tōron shūkai ni atsumare!" In Mizoguchi A., Saeki Y. and Miki S. eds. (1992), 165.

Meyer, C.L., and Oberman M. (2001) *Mothers Who Kill Their Children: Understanding the Acts of Moms from Susan Smith to the "Prom Mom"*. New York: New York University Press.

Mitsutani, M. (1986) "Reinassance in Women's Literature." *Japan Quarterly* 33(3), 313–19.

Miyoshi, M., and H.D. Harootunian, eds. (2002) *Learning Places: The Afterlives of Area Studies*. Durham, NC: Duke University Press.

Mizoguchi, A. et al. (1971) "Ūman ribu wo arainaosu." *Asahi Jānaru*, June 25, 1971: 4–28.

Mizoguchi, A., Y. Saeki, and S. Miki, eds. (1992) *Shiryō nihon ūman ribu shi*, Vol. 1. Kyoto: Shōkadō.
Mizoguchi, A., Y. Saeki, and S. Miki, eds. (1994) *Shiryō nihon ūman ribu shi*, Vol. 2. Kyoto: Shōkadō.
Mizoguchi, A., Saeki Y. and Miki S., eds. (1995) *Shiryō nihon ūman ribu shi*, Vol. 3. Kyoto: Shōkadō.
Mizuta, N. (1995) "Women's Self-Representation and Transformation of the Body." *Josai International Review* 3, 85–102
Mohanty, C. (1988) "Under Western Eyes: Feminist Scholarship and Colonial Discourse." *Feminist Review* 30, 61–88.
Mohanty, C. (2003) "'Under Western Eyes' Revisited: Feminist Solidarity through Anticapitalist Struggles." *Signs* 28(2), 499–535.
Moraga, C., and G. Anzaldúa (eds.) (1981) *This Bridge Called My Back: Writings by Radical Women of Color*. Albany: Kitchen Table Press.
Mori, M.T. (1994) "The Subversive Role of Fantasy in the Fiction of Takahashi Takako." *Journal of the Association of Teachers of Japanese* 28(1), 29–56.
Mori, M.T. (1996) "The Quest for *Jouissance* in Takahashi Takako's Texts." In P.G. Schalow and J.A. Walker, eds. (1996), 205–35.
Mori, M.T. (2000) "The Liminal Male as Liberatory Figure in Japanese Women's Fiction." *Harvard Journal of Asiatic Studies* 60(2), 537–94.
Mori, M.T. (2004) "Introduction." In *Lonely Woman*, Takahashi, Translated by Maryellen T. Mori, ix–xl. New York: Columbia University Press.
Morrissey, B. (2003) *When Women Kill: Questions of Agency and Subjectivity*. London: Routledge.
Motz, A. (2001) *The Psychology of Female Violence: Crimes against the Body*. East Sussex: Brunner-Routledge
Muto, I. (1997) "The Birth of the Women's Liberation Movement in the 1970s." In *The Other Japan: Conflict, Compromise and Resistance since 1945*, ed. J. Moore, 147–71. Armonk, NY: M.E.Sharpe.
Nakagawa, G. (1993) "Deformed Subjects, Docile Bodies: Disciplinary Practices and Subject-constitution in Stories of Japanese-American Internment." In *Narrative and Social Control: Critical Perspectives*, ed. D.K. Mumby, 143–63. Newbury Park, CA and London: Sage.
Nakayama, K. ([1986] 2006) "The Subject of Women's Literature and the Transformation of Its Consciousness." In *Woman Critiqued*, ed. R. Copeland, 145–52. Honolulu: University of Hawai'i Press.
Niikuni Wilson, M. (1996) "Becoming, or (Un)Becoming: The Female Destiny Reconsidered in Ōba Minako's Narratives." In P.G. Schalow and J.A. Walker, eds. (1996), 293–326.

Niimi, M. (1974) "Kono sakebi wo ba kike! Kogoroshi onna wa watashi deari, anata da." In Ribu Shinjuku Sentā Shiryō Hozon Kai, ed. (2008c), 139.

Ning, W., and S. Yifeng, eds. (2008) *Translation, Globalisation and Localisation: A Chinese Perspective*. Clevedon, UK and Buffalo, NY: Multilingual Matters.

Nishikawa, Y. (1999) "The Modern Family and Changing Forms of Dwellings in Japan: Male-Centered Houses, Female-Centered Houses, and Gender-Neutral Rooms." In *Gender and Japanese History: The Self and Expression, Work and Life*, Vol. 2, eds. H. Wakita, A. Bouchy, and C. Ueno, 477–507. Osaka: Osaka University Press.

Nishimura, M. (2006) *Onnatachi no kyōdōtai*. Tokyo: Shakai Hyōronsha.

Nolte, S.H., and S.A. Hastings (1991) "The Meiji State's Policy toward Women, 1890–1910." In *Recreating Japanese Women, 1600–1945*, ed. G.L. Bernstein, 151–74. Berkeley: University of California Press.

Norgren, T. (2001) *Abortion before Birth Control: The Politics of Reproduction in Postwar Japan*. Princeton, NJ: Princeton University Press.

Nori (1972) "Koumi kikai = kyōsei boteki jōkyō wo toppa seyo!" In Mizoguchi A., Saeki Y. and Miki S., eds. (1994), 16–17.

Oakley, A. (1979) *Becoming a Mother*. Oxford: Martin Robertson.

Ōba, M. ([1968] 1982) "The Three Crabs." Translated by Yukiko Tanaka and Elisabeth Hanson in *This Kind of Woman. Ten Stories by Japanese Women Writers 1960–1976*, eds. Y. Tanaka and E. Hanson, 87–113. New York: Perigee Books.

Ōba, M. (1970) *Funakui mushi*. Tokyo: Kōdansha.

Ōba, M. (1971) *Tsuga no yume*. Tokyo: Bunshun bunko.

Ōba, M. ([1976] 1991) "The Smile of a Mountain Witch." Translated by Noriko Mizuta Lippit in *Japanese Women Writers. Twentieth Century Short Fiction*, trans. and eds. N. Mizuta Lippit and K. Iriye Selden, 194–206. Armonk, NY: M.E. Sharpe.

Ōba, M., and T. Takahashi (1979) *Taidan—Sei to shite no onna*. Tokyo: Kōdansha.

Oberman, M., and C.L. Meyer (2008) *When Mothers Kill: Interviews from Prison*. New York: New York University Press.

Ochiai, E. (1997) *The Japanese Family System in Transition: A Sociological Analysis of Family Change in Postwar Japan*. Tokyo: International Library Foundation.

Ochiai, E. (2005) "The Postwar Japanese Family System in Global Perspective: Familism, Low Fertility, and Gender Roles." *U.S.-Japan Women's Journal* 29, 3–36.

Ogino, M. (1994) "Abortion and Women's Reproductive Rights: The State of Japanese Women, 1945–1991." In *Women of Japan and Korea: Continuity and Change*, eds. J. Gelb and M. Lief Palley, 69–94. Philadelphia: Temple University Press.

Ōgawara, M. (1973) "'Ikigurushii otoko no atsumari' annai." In Mizoguchi A., Saeki Y. and Miki S., eds. (1994), 381.

Ōgoshi, A. ([1996] 2005) *Feminizumu nyūmon*. Tokyo: Chikuma Shobō.

Ohinata, M. (1995) "The Mystique of Motherhood: A Key to Understanding Social Change and Family Problems in Japan." In Fujimura-Fanselow and Kameda, eds. (1995), 199–211.

Ohinata, M. (2000) *Boseiai no shinwa no wana*. Tokyo: Nihon Hyōronsha.

Oliver, K. (1993) *Reading Kristeva: Unraveling the Double-bind*. Bloomington and Indianapolis: Indiana University Press.

Onnatachi no ima wo tou kai, ed. (1996) *Zenkyōtō kara ribu e*. Tokyo: Inpakuto Shuppankai.

Orbaugh, S. (1996) "The Body in Contemporary Japanese Women's Fiction." In P.G. Schalow and J.A. Walker, eds. (1996), 119–64.

Orbaugh, S. (1999) "Arguing with the Real: Kanai Mieko." In *Ōe and Beyond: Fiction in Contemporary Japan*, eds. S. Snyder and P. Gabriel, 245–77. Honolulu: University of Hawai'i Press.

Orbaugh, S. (2002) "The Construction of Gendered Discourse in the Modern Study of Japanese Literature." In *Across Time and Genre: Reading and Writing Women's Texts*, eds. J. Brown and S. Arntzen, 1–9. Conference Proceedings. University of Alberta.

Orbaugh, S. (2003) "Gender, Family, and Sexualities in Modern Literature." In *The Columbia Companion to Modern East Asia Literature*, ed. J. Mostow, 43–51. New York: Columbia University Press.

O'Reilly, A., ed. (2004) *From Motherhood to Mothering: The Legacy of Adrienne Rich's of Woman Born*. Albany: State University of New York Press.

Orpett Long, S. (1996) "Nurturing and Femininity: The Ideal of Caregiving in Postwar Japan." In *Re-Imagining Japanese Women*, ed. A.E. Imamura, 156–176. Berkeley: University of California Press.

Paker, S. (2002) "Translation as *Terceme* and *Nazire*. Culture-bound Concepts and Their Implications for a Conceptual Framework for Research on Ottoman Translation History." In *Crosscultural Transgressions. Research Models in Translation Studies II: Historical and Ideological Issues*, ed. T. Hermans, 120–43. London and New York: Routledge.

Papastergiadis, N. (2000) *The Turbulence of Migration: Globalization, Deterritorialization and Hybridity*. Malden, MA: Polity Press.

Parker, R. ([1995] 2010) *Torn in Two: The Experience of Maternal Ambivalence*. London: Virago.

Paul, C., and J.J. Kim (2004) *Reporters on the Battlefield: The Embedded Press System in Historical Context*. Santa Monica, CA: Rand Corporation.
Polezzi L. (2006) "Translation, Travel, Migration." *The Translator* 12(2), 169–88.
Polezzi, L. (2012) "Translation and Migration." *Translation Studies* 5(3), 345–56.
Ponzanesi, S. (2015) "Translating Selves: On Polyglot Cosmopolitanism." In *The Subject of Rosi Braidotti: Politics and Concepts*, eds. B. Blaagaard and I. van der Tuin, 190–7. London: Bloomsbury Academic.
Pound, L. (1985) "Mother's Tragic Crime Exposes a Culture Gap." *Chicago Tribune*. Retrieved from http://articles.chicagotribune.com/1985-06-10/features/8502060678_1_first-degree-murder-suicide-fumiko-kimura
Pounds, W. (1990) "Enchi Fumiko and the Hidden Energy of the Supernatural." *The Journal of the Association of Teachers of Japanese* 24(2), 167–83.
Reader, I. (1998) "Review: Studies of Japan, Area Studies, and the Challenges of Social Theory." *Monumenta Nipponica* 53(2), 237–55.
Reddy, S. (2002) "Temporarily Insane: Pathologising Cultural Difference in American Criminal Courts." *Sociology of Health and Illness* 24(5), 667–87.
Reich, P.C., and A. Fukuda, eds. (1976) "Japan's Literary Feminists: The 'Seitō' Group." *Signs* 2(1), 280–91.
Reider, N.T. (2005) "*Yamauba*: Representation of the Japanese Mountain Witch in the Muromachi and Edo Periods." *International Journal of Asian Studies* 2(2), 239–64.
Ribu Gasshuku Jikkō I'inkai (1971) "Ribu gasshuku wa naze gasshuku ka." In Mizoguchi A., Saeki Y. and Miki S., eds. (1992), 319–23.
Ribu Shinjuku Sentā (1973) "Kogoroshi onna wa anata da… Asahi shinbun ni kōgi shiyō!" In Mizoguchi A., Saeki Y. and Miki S., eds. (1994), 68–9.
Ribu Shinjuku Sentā (1974) "Kogoroshi onna wa sochi nyūin?! Hoan shobun no sakidori wo yurusu na." In Ribu Shinjuku Sentā Shiryō Hozon Kai, ed. (2008c), 139.
Ribu Shinjuku Sentā Shiryō Hozon Kai, ed. (2008a) *Ribu Shinjuku Sentā shiryō shūsei—bira hen*. Tokyo: Inpakuto Shuppankai.
Ribu Shinjuku Sentā Shiryō Hozon Kai, ed. (2008b) *Ribu Shinjuku Sentā shiryō shūsei—panfuretto hen*. Tokyo: Inpakuto Shuppankai.
Ribu Shinjuku Sentā Shiryō Hozon Kai, ed. (2008c) *Ribu nyūsu, kono michi hitosuji. Ribu Shinjuku Sentā shiryō shūsei*. Tokyo: Inpakuto Shuppankai.
Rich, A. ([1976] 1979) *Of Woman Born: Motherhood as Experience and Institution*. London: Virago Press.

Rich, A. ([1978] 1980) "Disloyal to Civilization: Feminism, Racism, Gynophobia." In *On Lies, Secrets and Silence. Selected Prose 1966–1978*, ed. A. Rich, 275–310. London: Virago Press.

Rich, A. ([1984] 1986) "Notes toward a Politics of Location (1984)." In *Blood, Bread, & Poetry: Selected Prose, 1979–1985*, A. Rich, 210–231. London: Virago Press.

Ricoeur, P. ([2006] 2008) *On Translation*. London and New York: Routledge.

Robins-Mowry, D. (1983) *The Hidden Sun: Women of Modern Japan*. Boulder, CO: Westview Press.

Ronald, R. (2007) "The Japanese Home in Transition." In *Housing and Social Transition in Japan*, eds. Y. Hirayama and R. Ronald, 165–92. New York: Routledge.

Ruch, B. (1994) "Beyond Absolution: Enchi Fumiko's *The Waiting Years* and *Masks*." In *Masterworks of Asian Literature in Comparative Perspective: A Guide for Teaching*, ed. B. Stoler Miller, 439–56. Armonk, NY: M.E. Sharpe.

Said, E. (2005) "The Public Role of Writers and Intellectuals." In *Nation, Language, and the Ethics of Translation*, eds. S. Bermann and M. Wood, 15–29. Princeton, NJ: Princeton University Press.

Sakai, N. (1997) *Translation and Subjectivity: On "Japan" and Cultural Nationalism*. Minneapolis and London: University of Minnesota Press.

Sakai, N. (2001) "'You Asians:' On the Historical Role of the West and Asia Binary." *South Atlantic Quarterly* 99(4), 789–817.

Sakai, N. (2005) "The West—A Dialogic Prescription or Proscription?", *Social Identities: Journal for the Study of Race Nation and Culture* 11(3), 177–95.

Sakai, N. (2009) "Dislocation in Translation." *TTR: Traduction, Terminologie, Redaction* 22(1), 167–87.

Sakai, N. (2010) "From Area Studies toward Transnational Studies." *Inter-Asia Cultural Studies* 11(2), 265–74.

Sakai, N. (2014) "The Figure of Translation: Translation as a Filter?" In *European-East Asian Borders in Translation*, eds. J.C.H. Liu and N. Vaughan-Williams, 12–37. London and New York: Routledge.

Sakai, N., and H.D. Harootunian (1999) "Japan Studies and Cultural Studies." *Positions* 7(2), 593–647.

Sakamoto, K. (1999) "Reading Japanese Women's Magazines: The Construction of New Identities in the 1970s and 1980s." *Media, Culture and Society* 21(2), 173–93.

Sakane, Y. (1998) "The Mother, the Self and the Other: The Search for Identity in Sylvia Plath's *The Bell's Jar* and Takahashi Takako's *Congruent Figures*." *U.S.-Japan Women's Journal* 14, 27–48.

Sakurada, D. (1997) "For Mutual Benefit: The Japan-US Security Treaty: From a Japanese Perspective." Centre for Strategic Studies Working Paper 07, accessed 05/06/2013. http://www.victoria.ac.nz/hppi/centres/strategic-studies/publications/working-papers/WP07.pdf

Sams, J.P. (1986) "The Availability of the 'Cultural Defense' as an Excuse for Criminal Behavior." *Georgia Journal of International and Comparative Law* 16(2), 335–54.

Sapporo Komu-unu (1974) "Kogoroshi no shakai haikei wo mushi shite hōdō suru――Otoko to masukomi no konsensu ni wa hara ga tatsu no desu." In Mizoguchi A., Saeki Y. and Miki S., eds. (1994), 24–5.

Sasaki-Uemura, W. (2001) *Organizing the Spontaneous: Citizens Protest in Postwar Japan*. Honolulu: University of Hawai'i Press.

Sasaki-Uemura, W. (2007) "Postwar Japanese Society." In *A Companion to Japanese History*, ed. W.M. Tsutsui, 315–32. Malden, MA: Blackwell.

Sasaki, Y., ed. (1980) *Nihon no kogoroshi no kenkyū*. Tokyo: Kōbundō Shuppansha.

Satō, B. (2010) *Ūman ribu ga yatte kita—70 nendai, mezame-hajimeta otokotachi*. Tokyo: Inpakuto Shuppankai.

Sayama S., and F. Aida (1972) "Tegami to bira de tsudzuru ribu――kono ni nen." In Ribu Shinjuku Sentā Shiryō Hozon Kai, ed. (2008c), 4–5.

Sayama, S. et al., (1973) "Kogoroshi shiryō-shū 1: kogoroshi kōhan kiroku." In Ribu Shinjuku Sentā Shiryō Hozon Kai, ed. (2008b), 190–222.

Schalow, P.G., and J.A. Walker, eds. (1996) *The Woman's Hand: Gender and Theory in Japanese Women's Writing*. Stanford, CA: Stanford University Press.

Scheufele, D.A., and D. Tewksbury (2007) "Framing, Agenda Setting, and Priming: The Evolution of Three Media Effects Models." *Journal of Communication* 57(1), 9–20.

Seal, L. (2010) *Women, Murder and Femininity: Gender Representations of Women Who Kill*. Basingstoke: Palgrave Macmillan.

Shigematsu, S. (2012) *Scream from the Shadow: The Women's Liberation Movement in Japan*. Minneapolis, MN: University of Minnesota Press.

Shih, S.M. (2002) "Towards an Ethics of Transnational Encounter, or 'When' Does a 'Chinese' Woman Become a 'Feminist'?" *Differences* 13(2), 90–126.

Shisō Shūdan Esuīekkusu (1971) "3-11 shūkai tōron shiryō." In Mizoguchi A., Saeki Y. and Miki S., eds. (1992), 176–7.

Shisō Shūdan Esuīekkusu and Tora (1972) "Appīru." In Mizoguchi A., Saeki Y. and Miki S., eds. (1992), 185–6.

Shohat, E. (2002) "Area Studies, Gender Studies, and the Cartographies of Knowledge." *Social Text* 20(3), 67–78.

Shohat, E., and R. Stam (2014) *Unthinking Eurocentrism: Multiculturalism and the Media*. Second ed. London and New York: Routledge.

Sievers, S.L. (1983) *Flowers in Salt: The Beginning of Feminist Consciousness in Modern Japan*. Stanford, CA: Stanford University Press.

Snell-Hornby, M. (2007) "'What's in a Name?': On Metalinguistic Confusion in Translation Studies." *Target* 19(2), 313–25.

Spivak, G.C. ([1987] 2012) "Who Claims Alterity?" In *An Aesthetic Education in the Era of Globalization*, G.C. Spivak, 57–72. Cambridge, MA: Harvard University Press.

Spivak, G.C. (1988) "Can the Subaltern Speak?" In *Marxism and Interpretation of Culture*, eds. C. Nelson and L. Grossberg, 271–313. Chicago: University of Illinois Press.

Spivak, G.C. (1993) "The Politics of Translation." In *Outside of the Teaching Machine*, G.C. Spivak, 179–200. New York: Routledge.

Spivak, G.C. (2012) "Translating into English." In *An Aesthetic Education in the Era of Globalization*, G.C. Spivak, 256–74. Cambridge, MA: Harvard University Press.

Stangle, H.L. (2008) "*Murderous Madonna*: Femininity, Violence, and the Myth of Postpartum Mental Disorder in Cases of Maternal Infanticide and Filicide." *William and Mary Law Review* 50(2), 699–734.

Steinhoff, P.G. (1984) "Student Conflict." In *Conflict in Japan*, eds. E.S. Krauss, T.P. Rohlen, and P.G. Steinhoff, 174–213. Honolulu: University of Hawai'i Press.

Stephens, L.F. (2005) "News Narratives about Nano S&T in Major U.S. and Non-U.S. Newspapers." *Science Communication* 27(2), 175–99.

Stewart, R.W. (1985a) "Accused Mother Preoccupied by Death: Friend of Woman Whose Children Drowned Testifies at Hearing." *Los Angeles Times*. Retrieved from http://articles.latimes.com/1985-03-29/local/me-20453_1_death-penalty

Stewart, R. W. (1985b) "Probation Given to Mother in Drowning of Her Two Children." *Los Angeles Times*. Retrieved from http://articles.latimes.com/1985-11-22/local/me-1070_1_probation-report

Suga (1971) "Onna no kogoroshi was nani wo tou ka." In Ribu Shinjuku Sentā Shiryō Hozon Kai, ed. (2008a), 310–11.

Swerdlow, A. (1993) *Women Strike for Peace: Traditional Motherhood and Radical Politics in the 1960s*. Chicago and London: The University of Chicago Press.

Szanton, D., ed. (2004) *The Politics of Knowledge: Area Studies and the Disciplines.* Berkeley, Los Angeles, and London: University of California Press.
Takahashi, T. (1969) "Kodomosama." *Gunzō* 7, 54–71.
Takahashi, T. (1970) "Byōbō." *Bungakukai* 11, 134–60.
Takahashi, T. (1971a) "Kanata no mizuoto." *Gunzō* 4, 44–82.
Takahashi, T. ([1971b] 1978) *Kanata no mizuoto.* Tokyo: Kōdansha.
Takahashi, T. "Sōjikei." In Takahashi T. (1971b) 5–48.
Takahashi, T. "Byōbō." In Takahashi T. (1971b), 99–146.
Takahashi, T. "Kodomosama." In Takahashi T. (1971b), 147–77.
Takahashi, T. "Kanata no mizuoto." In Takahashi T. (1971b), 179–244.
Takahashi, T. (1972) *Hone no shiro.* Kyoto: Jinbun Shoin.
Takahashi, T. "Keshin." In Takahashi T. (1972), 33-55.
Takahashi, T. "Byakuya." In Takahashi T. (1972), 57-79.
Takahashi, T. "Me." In Takahashi T. (1972), 81–101.
Takahashi, T. (1973a) "Natsu no fuchi." *Bungakukai* 11, 96–121.
Takahashi, T. (1973b) *Sora no hate made.* Tokyo: Shinchōsha.
Takahashi, T. (1974) *Ushinawareta e.* Tokyo: Kawade Shobō Shinsha.
Takahashi, T. (1975) *Tamashii no inu.* Tokyo: Kōdansha.
Takahashi, T. "Satsui no bungaku." In Takahashi T. (1975), 13–6.
Takahashi, T. "Dopperugengeru-kō." In Takahashi T. (1975), 33–55.
Takahashi, T. "Otoko no naka no tada hitori." In Takahashi T. (1975), 207–11.
Takahashi, T. "Unmei no wakareme." In Takahashi T. (1975), 212–14.
Takahashi, T. "Onna-girai." In Takahashi T. (1975), 229–32.
Takahashi, T. "Umu umanu no jiyū." In Takahashi T. (1975), 254–5.
Takahashi, T. (1976) *Yūwakusha.* Tokyo: Kōdansha.
Takahashi, T. (1977a) *Takahashi Kazumi no omoide.* Tokyo: Kōsōsha.
Takahashi, T. "'Hi no utsuwa' jushō zengo." In Takahashi T. (1977a), 77–84.
Takahashi, T. "Takahashi Kazumi to sakka to shite no watashi." In Takahashi T. (1977a), 91–8.
Takahashi, T. (1977b) *Kioku no kurasa.* Kyoto: Jinbun Shoin.
Takahashi, T. "Senzai sekai e no gyakkō." In Takahashi T. (1977b), 29–33.
Takahashi, T. "Senzai ishiki no kōkei." In Takahashi T. (1977b), 81–5.
Takahashi, T. "Sei—onna ni okeru mashō to bosei." In Takahashi T. (1977b), 86–99.
Takahashi, T. "Ibu to Maria." In Takahashi T. (1977b), 110–14.
Takahashi, T. "Danjo kyōgaku." In Takahashi T. (1977b), 158–60.
Takahashi, T. "Watashi no donkansa." In Takahashi T. (1977b), 170–3.
Takahashi, T. "Karumeru-kai shudōin." In Takahashi (1977b), 174–8.

Takahashi, T. ([1977c] 1988) *Ronrii ūman*. Tokyo: Shūeisha. Translated by Maryellen T. Mori as *Lonely Woman* (2004). New York: Columbia University Press.
Takahashi, T. (1980) *Odoroita hana*. Kyoto: Jinbun Shoin.
Takahashi, T. "Shōsetsu wo kaku kekka." In Takahashi T. (1980), 35–8.
Takahashi, T. "Muishiki wo horu." In Takahashi T. (1980), 94–8.
Takahashi, T. (1984) "Kou." *Shinchō* 1, 152–75.
Takahashi, T. (1985) *Ikari no ko*. Tokyo: Kōdansha.
Takahashi, T. (1991) "Congruent Figures." Translated by Noriko Mizuta Lippit in *Japanese Women Writers: Twentieth Century Short Fiction*, eds. N. Mizuta Lippit and K. Iriye Selden, 168–193. Armonk, NY: M.E. Sharpe.
Takahashi, T. (1997a) *Takahashi Kazumi to iu hito. Nijūgonen no nochi ni*. Tokyo: Kawade Shobō Shinsha.
Takahashi, T. (1997b) *Sakai ni nite*. Tokyo: Kōdansha.
Takahashi, T. "Watashi no noirōze no koto." In Takahashi (1997b), 122–9.
Takahashi, T. "Shakaiteki atsuryoku unnun no koto." In Takahashi (1997b), 130–2.
Takahashi, T. (2003) *Kirei na hito*. Tokyo: Kōdansha.
Takahashi Y., and D. Berger (1996) "Cultural Dynamics and Suicide in Japan." In *Suicide and the Unconscious*, eds. A. Leenaars and D. Lester, 248–258. Northvale: Jason Aronson.
Take (1971) "Kogoroshi: Shiryō. …san e tayori shita watashi kara." In Ribu Shinjuku Sentā Shiryō Hozon Kai, ed. (2008a), 307–9.
Tama, Y. (1994) "The Logic of Abortion: Japanese Debates on the Legitimacy of Abortion as Seen in Post-World War II Newspapers." *U.S.-Japan Women's Journal* 7, 3–30.
Tama, Y. ([2001] 2008) *Boseiai to iu seido. Kogoroshi to chūzetsu no poritikusu*, Tokyo: Keisō Shobō.
Tanaka, K. (1995) "The New Feminist Movement in Japan, 1970–1990." In Fujimura-Fanselow and Kameda, eds. (1995), 343–52.
Tanaka, M. (1970) "Benjo kara no kaihō." In Mizoguchi A., Saeki Y. and Miki S., eds. (1992), 201–7.
Tanaka, M. ([1972] 2010) *Inochi no onnatachi e—Torimidashi ūman ribu-ron*. Tokyo: Pandora Gendai Shokan.
Tanaka, M. (1972) "Aete teiki suru = chūzetsu wa kitoku no kenri ka?" In Mizoguchi A., Saeki Y. and Miki S., eds. (1994), 61–4.
Tanaka, M. (1973) "Kogoroshi no saiban wo bōchō shite." In Ribu Shinjuku Sentā Shiryō Hozon Kai, ed. (2008c), 31.

Tanhan, D.A. (2014) *The Japanese Family: Touch, Intimacy and Feeling*. London and New York: Routledge.
Tansman, A. (2004) "Japanese Studies: The Intangible Act of Translation." In *The Politics of Knowledge: Area Studies and the Disciplines*, ed. D. Szanton, 184–216. Berkeley, Los Angeles, and London: University of California Press.
Tipton, E.K. ([2002] 2008) *Modern Japan: A Social and Political History*. New York: Routledge.
Tipton, E.K. (2009) "How to Manage a Household: Creating Middle Class Housewives in Modern Japan." *Japanese Studies* 29(1), 95–110.
Tokyo Komu-unu (1974) "Tokyo komu-unu ga bebī kā mondai wo tsuku." In Ribu Shinjuku Sentā Shiryō Hozon Kai, ed. (2008b), 317–341.
Tokyo Komu-unu (1975) "Seikatsu shashin-shū: 'Tokyo komu-unu' no kodomotachi." In Ribu Shinjuku Sentā Shiryō Hozon Kai, ed. (2008b), 370–402.
Tomida, H. (2004) *Hiratsuka Raichō and Early Japanese Feminism*. Boston: Brill.
Trivedi, H. (2005) "Translating Culture vs Cultural Translation." In *In Translation – Reflections, Refractions, Transformations*, eds. P. St-Pierre and P.C. Kar, 277–88. Amsterdam and Philadelphia: John Benjamins.
Tsurumi, Y. (1969) "Beheiren." *Japan Quarterly* 16(4), 444–48.
Tucker, L.R. (1998) "The Framing of Calvin Klein: A Frame Analysis of Media Discourse about the August 1995 Calvin Klein Jeans Advertising Campaign." *Critical Studies in Mass Communication* 15(2), 141–157.
Tuosto, K. (2008) "The 'Grunt Truth' of Embedded Journalism: The New Media/Military Relationship." *Stanford Journal of International Relations* 10(1), 20–31.
Tyler, I. (2008) "Why the Maternal Now?" Published by the Department of Sociology, Lancaster University, Lancaster, UK at http://www.lancs.ac.uk/fass/sociology/papers/whythematernal.pdf
Tyler, I. (2009) "Against Abjection." *Feminist Theory* 10(1), 77–98.
Tyler, I. (2013) *Revolting Subjects: Social Abjection and Resistance in Neoliberal Britain*. London and New York: Zed Books.
Tymoczko, M. (2006) "Reconceptualizing Western Translation Theory: Integrating Non-Western Thought about Translation." In *Translating Others*, Vol. II, ed. T. Hermans, 13–32. Manchester: St, Jerome.
Ueno, C. (1988) "The Japanese Women's Movement: The Counter-Values to Industrialism." In *The Japanese Trajectory: Modernization and Beyond*, eds. G. McCormack and Y. Sugimoto, 167–85. Cambridge: Cambridge University Press.

Ueno, C. (2011) "Nihon no ribu. Sono shisō to haikei." In *Nihon no feminizumu*, Vol. 1, eds. M. Amano et al., 1–52. Tokyo: Iwanami Shoten.
Uno, K.S. (1991) "Women and Changes in the Household Division of Labor." In *Recreating Japanese Women, 1600–1945*, ed. G.L. Bernstein, 17–41. Berkeley: University of California Press.
Uno, K.S. (1993) "The Death of 'Good Wife, Wise Mother'?" In *Postwar Japan as History*, ed. A. Gordon, 293–322. Berkeley: University of California Press.
Uno, K.S. (1999) *Passages to Modernity. Motherhood, Childhood, and Social Reform in Early Twentieth Century Japan*. Honolulu: University of Hawai'i Press.
Urawa, K. et al. (1975) 'Iwatsuki no "kogoroshi no jiken" ni yosete' in Mizoguchi A., Saeki Y. and Miki S., eds. (1995), 34–36.
Vatanabadi, S. (2009) "Translating the Transnational: Teaching the 'Other' in Translation." *Cultural Studies* 23(5–6), 795–809.
Venuti, L. (1986) "The Translator's Invisibility." *Criticism* 28(2), 179–212.
Venuti, L. (1991) "Genealogies of Translation Theory: Schleiermacher." *TTR: traduction, terminologie, redaction* 4(2), 125–50.
Venuti, L. (1995) *The Translator's Invisibility: A History of Translation*. London and New York: Routledge.
Viswanathan, M. (1996) "In Pursuit of the Yamamba: The Question of Female Resistance." In P.G. Schalow and J.A. Walker, eds. (1996) 239–61.
Vogel, S. (1978) "Professional Housewife: the Career of Urban Middle Class Japanese Women." *Japanese Interpreter* 12(1), 17–43.
Wakabayashi, J., and R. Kothari (2009) *Decentering Translation Studies: India and Beyond*. Amsterdam and Philadelphia: John Benjamins Publishing Company.
Wakakuwa, M. ([2000] 2004) *Sensō ga tsukuru joseizō: dainiji sekai taisenka no nihon josei dōin no shikakuteki puropaganda*. Tokyo: Chukuma Shobō.
Warner, M. (2005) *Publics and Counterpublics*. Brooklyn, NY: Zone Books.
Waswo, A. (2002) *Housing in Postwar Japan: A Social History*. London: Routledge Curzon.
Welker, J. (2012) "Translating Women's Liberation, Translating Women's Bodies in 1970s–1980s Japan." *Rim: Journal of the Asian-Pacific Studies Association* 13(2), 28–37.
Welker, J. (2015) "The Revolution Cannot Be Translated: Transfiguring Discourses of Women's Liberation in 1970s–1980s Japan." In *Multiple Translation Communities in Japan*, eds. B. Curran, N. Sato-Rossberg, and K Tanabe, 60–78. New York and London: Routledge.

Welldon, E.V. (1988) *Mother, Madonna, Whore: The Idealization and Denigration of Motherhood*. New York and London: The Guilford Press.
Wetherall, W. (1986) "The Trial of Fumiko Kimura." Retrieved from http://www.yoshabunko.com/suicide/Kimura_trial.html
Whittemore, E.P. (1961) *The Press in Japan Today... A Case Study*. Columbia: University of South Carolina Press.
Wilczynski, A. (1991) "Images of Women Who Kill Their Infants: The Mad and the Bad." *Women & Criminal Justice* 2(2), 71–80.
Wilczynski, A. (1997a) "Mad or Bad? Child killers, Gender and the Courts." *British Journal of Criminology* 37(3), 419–36.
Wilczynski, A. (1997b) *Child Homicide*. London: Greenwich Medical Media.
Wolf, N. (2002) *Misconceptions: Truth, Lies and the Unexpected on the Journey to Motherhood*. London: Vintage.
Yamakado, G. (1975) "Otoko wa te wo yogosanai!" In Mizoguchi A., Saeki Y. and Miki S., eds. (1995), 406.
Yamamoto, R. (2012) "Bridging Crime and Immigration: Minority Signification in Japanese Newspaper Reports of the 2003 Fukuoka Family Murder Case." *Crime, Media, Culture* 9(2), 153–70.
Yamamura, Y. (1986) "The Child in Japanese Society." In *Child Development and Education in Japan*, eds. H. Stevenson, H. Azuma, and K. Hakuta, 28–38. New York: W.H. Freeman and Company.
Yamaori, T. (1997) "The Image of the '*rōjo*' or Elderly Women in Japanese Legend." *Japan Review* 9, 29–40.
Yoda, T. (2000) "The Rise and Fall of Maternal Society: Gender, Labor, and Capital in Contemporary Japan." *The South Atlantic Quarterly* 99(4), 865–902.
Yoshitake, T (2006) *Onnatachi no undōshi—watashi no ikita sengo*. Tokyo: Mineruba Shoten.
Yoshizumi, K. (1995) "Marriage and Family: Past and Present." In Fujimura-Fanselow and Kameda, eds. (1995), 183–97.

Newspaper Articles (in Chronological Order)

"Tsuyoku natta josei, yowaku natta hahaoya." *Asahi shinbun*, 12 April, 1970, p. 5. Morning ed.
"Aomori de mo boshi sannin shinjū." *Yomiuri shinbun*, 15 May, 1970, p. 15. Morning ed.
"Gunma de mo boshi shinjū." *Asahi shinbun*, 5 June, 1970, p. 11. Evening ed.

"Akachan junan no sesō. Kōkai nai 'kekkan hahaoya'." *Yomiuri shinbun*, 18 August, 1970, p. 13. Morning ed.

"Kore ga oya ka. Jisshi wo korosu" *Asahi shinbun*, 4 September, 1970, p. 22. Morning ed.

"Haha ga yōjo nageotosu." *Asahi shinbun*, 4 September, 1970, p. 22. Morning ed.

"Matsudo de wa chichioya ga kōsatsu." *Asahi shinbun*, 4 September, 1970, p. 22. Morning ed.

"Akachan junan jidai." *Asahi shinbun*, 5 September, 1970, p. 17. Morning ed.

"Kogoroshi no keifu." *Asahi shinbun*, 6 September, 1970, p. 5. Morning ed.

"Mata shi no sekkan." *Asahi shinbun*, 13 September, 1970, p. 22. Morning ed.

"Akachan junan itsu made." *Asahi shinbun*, 19 September, 1970, p. 22. Morning ed.

"Akachhan mata junan." *Asahi shinbun*, 22 September, 1970, p. 11. Evening ed.

"Mata akachan-goroshi." *Yomiuri shinbun*, 28 September, 1970, p. 14. Morning ed.

"Ūman ribu—dansei tengoku jōriku." *Asahi shinbun*, 4 October, 1970, p. 24. Morning ed.

"Kawaru yo no naka." *Yomiuri Shinbun*, 10 October, 1970, p. 1. Evening ed.

"Akachan mata junan." *Yomiuri shinbun*, 11 October, 1970, p. 14. Morning ed.

"Mata, hidoi hahaoya." *Yomiuri shinbun*, 17 November, 1970, p. 13. Morning ed.

"Yokohamasen de mo sanninn. Noirōze. Haha ga michizure." *Asahi shinbun*, 17 November, 1970, p. 22. Morning ed.

"'Onna no tsūkaku' wo shuppatsuten ni."*Asahi shinbun*, 17 November, 1970, p. 17. Morning ed.

"Hahaoya… Kono musekinin, mushinkei." *Asahi shinbun*, 19 November, 1970, p. 22. Morning ed.

"Hijō na mama—Mata ni-ken." *Yomiuri Shinbun*, 23 November, 1970, p. 15. Morning ed.

"'Oni-fūfu' ni jikkei hanketsu." *Yomiuri shinbun*, 19 December, 1970, p. 9. Evening ed.

"Wagako no inochi naze ubau." *Asahi shinbun*, 21 December, 1970, p. 18. Morning ed.

"Katei no naka mo ningen fuzai." *Asahi shinbun*, 21 December, 1970, p. 18. Morning ed.

"Akachan gonan." *Asahi shinbun*, 8 February, 1971, p. 9. Evening ed.

"Mata haha ga niji wo korosu." *Asahi shinbun*, 11 February, 1971, p. 18. Morning ed.

"Kore de mo oya ka." *Yomiuri shinbun*, 13 March, 1971, p. 15. Morning ed.
"Nichiyō... Shinjū ya jisatsu aiitsugu." *Asahi shinbun*, 5 April, 1971, p. 22. Morning ed.
"Saishi-goroshi tobikomu." *Asahi shinbun*, 5 April, 1971, p. 22. Morning ed.
"Hokkaidō de mo ko-michizure." *Asahi shinbun*, 5 April, 1971, p. 22. Morning ed.
"Wagako koroshite / Haha, jisatsu hakaru." *Asahi shinbun*, 5 April, 1971, p. 22. Morning ed.
"Adachi de kappuku hakaru." *Asahi shinbun*, 5 April, 1971, p. 22. Morning ed.
"Gasu chūdoku / Yōji shinu / Boshi shinjū ka." *Asahi shinbun*, 5 April, 1971, p. 22. Morning ed.
"Tonai de yōji suishi futari." *Asahi shinbun*, 5 April, 1971, p. 22. Morning ed.
"Zankoku mama, yōji wo kerikorosu." *Yomiuri shinbun*, 11 April, 1971, p. 15. Morning ed.
"Niji to muri shinjū." *Yomiuri shinbun*, 28 May, 1971, p. 11. Evening ed.
"Mujō no haha yo," *Yomiuri shinbun*, 11 January, 1972, p. 3. Evening ed.
"Koredemo haha ka!" *Yomiuri shinbun*, 10 April, 1972, p. 8. Evening ed.
"'Musekinin-mama' sōken."*Asahi shinbun*, 3 June, 1972, p. 8. Evening ed.
"Naze? Kodomo-goroshi aitsugu." *Asahi shinbun*, 4 August, 1972, p. 11. Evening ed.
"Kono kokuhaku na oyatachi." *Asahi shinbun*, 24 August, 1972, p. 11. Morning ed.
"Oni no hosutesu-mama." *Yomiuri shinbun*, 8 September, 1972, p. 15. Morning ed.
"Mugoi haha no satsujin mata." *Asahi shinbun*, 11 October, 1972, p. 23. Morning ed.
"Bosei sōshitsu jidai." *Yomiuri shinbun*, 22 October, 1972, p. 18. Morning ed.
"Mikon no haha mata satsujin." *Asahi shinbun*, 23 October, 1972, p. 23. Morning ed.
"'Tōmei kōsoku' hijō kosute." *Yomiuri shinbun*, 30 October, 1972, p. 15. Morning ed.
"Boshi-ryō de sannin shinjū." *Yomiuri shinbun*, 30 October, 1972, p. 15. Morning ed.
"Haha ni nagerare shinu." *Yomiuri shinbun*, 30 October, 1972, p. 15. Morning ed.
"Tsuma ni sarare shinjū ni-ken." *Yomiuri shinbun*, 14 November, 1972, p. 11. Evening ed.
"Tsuma ni nigerare fushi shinjū hakaru." *Yomiuri shinbun*, 20 February, 1973, p. 11. Evening ed.

"Mata mugoi waga-kogoroshi. Mendō miru iya. Sakuran no haha." *Yomiuri shinbun*, 26 February, 1973, p. 10. Evening ed.
"Oni no haha wa…" *Yomiuri shinbun*, 4 April, 1973, p. 11. Evening ed.
"'Oni no hahaoya' to iu keredo uchiki de noirōze." *Yomiuri shinbun*, 5 April, 1973, p. 16. Morning ed.
"Kosute kogoroshi no sesō." *Yomiuri shinbun*, 10 April, 1973, p. 7. Evening ed.
"Oya-gokoro sōshitsu." *Yomiuri shinbun*, 11 June, 1973, p. 11. Evening ed.
"Tsuma ni sarare muri shinjū." *Asahi shinbun*, 12 June, 1973, p. 11. Evening ed.
"Akisame no naka ni shi ni isogu." *Asahi shinbun*, 6 September, 1973, p. 11. Evening ed.
"Aa akachan junan." *Yomiuri shinbun*, 13 July, 1973, p. 23. Morning ed.
"Ritsudai jokyōju ikka ga shinjū / Niji wo michizure jusui." *Asahi shinbun*, 6 September, 1973, p. 11. Evening ed.
"Jigyō shippai no ikka mo / Yahari niji michizure." *Asahi shinbun*, 6 September, 1973, p. 11. Evening ed.
"Gasu de boshi sannin." *Asahi shinbun*, 6 September, 1973, p. 11. Evening ed.
"Hahaoya, mijukuji ni shi no sekkan." *Asahi shinbun*, 6 September, 1973, p. 11. Evening ed.
"Mata 'Irōzaki shinjū'. Boshi sannin." *Yomiuri shinbun*, 16, October, 1973, p. 11. Evening ed.
"Tsuma ni nigerare sekkan satsujin." *Yomiuri shinbun*, 28 November, 1973, p. 11. Evening ed.

Index

A

abjection, 14, 70, 81, 138–40, 144, 164, 221
abortion, 29, 53n13, 77, 87, 103, 112–15, 115n44, 116, 120, 135–6n13, 147, 197, 225. *See also* Eugenic Protection Law
Abu-Lughod, Lila, 229
Ahmed, Sara, 28n32, 229, 230
Aki Shobō, 98
Akiyama, Yōko, 30, 84, 84n5, 84n6, 85, 85n9, 89–95, 98, 103n32, 110–12, 115
Alcoff, Linda, 16n19
Allinson, Gary D., 87n15, 114
Almond, Barbara, 14n17, 15
Alvarez, Sonia E., 28, 229
Alvis, Andra, 212n31
Anzaldúa, Gloria, 16n19

Aoi shiba no kai, 115
Apter, Emily, 22, 126n8, 230, 231
area studies
  colonial structure, 18
  cultural essentialism, 19
  decentering, 26
  imperialism, 18
  language training, 19
  reflexivity, 19
  translation, 7, 19
Avenell, Simon Andrew, 90
Ayres, Susan, 9n9, 150, 161

B

Bachmann-Medick, Doris, 18, 22n26, 230
Baraitser, Lisa, 14n16
Bargen, Doris G., 196n25
Barnett, Barbara, 9n9, 41n2, 42, 43

Note: Page number followed by 'n' refers to notes.

Bassnett, Susan, 22
Beaudry, Mary C., 9n8
Beheiren (anti-Vietnam war movement)
  antihierarchical structure, 90
  direct action, emphasis on, 89
  "personalization of politics," 90
  self-reflexivity, 89
Bellos, David, 25
Benjamin, Walter, 26
Berger, Douglas, 49, 51
Berman, Antoine, 24n28, 26, 26n30, 26n31, 27
Bermann, Sandra, 219, 229
Bhabha, Homi, 22n26
Borovoy, Amy, 109n38
boshi-shinjū, 40, 46–54, 54n14, 64, 66, 70, 73, 74, 81, 127, 185, 221–5
Boston Women's Health Book Collective, 95
Boyer, Edward J., 2, 5
Braidotti, Rosi, 139, 231n2
Brookman, Fiona, 32n34
Bryant, Tamie L., 48, 50, 50n11, 51, 106, 107, 107n35
Buckley, Sandra, 30, 87, 93n19, 97n24, 103–5, 111n41, 114
Bullock, Julia, 13n15, 92, 164n1, 166, 166n2, 200
Butler, Judith, 4, 5, 6n7, 7, 16, 16n19, 25, 26, 41n3, 44–6, 81, 169
  framing, 7, 41–6
  schemas of intelligibility, 7, 16, 46

C

Castellini, Alessandro, 123, 158
Cavaglion, Gabriel, 9n9, 41n2, 42, 43

Cavanagh, Kate, 15
Cerwonka, Allaine, 17n21, 28
Chakrabarty, Dipesh, 22
Cheever, Susan, 15
Cheung, Martha, 23n27
Chifuren (National Federation of Women's Organization), 87
child
  death of, 57, 168, 175, 177, 185
  killing of, 32, 32n34, 47, 50–4, 59, 65, 66, 131, 133, 136–8, 159, 222
  loss of, 61, 176, 187, 188
  mother's identification with, 50, 114
  as non-person, 222
child-killing, 40, 125, 126n8, 137, 222
child-killing *onna*, 11, 123, 125–7, 132–42, 147, 163, 169, 220, 227. See also *kogoroshi no onna*
Chow, Rey, 17, 18, 19n23, 19n24, 28
Chūpiren, 137, 138, 149
Cohen, Stanley, 8, 43
Connell, Raewyn, 20n24, 28
consciousness transformation, 96–100, 166n2. See also *ishiki henkaku*
Cook, Lauren J., 9n8
Copeland, Rebecca L, 167
Covino, Debora Caslav, 140
Coward, Ros, 41n2
cultural representations, 8, 9, 13, 14, 23, 25, 163

D

Davis, Kathy, 95n23
de Beauvoir, Simone, 92

De Lange, William, 30n33
de Lima Costa, Claudia, 28, 229
de Man, Paul, 25
Derrida, Jacques, 6, 25, 29
dialogue, 7, 16, 21, 26, 95, 160, 161, 193
difference
    cultural difference, 3n3, 3n4, 16, 17, 229
    fetishization, 17
    translation, 22, 229
Di Marco, Francesca, 51, 73, 74
Dizdar, Dilek, 22
Dobash, R.E.
Dobash, R.P.
Dodane, Claire, 165
Doi, Takeo, 50
Dolan, Maura, 2, 2n1, 3, 3n4, 4, 4n5, 4n6
Dongchao, Min, 13n14
Douglas, Susan, 41n2

E

Ehara, Yumiko, 84n6, 84n7, 101–3, 108, 110, 115, 123n5
Enchi, Fumiko, 167n3, 196n25
Endō, Misaki, 108n36
Endo, Orie, 100
Entman, Robert M, 42
Ericson, Joan E., 109, 167
Eugenic Protection Law, 29, 112–16, 135n13, 197

F

Fahmy, Shahira, 41n3
fathers who kill, 146, 149

Feldman, Ofer, 40n1
Feldman, Paul, 3, 30n33
feminism
    Anglo-American feminism, 18
    economy of knowledge, 20n24
    western feminism, 11, 16–18, 20n24, 91–5
fictional representations, 8, 164
filicide. *See* maternal filicide
Firestone, Shulamith, 84, 85n9, 92, 93, 94n21
Fisher, Susan, 215n32
Foucault, Michel
    discourse, 8, 9n8, 10, 10n10, 10n11
    power, 8, 10
    silence, 10, 10n11
Friedan, Betty, 92, 106
Friedman, Susan, 16n19
Fujieda, Mioko, 11n12, 13n13, 13n14, 84n6, 84n7
Fujimura-Fanselow, Kumiko, 11n12, 13n13, 13n14, 84n6, 84n7
Fukuda, Atsuko, 87n12

G

Gamson, William A., 42
Gao, Bai, 87
Goc, Nicola, 9n9, 41n2, 42, 43
Goel, Rashmi, 3n3, 3n4
Goodman, Roger, 30, 48, 50, 72n81
Greer, Germaine, 92
Grewal, Inderpal, 16n19
Gurūpu Tatakau Onna (*ribu* group), 102, 128n11, 129, 129n12, 130, 133, 134, 138, 142, 150, 153, 153n21

H

Hahaoya taikai (Mothers' Convention), 87, 127n9
Hara, Kimi, 109n38
Hara, Yoshihisa, 83n1
Harootunian, Harry D., 18, 19, 19n22
Hartley, Barbara, 167n4
Hastings, Sally Ann, 109, 109n38
Hayashi, Kaori K., 2, 2n1, 2n2, 30, 30n33, 31, 40n1
Heine, Steven, 48, 51
Hemmings, Clare, 18, 230
High Economic Growth Era, 87
Hillenbrand, Margaret, 229
Hook, Derek, 9n8
Hoshino, Ikumi, 209n30
Huckerby, Jayne, 9n9
Hulvey, Yumiko, 215n32

I

Ikeda, Sachiko, 233
infanticide, 32, 32n34, 43, 46, 50, 50n11, 53n13, 54, 55, 62, 107, 113, 165
Inoue, Teruko, 96, 108
ishiki henkaku (consciousness transformation), 96, 100, 166n2

J

Jackson, Peter A., 19, 20
Jakobson, Roman, 22
Johnson, Barbara, 23
Johnson-Cartee, Karen S., 42
Johnson, Thomas J., 41n3
Jones, Ann, 43
Jones, Gretchen, 165
Jones, Tamara, 3, 3n4, 4
josei kaihō undō (women's liberation movement), 85, 85n10, 94, 98n29

K

Kameda, Atsuko, 239–41, 247, 253, 256
Kan, Hideki, 83n1
Kanno, Sugako, 87
Kanō, Mikiyo, 166n2
Kaplan, Caren, 16n19
Kato, Masae, 113n42, 115, 116, 136n13
Kato, Shuichi, 48
Kawanishi, Yuko, 49–51
Kearney, Richard, 27
Kersten, Rikki, 83n1, 89
Kim, James, 41n3
Kim, Nancy S., 3n3
Kimura case
  cultural alterity, 5, 6
  cultural essentialism, 4
  cultural translation, 5
  framing, 7
  insanity defence, 3
  intelligibility, 5, 7, 184
  intercultural understanding, 5, 6
  Japanese culture, 3n4, 4, 6
  language, 4, 7
  maternal violence, conceptualizations of, 7
  murder, 2, 7
  news media, 3n4
  orientalism, 17

oyako shinjū (parent-child suicide), 2, 3n4, 5
representation, 3n4, 7
stereotyping, 3n4, 4n5
suicide, 2, 5
translation, 4–7, 176
violence, 1, 5–7, 184
Kobayashi, Fukuko, 166
Koedt, Anne, 84, 94n21
Kogoroshi, 32, 32n35, 40, 45–54, 62, 63, 70, 73–6, 81, 100, 113, 119, 121, 125–7, 129, 135n13, 145, 147, 148, 220, 221, 224, 225. See also infanticide; maternal filicide
kogoroshi no onna. See also child-killing *onna*; *onna*
abjection, 121, 220
agency, 132–3
alienation, 121, 121n3, 136, 169
continuum of women, 142–5
criminalization, 74, 99, 113, 223
discourse, 45, 129, 220
Hannya mask, 141, 141n16, 142
intelligibility, 45, 220
maternal love, myth of, 220, 221
maternal potential for violence, 45, 123, 220
maternal violence, 45, 121, 125–7, 220
men's responsibility, 148
men's *ribu*, 45, 121, 125–7, 147
mental disorder, 154–6
news media, 40, 54, 63, 73, 75, 81, 220, 221, 225
non-existing *onna*, 126
pathologization, 73–5, 223
resentment, 134, 144, 145
revolutionary subject, 100, 112, 125, 142
social conditions, 62, 78n87
solidarity, 121, 126, 128, 223
stigmatization, 100, 127, 223
victim, 32, 75
woman's grudge, 134
Kōno, Taeko, 165–7
koseki seido (family registration system), 106
Kothari, Rita, 23n27
Kouno, Akihisa, 30
Kristeva, Julia, 139

L

Lai, Ming-Yan, 19n23
Lang, Lucy Jane, 32n34
Lazarre, Jane, 15
Lebra, Takie Sugiyama, 50, 51
Lee, Jung Bock, 30, 31n33
Lewis, R., 236
Lin, Chun, 13
linguistic hospitality. See translation
Liu, Lydia H, 28
Loftus, Ronald P., 77, 97n24, 105, 134, 158, 166
Lowy, Dina, 87n12
Lule, Jack, 43

M

Mackie, Vera, 12, 13n13, 84, 87, 87n14, 88, 93n19, 97n24, 104n33, 109, 111n41, 113, 146n18
mai hōmu shugi [my-homism], 105
Marotti, William, 89

Marvin, Stephen E., 141n16
maternal ambivalence, 15, 168, 175–97, 210, 215, 229
maternal animosity, 8, 37, 163–217, 219, 225, 226
maternal filicide, 6–11, 23, 25, 30, 31, 33, 37, 39, 40, 41n2, 43–6, 51, 53, 64, 69, 75, 78, 79, 81, 120, 121, 122n4, 123n5, 124, 125, 127, 130, 133, 135–8, 144, 145, 149, 151, 152, 154–8, 160–4, 167, 194, 219–25. *See also* maternal potential for violence
media coverage, 7, 31, 39, 43, 46, 53, 149, 150, 152, 153, 157, 163, 219, 221, 223, 224
maternal love, myth of, 109–12, 125, 133, 135, 179, 217, 220, 221, 226
maternal potential for violence. *See also* child-killing *onna*
"bad" and "mad" mother, 9, 40, 54, 81
conditions of appearance, 7, 8, 44, 46, 54, 163, 168, 185, 226
as counter-discourse, 8, 161, 163, 220, 226, 227
cultural intelligibility of, 5, 7, 10n10, 14, 16, 45, 52, 70, 75, 163, 168, 169, 184, 194, 220, 228
cultural representations, 9, 14, 23, 25, 163
cultural taboo, 15, 220, 228
and feminist theory, 29

fictional representations, 8, 164
liberatory potential, 206
maternal subjectivity, 15, 164, 168
monsterization, 8, 14
pathologization, 14, 73–5, 194, 223
representation (*see* cultural representations; fictional representations)
and silencing, 9, 45, 46, 184
stigmatization, 8, 223
maternal violence. *See* maternal potential for violence
Matsui, Machiko, 84n7, 86, 93n19, 96
Matsumoto, Alison, 3, 3n3
Mauriac, François, 171, 173, 207
McCombs, Maxwell, 41
Mead, Margaret, 92
men's *ribu*, 118
mental disorder, 154–6
mental instability, 3n3, 72, 154–7, 194
Metropolitan (*ribu* group), 20n24, 64, 119, 137
Meyer, Cheryl L., 9n9, 15n18
Michaels, Meredith, 41n2
Miki Sōko, 34, 161
mikon no haha (unmarried mothers), 56n24, 79, 108, 112
Mitchell, Juliet, 92
Mitsutani, Margaret, 165
Miyoshi, Masao, 18
Mizoguchi, Akiyo, 34, 35, 102n31, 111, 112, 118, 119, 128n11, 130, 136, 161
Mizuta, Noriko, 167n4, 210, 212
Modigliani, Andre, 42

Mohanty, Chandra Talpade, 16n19
monsterification, 72, 75, 79, 150
Moraga, Cherríe, 16n19
Mori, Maryellen Toman, 13n15, 165, 167n4, 171–4, 201, 203, 204, 206
Morrissey, Belinda, 43
mother-child bond, 110, 125, 128–32, 169, 202. *See also ribu*; Takahashi, Takako
mother-child relationship, 51, 112
mother-child suicide, 40, 46, 47, 50, 52, 54, 55, 60, 61, 64, 66, 73, 74, 127
motherhood
   and aggression, 14, 164, 204
   and ambivalence, 15, 132, 133, 168, 190, 192, 197–205, 229
   cultural idealization, 74, 190
   hatred of, 165, 191
   as institution, 53n13, 110, 116, 117, 166, 226
   loss of, 31, 33, 39, 62, 63, 75, 76, 78, 79, 81, 151, 221
   and myth (*see* maternal love, myth of)
   as non-violent, 7
   as nurturing, 7, 129
   and rage, 14, 65, 204
   rearticulation of, 8
   refusal of, 132, 165, 167
   and social norms, 8, 174
   and violence, 7, 15, 16, 26, 46, 163, 164, 180, 181, 190, 192, 197, 219, 225 (*see also* maternal animosity; maternal filicide; maternal potential for violence; mothers who kill)

mothers who kill, 7–9, 11, 13, 14, 37, 39–80, 82, 99, 100, 107, 110, 119–63, 219, 220, 223, 224, 226–8
Motz, Anna, 14n16
Mrozowski, Stephen A., 9n8
murder, 2, 8, 43, 47–9, 49n9, 54, 54n14, 56, 113, 127, 147, 162, 165, 200, 207, 208
Muto, Ichiyo, 30, 83, 84n7, 86, 88, 89, 96, 98, 98n27, 105

N

Nakagawa, Gordon, 46
Nakayama, Kazuko, 166, 166n2
New Left, Japanese, 88, 89, 102
Niikuni Wilson, Michiko, 167n4
Ning, Wang, 18
Nishikawa, Yūko, 105
Nishimura, Mitsuko, 107–8n36, 112
noirōze (neurosis), 33, 55n20, 59, 72, 74n82, 171n11
Nolan, Jane, 32n34
Nolte, Sharon H., 109, 109n38
Norgren, Tiana, 113, 114

O

Oakley, Ann, 15
Ōba, Minako, 165, 167, 167n3, 174, 174n19
Oberman, Michelle, 9n9, 15n18
Ochiai, Emiko, 84n7, 85, 96, 104, 111n41
Ogino, Miho, 103, 109, 113, 114, 114n43
Ōgoshi, Aiko, 110
Ohinata, Masami, 110

Oliver, Kelly, 139
onna, 11, 98, 98n28, 100–4, 111, 112, 116, 117, 121, 123, 125, 126n8, 129, 135, 152, 162, 198, 225, 227. See also *kogoroshi no onna; ribu*
Orbaugh, Sharalyn, 117n45, 165, 166, 167n4
O'Reilly, Andrea, 110
orientalism, 17, 28n32
Orpett Long, Susan, 110
oyako shinjū, 2, 2n1, 3n4, 5, 40, 45–53, 63

P

Paker, Saliha, 23n27
Papastergiadis, Nikos, 22n26
parent-child suicide, 2, 5, 40, 45–7, 49, 49n10, 51, 52, 63. See also *oyako shinjū*
Parker, Roszika, 14n17, 15
paternal filicide, 53, 68
paternal responsibility, 53
pathologization, 3n3, 14, 73–5, 150, 194, 223
Paul, Christopher, 41
Polezzi, Loredana, 22n26
Ponzanesi, Sandra, 231n2
Pound, Leslie, 2, 3
Pound, Wayne, 196n25

R

Reddy, Sita, 3n3
Reich, Pauline C., 87n12
Reider, Noriko T., 215n32
representability, 7, 45, 46, 74, 81, 132, 145, 163, 166, 168

ribu
  abortion, 29, 77, 87, 103, 112–15, 115n44, 116, 120, 147, 197, 225
  adoption, stigma against, 7, 8, 13n14, 51, 79, 100, 102, 106–8, 110, 120, 127, 223
  alternative media of, 103
  anti-imperialism, 117
  collectives, 97, 107, 107n36
  communes, 90, 103, 111, 118
  consciousness transformation, 96–100, 166n2 (*see also ishiki henkaku*)
  counter-discourse, 8, 79, 82, 161, 163, 220, 226, 227
  criminalized women, identification with, 99
  disabled persons, solidarity with, 8, 82, 89, 92, 95, 99, 107, 110, 115, 119, 121, 122, 126, 128, 131, 142, 155, 162, 163, 219, 223
  discursive intervention, 37, 82, 113, 121, 125, 145, 152
  family system, critique of, 104–8, 125, 128–32
  female body, knowledge of, 103
  feminizumu, distinction from, 12, 84n4, 94
  gender critique of, 82
  imperialism, Japanese women's complicity in, 90
  internalized female consciousness, 83
  jiko hitei (self-criticism), 89
  kogoroshi no onna, solidarity with (*see kogoroshi no onna*)
  language, 224, 226

logic of productivity, 96, 104, 115, 117, 156
mass media, 45, 104, 151, 161
maternal love, myth of, 109–12, 125, 133, 135, 220, 226
men's liberation (*see* men's *ribu*)
mini-komi, 34, 35, 103, 104, 146n18, 161
motherhood, 7, 8, 11, 13, 78, 79, 109, 110, 114, 116, 117, 126, 130, 132, 133, 161, 164, 166, 197–205, 220, 226
mothers who kill their children (*see kogoroshi no onna*)
New Left, 88, 89, 102
as non-western movement, 28, 29
onna, 101, 117, 126, 129, 147, 220
other Japanese feminist movements, distinction from, 13n14, 20, 21, 101, 129, 144, 226
as Pan-Asian movement, 117
relationality, 96–101, 111, 117, 121, 122, 125, 130, 142, 159n27, 220, 223, 224
ryōsai kenbo, rejection of, 109
sexuality, liberation of, 102, 104, 135
sex workers, 99, 117
translation, 7, 23, 29, 84, 92, 93, 93n19, 95, 99n29, 100n30, 103, 126, 153, 154, 220
United Red Army, 99, 123, 123n5
unmarried mothers, 79, 99, 108, 112, 225
violence, 86, 128–32, 224
as western import, 86n11, 92
woman's logic, 96
and Women's Lib, U.S., 84, 85n9, 91, 92, 93n19
Ribu Shinjuku Center, 35, 90, 91, 107n36, 115n44, 118, 119, 122, 134, 158n25, 161
Rich, Adrienne, 14, 15, 15n18, 16n19, 17n20, 19n22, 110, 166, 185
Ricoeur, Paul, 1, 25, 26n30, 27
Robins-Mowry, Dorothy, 87, 87n12, 88, 105
Ronald, Richard, 77, 209n30
Rosenzweig, Franz, 26
Ruch, Barbara, 167n3
ryōsai kenbo (good wife, wise mother), 109. *See also See also ribu*

S

Saeki, Yōko, 16, 34
Sakai, Naoki
 cultural studies, 20
 schema of co-figuration, 20, 21
 translation as filter, 21
 untranslatables, 21n25
Sakamoto, Kazue, 146n18
Sakane, Yōko, 212
Sakurada, Daizo, 83n1
Sams, Julia P., 3
Sapporo Komu-unu (*ribu* group), 149, 151, 152
Sasaki-Uemura, Makoto Wesley, 83n1, 87n15, 88, 105, 114, 158, 161
Sasaki, Yasuyuki, 29, 54
Satō, Bunmei, 87n13, 118

Seal, Lizzie, 9, 43
Seitō (Bluestockings), 86, 87n12
sengyō shufu (professional housewife), 105
Shigematsu, Setsu, 11n12, 12, 13n13, 13n14, 30, 83n2, 84n5, 84n6, 85, 86, 86n11, 87, 87n13, 88–91, 91n17, 98, 98n27, 99, 100, 100n30, 102, 102n31, 104n33, 107–8n36, 108, 109, 111, 112, 114, 115n44, 116–19, 121, 121n3, 122, 123, 123n6, 124, 126, 126n8, 127, 129n12, 135, 135n13, 136, 137, 223, 225
Shih, Shu-Mei, 13n14
shinjū, 2n1, 33, 47–9, 49n9, 49n10, 52, 56, 59, 60, 62, 64, 66, 67, 73, 222, 223, 225
Shisō Shūdan Esuīekkusu (*ribu* group), 128n11, 134, 137, 138
Shohat, Ella, 17
Shufuren (Housewives Association), 87
Sievers, Sharon L., 87n12
silence, 1, 6–11, 25, 26, 29, 158, 160, 164, 168, 177, 179–81, 184, 188, 194, 220, 224, 228
Snell-Hornby, Mary, 23
Spivak, Gayatri Chakravorty, 6n7, 16n19, 17, 23, 24, 28
Stam, Robert, 17
Stangle, Heather Leigh, 9n9
Steinhoff, Patricia G., 89
Stewart, Robert W., 2, 3, 5
stigmatization, 8, 79, 100, 127, 223
suicide, 2, 2n1, 5, 8, 33, 40, 45–8, 48n7, 48n8, 49, 49n9, 49n10, 50–2, 54, 55, 59–67, 73, 74, 127, 222. *See also shinjū, boshi shinjū, oyako shinjū*
Swerdlow, Amy, 87n14
Szanton, David, 19, 19n24

T

Takahashi, Takako
abortion, 197, 225
alienation, woman's, 165, 169, 175, 189, 209, 210
anti-social behavior, 164, 205, 208, 212
biography, 168
"Byakuya" (White Night), 36, 200
"Byōbō" (Boundlessness), 36, 169, 201–205
Christianity, 173, 199
coeducation, 170
confession, 168, 177, 180, 181, 185, 190, 195, 196
crime, 7, 8, 195, 207, 228
cultural prescriptions, critique of, 164, 174, 225
"Danjo kyōgaku" (Coeducation), 170n6
demonic woman, 169, 205–8, 217, 220, 226, 227
"Dopperugengeru-kō" (Thought on the doppelgänger), 189
double, 45, 49, 49n9, 165, 173, 180, 189, 192, 202, 208, 212

family, critique of, 226
father, absence of, 64, 66, 68
femininity, 13, 165, 166, 169, 203, 206, 208, 220, 225
gender norms, challenge to, 169, 171, 174, 205, 206, 216
Hone no shiro (Castle of Bones), 36
"Ibu to Maria" (Eve and Mary), 199, 207
Ikari no ko (Child of Wrath), 172
Japanese language, 13, 199
"*Kanata no mizuoto*" (Yonder Sound of Water), 36, 169, 209–211
"Keshin" (Incarnation), 36, 168, 185–197
Kirei na hito (Beautiful Person), 173
"Kodomosama" (Honorable Child), 36, 201n28
"Kou" (To Yearn), 172
marriage, 170, 171, 183, 207
maternal ambivalence, 168, 175–97, 210, 215
maternal animosity, 8, 37, 163–217, 219, 225, 226
maternal potential for violence, 7, 11, 45, 163–217, 219–23, 226–9
maternal, refusal of, 165, 167
maternal subjectivity, 164, 168
maternal violence, 7, 8, 11, 12, 23, 36, 45, 163, 164, 167, 167n5, 169, 185, 217, 219, 220, 225–7
maternal voice, 164
"Me" (Eyes), 36, 200
mother and child, 51, 184, 198

mother-child bond, critique of, 169, 202
motherhood, hostility to, 7, 8, 11, 13, 23, 163, 164, 166–8, 174, 180, 181, 185, 190, 192, 197–205, 207, 208, 211, 219, 220, 225, 226
"Natsu no fuchi" (Summer Abyss), 36, 168, 175–185
"Onna-girai" (Woman-hating), 198
"Otoko no naka no tada hitori" (The only one among men), 170n6
pregnancy, hostility to, 164, 167, 169
reproduction, 167, 169, 174, 197–205, 216
"*Ronrii ūman*" (Lonely Woman), 172, 200
"Satsui no bungaku" (A literature of murder), 228
Sei —— onna ni okeru mashō to bosei" (Sexuality —— The demonic and the maternal in women), 205, 207
sexuality, 165, 167, 205, 207, 226
"Sōjikei" (Congruent Figures), 36, 169, 209, 211–216
Sora no hate made (To the end of the sky), 172
"Takahashi Kazumi to sakka to shite no watashi" (Takahashi Kazumi and my literary career), 171n9
Tamashii no inu (*Soul Dogs*), 170n6, 197

Takahashi, Takako (*cont.*)
  Thérèse Desqueyroux, 171, 207, 227
  translation, 7, 10, 23, 49, 171, 176, 199, 205, 206, 210, 212, 219, 220
  "*umu umanu no jiyū*" (The freedom to give or not to give birth), 197
  unconscious, 169, 173, 174, 180, 181, 202, 207, 208, 211, 220, 227, 228
  "Unmei no wakareme" (Fateful departure), 170
  "Watashi no noirōze no koto" (Concerning my neurosis), 171n11
  "*Yūwakusha*" (The Temptress), 172
Takahashi Yoshitomo, 253
Takamure, Itsue, 87
Tama, Yasuko, 29, 30, 37, 53, 53n13, 54, 63, 71, 79, 113n42
Tanaka, Kazuko, 11n12, 30, 96, 98n27, 105
Tanaka, Mitsu, 79, 91, 91n17, 101, 115, 121, 123, 126, 134
Tanhan, Diana Adis, 51
Tansman, Alan, 19
Tipton, Elise K., 88, 109n38, 111n41, 116
Tokyo Komu-unu (*ribu* group), 111, 112, 118, 159n27
Tomida, Hiroko, 87n12
translation. *See also ribu*; *Urufu no kai*
  across media, 23
  and alterity, 4–6, 21n25, 27, 28
  betrayal, 24, 25
  cognitive boundaries, 21
  constitutional failure of, 25
  cultural translation, 5, 22, 49
  decentering, 26
  and dialogue, 7, 21, 26, 95
  directionality of, 18, 28
  and ethical responsibility, 49n9
  ethics, 22, 23, 26, 28, 219, 220, 229
  fidelity, 23, 24, 25n29
  as filter, 21
  hegemony of English, 18
  hermeneutic dimension of, 21
  and incommunicability, 21, 210
  interventionist, 24n28, 25n29, 94
  linguistic hospitality, 28
  metaphorical uses of, 22
  monolinguality, 29
  non-western conceptualizations, 23n27, 229
  original, 5, 7, 22–5, 25n29, 26, 26n30, 49, 92, 94, 95, 153, 176n21, 205
  and otherness, 27
  provincialization of the west, 27
  and silence, 6, 10, 25, 26, 29, 220
  transcultural dialogue, 7
  translational encounter, 21–9
  translation turn, 22
  untranslatability, 21, 25, 126n8, 230
  and violence, 5–7, 10, 21–6, 28, 29, 40, 41, 46, 49, 126, 199, 219, 220, 229
translator. *See also* Spivak, Gayatri Chakravorty
  agentic subject, 24n28
  into English, 23, 28
  as mediator, 24n28
  psychological ambivalence, 24n28

Trivedi, Harish, 22
Tsurumi, Yoshiyuki, 90
Tucker, Lauren R., 42
Tuosto, Kylie, 41n3
Tyler, Imogen, 14n16, 15, 139, 140, 223
Tymoczko, Maria, 23n27, 94

U
Ueno, Chizuko, 84n6, 102, 104, 105, 106n34, 110, 111n41
ūman ribu. See ribu
Uno, Kathleen S., 109, 109n38, 109n39
untranslatability, 21, 25, 49n9, 126n8, 230
untranslatables, 1, 21n25, 67, 100, 126n8, 231
Urufu no kai (WOLF group), 93. See also *ribu*, translation

V
Vatanabadi, Shouleh, 28
Venuti, Lawrence, 24, 24n28, 25, 25n29, 27, 49, 49n9
violence. See Kimura case; *kogoroshi no onna*; maternal filicide; maternal potential for violence; motherhood; mothers who kill; Takahashi, Takako
Viswanathan, Meera, 215n32
Vogel, Suzanne H., 105

W
Wakabayashi, Judy, 23n27

Wakakuwa, M. ([2000] 2004) *Sensō ga tsukuru joseizō: dainiji sekai taisenka no nihon josei dōin no shikakuteki puropaganda.* Tokyo: Chukuma Shobō, 109
Warner, Michael, 150n19
Waswo, Ann, 209
Welker, James, 84, 84n8, 93, 93n19, 93n20, 94, 95, 95n23, 103n32, 106
Welldon, Estela V., 14n16
Wetherall, William, 5
Whittemore, Edward P., 40n1
Wilczynski, Ania, 9n9
Winters Carpenter, Juliet, 239
women's lib, U.S., 7, 11n12, 13, 30, 31, 34, 70, 76, 78–118, 134, 166n2, 220

Y
Yamamoto, Ryoko, 30, 42
Yamamura, Yoshiaki, 50
Yamaori, Tetsuo, 215n32
Yifeng, Sun, 18
Yoda, Tomiko, 105, 106, 108n37
Yoshitake, Teruko, 97n25, 134, 158
Yoshizumi, Kyoko, 105

Z
Zenkyōtō student movement
 gender discrimination, 88
 jiko hihan (self-criticism), 89
 jiko hitei (self-denial), 89
 self-reflexivity, 89
 sexism, 89
 violence, 88, 89